DATA MINING

DR. S. UMA | DR. M. AMUTHA | MR. M. RAVIKUMAR

Made with ♥ on the Notion Press Platform
www.notionpress.com

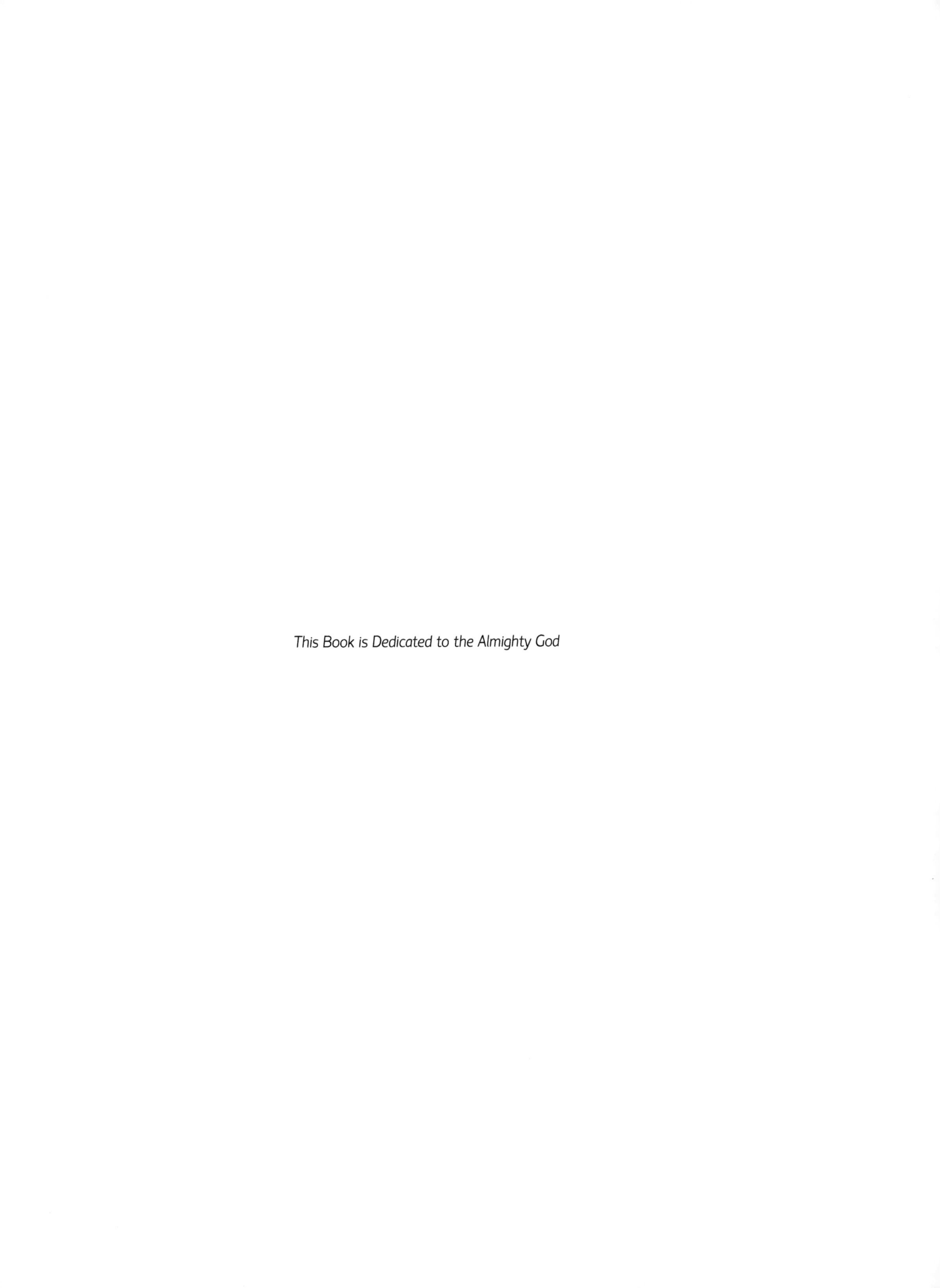

This Book is Dedicated to the Almighty God

Contents

Preface

With the rapid development of information technology, the capacity to produce and gather data across all areas has risen tremendously. Retailers and e-commerce have created incredibly big databases on commercial transactions in the corporate world. Numerous scientific domains have also produced a significant amount of data. Another example is the World Wide Web, which has billions of web pages with text and multimedia content that are used by millions of users. It is still difficult to analyse large amounts of data in ways that can be recognized and used effectively.

This issue is addressed by data mining, which offers methods and tools for automatically analysing and exploring massive and complex data sets. Many different domains, including statistics, computer science, machine learning, database administration, and data visualisation, to mention a few, are conducting research on data mining.

Massive amounts of data must first be mined for patterns, and then those patterns must be comprehended in the context of particular problems in order to be transformed into meaningful information and knowledge. Numerous data mining techniques are available to automate the initial stage of mining different sorts of data patterns from enormous amounts of data. Data pattern interpretation typically requires specialised topic knowledge and analytical skills which are discussed in this book.

This book is written with reference from a number of sources on data mining yet Data mining by Kenneth and Hamber provided us with a good understanding of the data minining concepts . Hence to give a clear picture on data mining concepts , we have cited some of the examples and figures from the above mentioned book.

Author name DR. S. UMA DR. M. AMUTHA MR. M. RAVIKUMAR
Date 08.11.2022

Prologue

This book discusses the fundamental concepts of data mining. This book is organized in five chapters that covers the major principles and concepts of data mining.

The first chapter deals with the process of data mining, its architecture, functionalities and data preprocessing.

A discussion of Data Warehouse, and OLAP technology are dealt in the second chapter. This chapter also gives details on the data warehouse components, OLAP servers, Query Tools, OLAP Operations, and Implementation of Data Warehouse Architecture. Mining Frequent Patterns, Associations and Correlations, Association Rule Mining and Apriori Algorithm and Mining Multilevel Association Rules from Relational Databases and Data warehouses are the other topics discussed in the second chapter.

Waikato Environment for Knowledge Analysis (Weka), developed at the University of Waikato, New Zealand, is a free software licensed under the GNU General Public License. Weka includes a number of data visualisation tools and methods for predictive modelling and data analysis, together with graphical user interfaces for quick access to these tasks, which aids in the learners' knowledge of data mining. Chapter three gives a detailed explanation on the installation and usage of the WEKA tool.

The fourth chapter deals with the classification, clustering, and prediction techniques.

Finally, mining of time series: trend analysis, pattern mining, mining text data, multimedia data and World Wide Web are discussed in detail in this book.

CHAPTER ONE

DATA MINING

DATA MINING

1. Introduction

Data mining is the process of finding new, relevant connections, patterns, and trends by sifting through a significant amount of data kept in repositories and using pattern recognition technology, using statistical and mathematical approaches. It involves selecting, examining, and modelling a vast amount of data to find previously undetected patterns or links in order to provide conclusions that are both clear and beneficial to the database owner.

It is not limited to using computer algorithms or statistical techniques. Information technology can be used in conjunction with this type of business intelligence to support corporate decisions.

Data Mining is similar to Data Science. It is carried out by a person in a specific situation, on a specific data set, with a specific goal in mind. This phase includes a variety of services such as text mining, web mining, audio and video mining, pictorial data mining, and social media mining. It is completed using simple or highly specific software.

Because of the widespread availability of massive amounts of data and the impending need to convert such data into useful data and knowledge, data mining has garnered a great deal of attention in the information market and society as a whole in recent years. The information and knowledge gained can be used in software applications ranging from industry analysis, fraud detection, and user retention to production control and scientific exploration.

Data mining can be viewed as a natural progression of data technology. The database system market has encouraged the evolution of the following functionalities: data collection and database creation, data management, and advanced data analysis.

For example, the recent development of a structure for data collection and database creation was required for the later development of an effective structure for data storage and retrieval, as well as query and transaction processing. Advanced data analysis has evolved into the next object as various database systems provide query and transaction processing as standard practise.

Data can be stored in various databases and data repositories. A repository of several heterogeneous data sources organised under a unified schema at a single site to support management decision making is one data repository structure that has appeared in the data warehouse.

Data warehouse includes data cleaning, data integration, and online analytical processing (OLAP), particularly analysis techniques with functions such as summarization, consolidation, and aggregation, as well as the ability to query data warehouses.

1.1 Steps in Data Mining

Data mining, sometimes referred to as knowledge discovery in databases, is a method for extracting informational value from massive amounts of data held in data warehouses and databases. This analysis is carried out for corporate decision-making procedures.

Numerous methods, including clustering, association, sequential pattern analysis, and decision trees, are used in data mining.

1.2.1 Process of Data Mining

Businesses employ the technique of data mining to transform unstructured data into information that is useful. Businesses can discover new information about their customers to create more efficient marketing campaigns, boost sales, and cut expenses by employing software to search for patterns in massive amounts of data.

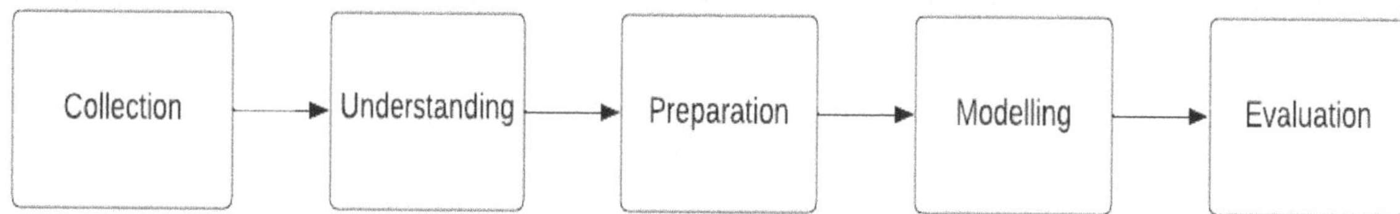

Figure 1.1 Process of Data Mining

The Data Mining process can be explored in 5 steps.

- **Collection** – First data is collected, organized, and filled into a data warehouse. The data is stored and managed either in the cloud or in-house servers.
- **Understanding** – Data scientists and business analysts examine the properties of the data and conduct an in-depth analysis from the context of a particular problem statement as defined by the company. This is addressed using querying, visualization, and reporting.
- **Preparation** – Once the data sources of the available data are confirmed, the data is cleared, constructed, and formatted into the required form. In this process, additional data can also be explored at a greater depth, which is well informed by the insights and uncovered in the previous stage.
- **Modelling** – In this stage, for the prepared dataset, modelling techniques are selected. A data model is just like a diagram that reflects and describes the relationships between different types of information that are stored in the database.
- **Evaluation** – In the context of the business objectives, the model results are evaluated. In this phase, due to new patterns that are discovered in the model results or other factors, new business requirements may be raised.

1.3 Architecture

Data mining is the technique of extracting interesting knowledge from a set of huge amounts of data stored in many data sources such as file systems, data warehouses, and databases. The significant components of data mining systems are a data source, data mining engine, data warehouse server, the pattern evaluation module, graphical user interface, and knowledge base.

1.3.1 Data Sources

A huge variety of present documents such as data warehouse, database, www or popularly called a World wide web become the actual data sources. Most of the times, it can also be the case that the data is not present in any of these golden sources but only in the form of text files, plain files or sequence files or spreadsheets and then the information needs to be processed in a very similar way as the processing would be done upon the data received from golden sources. Most of the major chunk of data today is obtained from the internet or the world wide web as everything present on the internet today is data in some form or another which forms some form of information repository units.

Before the data is processed ahead the different processes through which it goes involves data cleansing, integration, and selection before finally the information is passed onto the database or any of the EDW (enterprise data warehouse) server. The major challenge that lies at times with this set of data is different sources and a wide array of data formats that form the data components. Therefore the data cannot be directly used for processing in its naïve state but processed, transformed and crafted in a much more usable way. This way, the reliability and completeness of the data are also ensured. The primary step involves data collection, cleaning and integration, and post that only the relevant data is passed forward. All this activity forms a part of a separate set of tools and techniques.

1.3.2 Data Warehouse Server or Database

The database server is the actual space where the data is contained once it is received from various data sources. The server contains the actual set of data which becomes ready to be processed, and therefore the server manages the data retrieval. All this activity is based on the request for data mining of the person.

1.3.3 Data Mining Engine

In data mining, the engine forms the core component and is the most vital part, or to say the driving force which handles all the requests and manages them and is used to contain several modules. The number of modules present includes mining tasks such as classification technique, association technique, regression technique, characterization, prediction and clustering, time series analysis, naive Bayes, support vector machines, ensemble methods, boosting and bagging techniques, random forests, decision trees, etc.

Figure 1.2 Architecture of Data Mining

1.3.4. Pattern Evaluation Modules

This evaluation technique of the modules is mainly responsible for measuring the interestingness of all those patterns used for calculating the basic level of the threshold value and is used to interact with the data mining engine to coordinate in the evaluation of other modules. The main purpose of this component is to look out and search for all the interesting and useable patterns that could make the data of comparatively better quality.

1.3.5. Graphical User Interface

When the data is communicated with the engines and among various pattern evaluation of modules, it becomes a necessity to interact with the various components present and make it more user friendly so that the efficient and effective use of all the present components could be made and therefore arises the need of a graphical user interface popularly known as GUI.

This is used to establish a sense of contact between the user and the data mining system, thereby helping users access and use the system efficiently and easily to keep them devoid of any complexity arising in the process. This is a form of abstraction where only the relevant components are displayed to the users. All the complexities and functionalities responsible for building the system are hidden for simplicity. Whenever the user submits a query, the module then interacts with the overall set of a data mining system to produce a relevant output easily shown to the user in a much more understandable manner.

1.3.6. Knowledge Base

This is the component that forms the base of the overall data mining process as it helps in guiding the search or in the evaluation of interestingness of the patterns formed. This knowledgebase consists of user beliefs and the data obtained from user experiences, which are helpful in the data mining process. The engine might get its input set from the created knowledge base, thereby providing more efficient, accurate and reliable results.

Data mining is one of the most important techniques today that deals with data management and data processing, which forms any organisation's backbone. Analysis of data in any organization will bring fruitful results. Each component of the data mining technique and architecture has its own way of performing responsibilities and completing data mining efficiently. The different modules are needed to interact correctly to produce a valuable result and complete the complex procedure of data mining successfully by providing the right set of information to the business.

1.4 Data Mining and Databases

Databases are a collection of organised data. Databases are the single most important tool used to store data by programmers and web developers. It can, for example, be used to store everything such as, the settings in an application, text on a website, graphics, status updates, personal messages and comments on social networks.

1.4.1 Data Mining

Data Mining is a process of finding potentially useful patterns from huge data sets. It is a multi-disciplinary skill that uses machine learning, statistics, and AI to extract information to evaluate future events probability

Data mining is also called Knowledge Discovery in Data (KDD), Knowledge extraction, data/pattern analysis, information harvesting, etc.

Data collected by large organizations in the course of everyday business is usually stored in databases. But database administrators may not be willing to allow data miners direct access to these data sources, and direct access may not be the best option from your point of view either. Direct access to operational (used for routine business operations) databases can be a bad idea because

Data miners use a lot of data. You could unintentionally tie up resources and interfere with ordinary business operations.

Legal and other business obligations matter. You could unintentionally violate a data privacy law or other data management requirement if your data access is not properly controlled.

1.4.2 Databases

A database is a systematic collection of data. They support electronic storage and manipulation of data. Databases make data management easy.

1.4.2.1 Types of Databases

Distributed databases:

A distributed database is a type of database that has contributions from the common database and information captured by local computers. In this type of database system, the data is not in one place and is distributed at various organizations.

Relational databases:

This type of database defines database relationships in the form of tables. It is also called Relational DBMS, which is the most popular DBMS type in the market. Database example of the RDBMS system include MySQL, Oracle, and Microsoft SQL Server database.

Object-oriented databases:

This type of computers database supports the storage of all data types. The data is stored in the form of objects. The objects to be held in the database have attributes and methods that define what to do with the data. PostgreSQL is an example of an object-oriented relational DBMS.

Centralized database:

It is a centralized location, and users from different backgrounds can access this data. This type of computers databases store application procedures that help users access the data even from a remote location.

Open-source databases:

This kind of database stored information related to operations. It is mainly used in the field of marketing, employee relations, customer service, of databases.

Cloud databases:

A cloud database is a database which is optimized or built for such a virtualized environment. There are so many advantages of a cloud database, some of which can pay for storage capacity and bandwidth. It also offers scalability on-demand, along with high availability.

1.5 Data warehouses:

Data Wraehouse is to facilitate a single version of truth for a company for decision making and forecasting. A Data warehouse is an information system that contains historical and commutative data from single or multiple sources. Data Warehouse concept simplifies the reporting and analysis process of the organization.

NoSQL databases:

NoSQL database is used for large sets of distributed data. There are a few big data performance problems that are effectively handled by relational databases. This type of computers database is very efficient in analyzing large-size unstructured data.

Graph databases:

A graph-oriented database uses graph theory to store, map, and query relationships. These kinds of computers databases are mostly used for analyzing interconnections. For example, an organization can use a graph database to mine data about customers from social media.

OLTP databases:

OLTP another database type which able to perform fast query processing and maintaining data integrity in multi-access environments.

Personal database:

Operational databases are not organized for data mining. You could spend a lot of time struggling to get the data you need, and still not be sure of getting it right.

3. **Data warehouses**

A data warehouse is a centralised storage system that enables data to be collected, processed, and interpreted in order to improve decision-making. Data warehouses regularly receive data from transactional systems, relational databases, and other sources.

1.5.1 **Characteristics of Data Warehouse**

The main characteristics of a data warehouse are as follows:

Subject-Oriented

A data warehouse is subject-oriented since it provides topic-wise information rather than the overall processes of a business. Such subjects may be sales, promotion, inventory, etc. For example, if you want to analyze your company's sales data, you need to build a data warehouse that concentrates on sales. Such a warehouse would provide valuable information like 'who was your best customer last year?' or 'who is likely to be your best customer in the coming year?'

Integrated

A data warehouse is developed by integrating data from varied sources into a consistent format. The data must be stored in the warehouse in a consistent and universally acceptable manner in terms of naming, format, and coding. This facilitates effective data analysis.

Non-Volatile

Data once entered into a data warehouse must remain unchanged. All data is read-only. Previous data is not erased when current data is entered. This helps you to analyze what has happened and when.

Time-Variant

The data stored in a data warehouse is documented with an element of time, either explicitly or implicitly. An example of time variance in Data Warehouse is exhibited in the Primary Key, which must have an element of time like the day, week, or month.

1.5.2 Data Warehouse Architecture

Usually, data warehouse architecture comprises a three-tier structure.

Bottom Tier

The bottom tier or data warehouse server usually represents a relational database system. Back-end tools are used to cleanse, transform and feed data into this layer.

Middle Tier

The middle tier represents an OLAP server that can be implemented in two ways.

The ROLAP or Relational OLAP model is an extended relational database management system that maps multidimensional data process to standard relational process.

The MOLAP or multidimensional OLAP directly acts on multidimensional data and operations.

Top Tier

This is the front-end client interface that gets data out from the data warehouse. It holds various tools like query tools, analysis tools, reporting tools, and dat mining tools.

1. 5.3 How Data Warehouse Works

Data Warehousing integrates data and information collected from various sources into one comprehensive database. For example, a data warehouse might combine customer information from an organization's point-of-sale systems, its mailing lists, website, and comment cards. It might also incorporate confidential information about employees, salary information, etc. Businesses use such components of data warehouse to analyze customers.

Data mining is one of the features of a data warehouse that involves looking for meaningful data patterns in vast volumes of data and devising innovative strategies for increased sales and profits.

1.5.4 Types of Data Warehouse

There are three main types of data warehouse.

Enterprise Data Warehouse (EDW)

This type of warehouse serves as a key or central database that facilitates decision-support services throughout the enterprise. The advantage to this type of warehouse is that it provides access to cross-organizational information, offers a unified approach to data representation, and allows running complex queries.

Operational Data Store (ODS)

This type of data warehouse refreshes in real-time. It is often preferred for routine activities like storing employee records. It is required when data warehouse systems do not support reporting needs of the business.

Data Mart

A data mart is a subset of a data warehouse built to maintain a particular department, region, or business unit. Every department of a business has a central repository or data mart to store data. The data from the data mart is stored in the ODS periodically. The ODS then sends the data to the EDW, where it is stored and used.

1.5.5 Data Warehouse Example

These are the examples of how companies use data warehouse as an integral part of their day-to-day operations.

Investment and Insurance companies use data warehouses to primarily analyze customer and market trends and allied data patterns. In sub-sectors like Forex and stock markets, data warehouse plays a significant role because a single point difference can result in huge losses across the board.

Retail chains use data warehouses for marketing and distribution, so they can track items, examine pricing policies and analyze buying trends of customers. They use data warehouse models for business intelligence and forecasting needs.

Healthcare companies, on the other hand, use data warehouse concepts to generate treatment reports, share data with insurance companies and in research and medical units. Healthcare systems depend heavily upon enterprise data warehouses because they need the latest, updated treatment information to save lives.

1.5.6 **Data Warehousing Tools**

These are software components used to perform several operations on an extensive data set. These tools help to collect, read, write and transfer data from various sources. What do data warehouses support? They are designed to support operations like data sorting, filtering, merging, etc.

Data warehouse applications can be categorized as:

Query and reporting tools

Application Development tools

Data mining tools

OLAP tools

Some popular data warehouse tools are Xplenty, Amazon Redshift, Teradata, Oracle 12c, Informatica, IBM Infosphere, Cloudera, and Panoply.

1.6Data Mining Functionalities

Some most popular functionalities of data mining, such as –

Classification

Association Analysis

Cluster Analysis

Data Charectization

Data Discrimination

Prediction

Outlier Analysis

Evolution Analysis

1.6.1 Classification

As the name suggests, classification is the technique to categorize elements in a collection, basis their predefined functionalities and properties. In classification, the model can classify new instances whose classification is unknown. These particular instances that are used to create the model are called training data. Such a mechanism of classification uses methods like if-then, decision trees, neural networks, or even a set of classification rules. These methods can be retrieved to identify future data.

1.6.2 Association Analysis

Association Analysis is also called Market Basket Analysis. It is a very popular data mining methodology with usage in sales. Association analysis helps to find relations between elements frequently occurring together. It is made up of a series of sets of elements and rules that describe how these are grouped within the cases. Association rules are used to predict the presence of an element in the database and are based on the manifestation of a specific element identified as important. Association analysis is based on 2 parts rule – antecedent (if) consequent(then) –

An antecedent (if) points towards a degree of discovering a consequent (then) in the data set. It suggests that they are associated.

One example to understand this better can be – If a person is buying popcorn in the theatre then there are 60% chances that he will buy a cold drink. This way, a prediction can be made on the shopping behavior of the consumer.

1.6.3 Cluster Analysis

The cluster analysis process is similar to that of classification. In cluster analysis, similar types of data are grouped, and the only difference is that the class label is unknown. Clustering algorithms divide the data basis similarities and the grouped data are similar to each other more than the other data in other groups. Cluster analysis is used in machine learning, deep learning, image processing, pattern recognition, and NLP, etc.

1.6.4 Data Characterization

The process of data characterization involves summarizing the generic data features, which can result in specific rules to define a target class. To characterize the data without much user intervention or interaction, an attribute-oriented induction technique is used and the resultant characterized data can be visualized in the form of different types of graphs, charts, or tables.

1.6.5 Data Discrimination

Data discrimination is a bias, which happens when a data set or source is treated differently than the others, be it intentional or unintentional. This data mining functionality helps to separate peculiar data sets, based on the ambiguity in attribute values.

1.6.6 Prediction

Prediction is among the most popular data mining functionalities that determine any missing or unknown element in a data set. Linear regression models based on the previous data are used to make numeric predictions, which help businesses forecast the results of any given event, in a positive or negative way. There are two types of predictions –

Numeric Predictions – Predict any missing or unknown element in a data set

Class Predictions – Predict the class label using a previously built class model

1.6.7 Outlier Analysis

If we are unable to group any data in any class, we use the outlier analysis technique. Outlier analysis helps to learn about data quality. Outlier means data abnormality in most cases. More outliers in your data sets, low the data quality. You cannot identify data patterns or derive any conclusions from data sets with a big number of outliers. The outlier analysis process helps in checking if there is any data that can be used to analyze after some clean-up. Nevertheless, it is still important to keep a track of unusual data and activities so that any anomalies can be detected beforehand and any business impact can be detected in advance.

1.6.2 Evolution Analysis

Evolution Analysis refers to the study of data sets that may have been through a phase of transformation or change. The evolution analysis models capture evolutionary trends in data, which further contributes to data characterization, classification, or discrimination and clustering for multivariate time series.

1.7. Data mining primitives

A data mining query is defined in terms of the following primitives

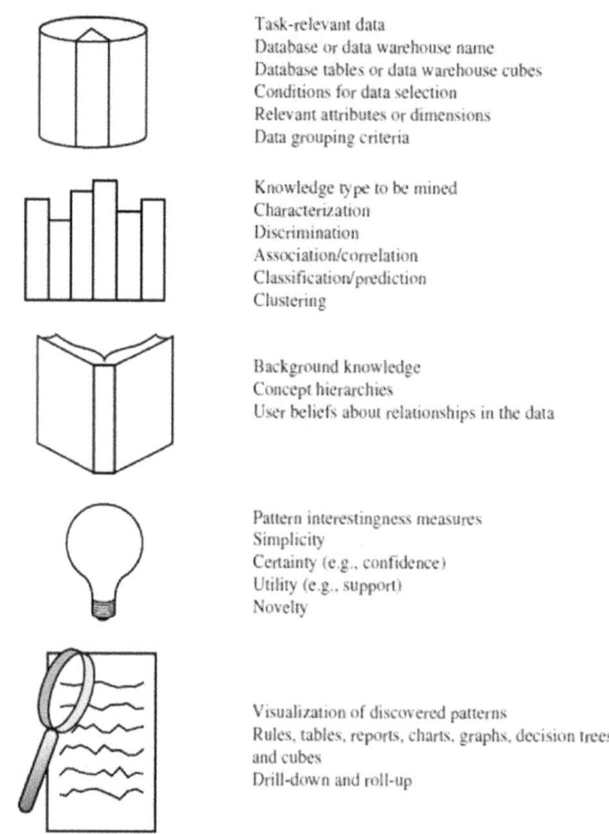

Figure 1.3 Primitives for Data Mining Tasks

1.7.1 Task-relevant data: This is the database portion to be investigated. For example, suppose that you are a manager of All Electronics in charge of sales in the United States and Canada. In particular, you wouldlike to study the buying trends of customers in Canada. Rather than mining on the entire database. These are referred to as relevant attributes

1.7.2The kinds of knowledge to be mined: This specifies the data mining functions to be performed, such as characterization, discrimination, association, classification, clustering, or evolution analysis. For instance, if studying the buying habits of customers in Canada, you may choose to mine associations between customer profiles and the items that these customers like to buy

1.7.3 Background knowledge: Users can specify background knowledge, or knowledge about the domain to be mined. This knowledge is useful for guiding the knowledge discovery process, and for evaluating the patterns found. There are several kinds of background knowledge.

1.7.4 Interestingness measures: These functions are used to separate uninteresting patterns from knowledge. They may be used to guide the mining process, or after discovery, to evaluate the discovered patterns. Different kinds of knowledge may have different interestingness measures.

1.7.5 Presentation and visualization of discovered patterns: This refers to the form in which discovered patterns are to be displayed. Users can choose from different forms for knowledge presentation, such as rules, tables, charts, graphs, decision trees, and cubes.

1.8 Data Preprocessing

Data preprocessing is the process of transforming raw data into an understandable format. It is also an important step in data mining as we cannot work with raw data. The quality of the data should be checked before applying machine learning or data mining algorithms.

1.8.1 Why Data preprocessing?

Preprocessing of data is mainly to check the data quality. The quality can be checked by the following

Accuracy: To check whether the data entered is correct or not.

Completeness: To check whether the data is available or not recorded.

Consistency: To check whether the same data is kept in all the places that do or do not match.

Timeliness: The data should be updated correctly.

Believability: The data should be trustable.

Interpretability: The understand ability of the data.

1.8.2 Major Tasks in Data Preprocessing:

- Data cleaning
- Data integration
- Data reduction
- Data transformation

1.8.2.1 Data Cleaning.

Before analyzing data, it is necessary to remove faulty data, structure the raw data, and fill in the null values.

Data cleaning is the process that removes data that does not belong in your dataset.

There are some techniques in data cleaning

- Handling missing values
- Noisy
- Removing unwanted or irrelevant observations
- Fixing structural error
- Filtering umwanted ouliers
- Validate and Qualty Analysis

The best approach for one-time requests is often for the administrator to extract the data for you and deliver it in a text file or other acceptable format.

Ongoing data access is another matter. The administrator may not want to provide data extracts over and over, and giving you direct access to business systems is risky. A common solution is to create an analytic database. This is an ordinary relational database that is separate from conventional business systems. Data is routinely (and automatically) transferred from business systems to the analytic database, and data miners can access it at any time.

If the database administrator insists that the data can't be stored this way, ask whether it's possible to create a view (a stored query that can be queried as if it were a conventional data table) with the organization that you need.

Many data-mining products are able to read data from databases. The steps required vary based on the

- Design of the data-mining application
- Structure of the source database

Middleware, usually called a driver (ODBC driver, JDBC driver), special software that mediates between the database and applications software

Documentation for your data-mining application should tell you whether it can read data from a database, and if so, what tool or function to use, and how. The administrator who sets up the analytics database can provide details about accessing the database.

Handling missing values:

Standard values like "Not Available" or "NA" can be used to replace the missing values.

Missing values can also be filled manually but it is not recommended when that dataset is big.The attribute's mean value can be used to replace the missing value when the data is normally distributed wherein in the case of non-normal distribution median value of the attribute can be used.While using regression or decision tree algorithms the missing value can be replaced by the most probable
value.

Noisy:

Noisy generally means random error or containing unnecessary data points. Here are some of the methods to handle noisy data.

Binning:

This method is to smooth or handle noisy data. First, the data is sorted then and then the sorted values are separated and stored in the form of bins. There are three methods for smoothing data in the bin. Smoothing by bin mean method: In this method, the values in the bin are replaced by the mean value of the bin;

Smoothing by bin median: In this method, the values in the bin are replaced by the median value;

Smoothing by bin boundary: In this method, the using minimum and maximum values of the bin values are taken and the values are replaced by the closest boundary value.

Regression: This is used to smooth the data and will help to handle data when unnecessary data is present. For the analysis, purpose regression helps to decide the variable which is suitable for our analysis.

Clustering: This is used for finding the outliers and also in grouping the data. Clustering is generally used in unsupervised learning.

Removing unwanted or irrelevant observations

Eliminate duplicate or irrelevant observations from your dataset. Duplicate data can be generated when you mix data sets from the several sources, scrape data, or get data from clients or other departments.

for instance, if you want to analyze data about millennial clients but your dataset also includes older generations. This can make analysis more efficient and minimize distraction from your primary target—as well as creating a more manageable and more performant dataset.

Fixing structural error

When you measure or transfer data and find strange naming patterns, typos, or incorrect capitalization, such are structural faults. Incorrectly labeled categories or classes may result from these inconsistencies. For instance, you might see both "N/A" and "Not Applicable," but they should be assessed as belonging to the same category.

Filtering umwanted ouliers

There will frequently be isolated findings that, at first look, do not seem to fit the data you are evaluating. Removing an outlier if you have a reasonable cause to, such as incorrect data entry, will improve the performance of the data you are working with. Never forget that an outlier doesn't necessarily indicate that something is wrong. To determine the reliability of the number, this step is necessary. If an outlier shows out to be incorrect or irrelevant for the analysis, you might want to remove it.

Validate and Qualty Analysis

At the end of the data cleaning process, you should be able to answer these questions as a part of basic validation:

Does the data make sense?

Does the data follow the appropriate rules for its field?

Does it prove or disprove your working theory, or bring any insight to light?

Can you find trends in the data to help you form your next theory?

If not, is that because of a data quality issue?

1.8.2.2Data Integration

The process of combining data from various dissimilar sources is known as data integration. You must address data duplication, inconsistency, and other issues as you integrate the data. Data integration is a record preparation technique used in data mining that involves combining data from a few disparate heterogeneous data sources into coherent data in order to preserve and present a cohesive perspective of the data. Databases, flat documents, and various record cubes could potentially be included in this list of assets. The triple (G, S, and M) approach is how the statistical integration strategy is explicitly described. S stands for the diverse sources of schema, G for the global schema, and M for the mapping between source and global schema queries.

The data integration methods are formally characterized as a triple **(G, S, M)**, where;

G represents the **global schema**,

S represents the **heterogeneous** source of schema,

M represents the **mapping** between **source** and **global** schema queries.

Why is the Data Integration Important?

Big data, with all of its advantages and disadvantages, is embraced by businesses that want to remain competitive and relevant. Market and consumer data gathering is one of the most popular uses for data integration services and technologies. Corporate intelligence and consumer data analytics help to drive real-time information delivery by supporting queries in these massive datasets. Enterprise reporting, predictive analytics, and corporate intelligence are made possible through enterprise data integration, which feeds integrated data into data centres.

Particularly in the healthcare sector, data integration is crucial. By combining data from numerous systems into a single, helpful view of information from which helpful insights may be deduced, integrated data from various patient records and clinics help clinicians diagnose medical problems and diseases. efficient data integration and gathering

Data Integration Approaches

There are mainly two types of approaches for data integration. These are as follows:

Tight Coupling

It is the process of using **ETL (Extraction, Transformation, and Loading)** to combine data from various sources into a single physical location.

Loose Coupling

Facts with loose coupling are most effectively kept in the actual source databases. This approach provides an interface that gets a query from the user, changes it into a format that the supply database may understand, and then sends the query to the source databases without delay to obtain the result.

Issues in Data Integration

When you integrate the data in Data Mining, you may face many issues. There are some of those issues:

Entity Identification Problem

As you understand, the records are obtained from heterogeneous sources, and how can you 'match the real-world entities from the data'. For example, you were given client data from specialized statistics sites. Customer identity is assigned to an entity from one statistics supply, while a customer range is assigned to an entity from another statistics supply. Analyzing such metadata statistics will prevent you from making errors during schema integration.

Structural integration is completed by guaranteeing that the functional dependency and referential constraints of a character in the source machine match the functional dependency and referential constraints of the identical character in the target machine. For example, assume that the discount is applied to the entire order in one machine, but in every other machine, the discount is applied to each item in the order. This distinction should be noted before the information from those assets is included in the goal system.

Redundancy and Correlation Analysis

One of the major issues in the course of data integration is redundancy. Unimportant data that are no longer required are referred to as redundant data. It may also appear due to attributes created from the use of another property inside the information set. For example, if one truth set contains the patronage and distinct data set as the purchaser's date of the beginning, then age may be a redundant attribute because it can be deduced from the use of the beginning date.

1.8.2.3 **Data Reduction:**

"Data reduction is the transformation of numerical or alphabetical digital information derived empirically or experimentally into a corrected, ordered, and simplified form."

- Dimensionality Reduction
- Numerosity Reduction
- Histogram
- Clustering
- Sampling
- Data Cube Aggregation
- Data Compression

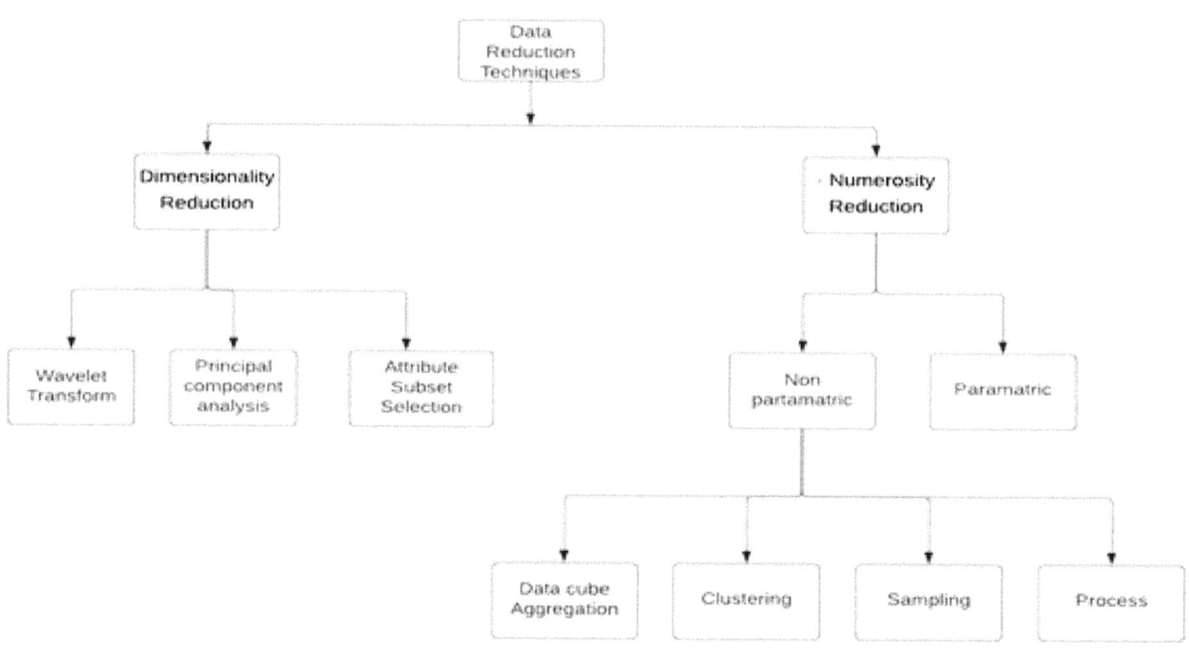

Figure 1.4 Data Mining Techniques

Dimensionality Reduction

Dimensionality Reduction is the process of reducing the number of dimensions the data is spread across. It means, the attributes or features, that the data set carries as the number of dimensions increases the sparsity. This sparsity is critical to clustering, outlier analysis and other algorithms. With reduced dimensionality, it is easy to visualize and manipulate data. There are three types of Dimensionality reduction.

Wavelet Transform

Wavelet Transform is a lossy method for dimensionality reduction, where a data vector X is transformed into another vector X', in such a way that both X and X' still represent the same length. The result of wavelet transform can be truncated, unlike its original, thus achieving dimensionality reduction. Wavelet transforms are well suited for data cube, sparse data or data which is highly skewed. Wavelet transform is often used in image compression.

Principal Component Analysis

This method involves the identification of a few independent tuples with 'n' attributes that can represent the entire data set. This method can be applied to skewed and sparse data.

Attribute Subset Selection

Here, attributes irrelevant to data mining or redundant ones are not included in a core attribute subset. The core attribute subset selection reduces the data volume and dimensionality.

Dimensionality Reduction

In the numerosity reduction, the data volume is decreased by selecting an alternative, smaller form of data representation. These techniques can be parametric or non-parametric

1.8.2.3.1 Parametric

This method assumes a model into which the data fits. Data model parameters are estimated, and only those parameters are stored, and the rest of the data is discarded. Regression and Log-Linear methods are used for creating such models.

Regression:

There are two types of linear regression: basic and multiple. Such a regression model is known as simple linear regression when there is just one independent attribute. Such regression models are referred to as multiple linear regressions if there are numerous independent attributes.

A linear relationship between two properties of the data set is modelled by linear regression. We must fit a linear regression model between the two variables x and y, where x is the independent variable or predictor variable and y is the dependent variable. The equation y=wx+b, where w and b are regression coefficients, can be used to express the model. We can define the variable y in terms of many predictor attributes using a multiple linear regression model.

Log-Linear Model: Based on a smaller subset of dimensional combinations, the log-linear model can be used to predict the likelihood of each data point in a multidimensional space for a collection of discretized attributes. As a result, a higher-dimensional data space can be built from attributes of lesser dimensions. The association between two or more discrete attributes is found using the log-linear model. Assume that we have a collection of tuples in n-dimensional space; the log-linear model aids in determining the probabilities of each tuple in this n-dimensional space.

1.8.3.2 Non-Parametric

A non-parametric numerosity reduction technique does not assume any model. The non-Parametric technique results in a more uniform reduction, irrespective of data size, but it may not achieve a high volume of data reduction like the Parametric one. There are at least four types of Non-Parametric data reduction techniques, Histogram, Clustering, Sampling, Data Cube Aggregation, Data Compression.

Histograms: The frequency-based data representation is called a histogram. It is a common method of data reduction and uses binning to roughly match distribution. Consider a histogram that separates the data distribution for an attribute A into distinct subsets or buckets. Singleton buckets are buckets that define only one specific attribute-value or frequency pair per bucket.

Clustering: Techniques for clustering treat tuples of data as objects. In order to make things within a cluster "similar" to one another and "dissimilar" to objects in other clusters, they divide the objects into groups or clusters. It is frequently described using a distance function to describe how "near" the objects are to one another in space.

Sampling: Sampling can be used as a data reduction approach because it enables a huge data set to be defined by a much smaller random sample or a subset of the information. Sampling can reduce large data sets into smaller sample data sets to represent the original data set. There are four types of sampling data reduction methods.

Simple Random Sample Without Replacement of sizes

Simple Random Sample with Replacement of sizes

Cluster Sample

Stratified Sample

Data Cube Aggregation: Data cube aggregation involves moving the data from a detailed level to fewer dimensions. The resulting data set is smaller in volume, without loss of information necessary for the analysis task. Data Cube Aggregation is a multidimensional aggregation that uses aggregation at various levels of a data cube to represent the original data set, thus achieving data reduction. Data Cube Aggregation, where the data cube is a much more efficient way of storing data, thus achieving data reduction, besides faster aggregation operations.

Data Compression: It employs modification, encoding, or converting the structure of data in a way that consumes less space. Data compression involves building a compact representation of information by removing redundancy and representing data in binary form. Data that can be restored successfully from its compressed form is called Lossless compression. In contrast, the opposite, where it is not possible to restore the original form from the compressed form, is Lossy compression.

1.8.2.4 DATA TRANSFORMATION:

In data transformation, the data are transformed or consolidated into forms appropriate for mining. Data transformation can involve the following:

Smoothing: Smoothing is a process used to remove the unnecessary, corrupt or meaningless data or 'noise' in a dataset. Smoothing improves the algorithm's ability to detect useful patterns in data.

Aggregation: Data aggregation is gathering data from a number of sources and storing it in a single format. Aggregation, in itself, is a process of improving the quality of the data where it helps gather info about data clusters and collect lots of data.

Discretization: Discretization is one of the transformation methods that break up continuous data into small intervals. Although data mining requires continuous data, the existing frameworks can only handle discrete data chunks.

Attribute construction: In attribute construction, new attributes are generated and applied in the mining process from the existing set of attributes. It improves mining efficiency by simplifying the original data.

Generalization: Generalization is used to convert low-level data attributes to high-level data attributes by the use of concept hierarchy. An example is an age in the numerical form of raw data (22, 52) is converted into (Young, old) categorical value.

Normalization: Normalization is an important step in data transformation and also called pre-processing. Here the data is transformed to categorize it under a given range.

1.9 Data Integration Techniques

There are various data integration techniques in data mining. Some of them are as follows:

Manual Integration

This approach generally avoids of automation for data integration. For the purpose of creating useful information, the data analyst gathers, purifies, and combines the data. This approach is appropriate for a small business with scant data. However, the extensive, sophisticated, and ongoing integration will take some time. It takes a long time because the entire process has to be done manually.

Middleware Integration

Data from many sources are combined, normalised, and stored in the final data set using middleware software. This method is employed when an organisation has to integrate data from historical systems into modern systems.

Software called middleware serves as a translator between antiquated and modern systems. You could bring an adapter that enables the connection of two systems with various interfaces. **Application-based integration**

It is using software applications to extract, transform, and load data from disparate sources. This strategy saves time and effort, but it is a little more complicated because building such an application necessitates technical understanding. This strategy saves time and effort, but it is a little more complicated because building such an application necessitates technical understanding.

Uniform Access Integration

This method combines data from a more disparate source. However, the data's position is not altered in this scenario; the data stays in its original location. This technique merely generates a unified view of the integrated data. The integrated data does not need to be stored separately because the end-user only sees the integrated view.

The term "hierarchy" refers to an organisational structure or mapping in which components are prioritised in accordance with their relative value. In other terms, a hierarchical notion is a series of mappings from a set of more fundamental concepts to more sophisticated ones. This indicates that low-level notions are mapped to high-level concepts. For instance, there are various kinds of hierarchical systems in computer science. The best example of a computer hierarchical tree model is when a document is placed in a folder in Windows at a certain location in the tree structure. Top-down mapping and bottom-up mapping are the two different styles of hierarchy.

Data Discretization

- Dividing the range of a continuous attribute into intervals.
- Interval labels can then be used to replace actual data values.
- Reduce the number of values for a given continuous attribute.
- Some classification algorithms only accept categorically attributes.

This leads to a concise, easy-to-use, knowledge-level representation of mining results.

Discretization techniques can be categorized based on whether it uses class information or not such as follows:

Supervised Discretization - This discretization process uses class information.

Unsupervised Discretization - This discretization process does not use class information.

1.10.1 Typical Methods of Discretization and Concept Hierarchy Generation for Numerical Data

1.10.1.1 Binning

Binning is a top-down splitting technique based on a specified number of bins.Binning is an unsupervised discretization technique because it does not use class information. In this, the sorted values are distributed into several buckets or bins and then replaced with each bin value by the bin mean or median.It is further classified into Equal-width (distance) partitioning and Equal-depth (frequency) partitioning.

1.10.1.2 Histogram Analysis

It is an unsupervised discretization technique because histogram analysis does not use class information. Histograms partition the values for an attribute into disjoint ranges called buckets. It is also further classified into Equal-width histogram Equal frequency histogram. The histogram analysis algorithm can be applied recursively to each partition to automatically generate a multilevel concept hierarchy, with the procedure terminating once a pre-specified number of concept levels has been reached.

1.10.1.3 Cluster Analysis

Cluster analysis is a popular data discretization method.

A clustering algorithm can be applied to discretize a numerical attribute of A by partitioning the values of A into clusters or groups. Clustering considers the distribution of A, as well as the closeness of data points, and therefore can produce high-quality discretization results. Each initial cluster or partition may be further decomposed into several subcultures, forming a lower level of the hierarchy.

1.10.1.4 Entropy-Based Discretization

Entropy-based discretization is a supervised, top-down splitting technique. It explores class distribution information in its calculation and determination of split points. Let D consist of data instances defined by a set of attributes and a class-label attribute. The class-label attribute provides the class information per instance. In this, the interval boundaries or split-points defined may help to improve classification accuracy. The entropy and information gain measures are used for decision tree induction.

1.10.1.5 Interval Merge by $\chi 2$ Analysis

It is a bottom-up method.Find the best neighboring intervals and merge them to form larger intervals recursively. The method is supervised in that it uses class information.

ChiMerge treats intervals as discrete categories. The basic notion is that for accurate discretization, the relative class frequencies should be fairly consistent within an interval. Therefore, if two adjacent intervals have a very similar distribution of classes, then the intervals can be merged. Otherwise, they should remain separate.

1.11. Concept Hierarchies

Discretization can be performed rapidly on an attribute to provide a hierarchical partitioning of the attribute values, known as a Concept Hierarchy.Concept hierarchies can be used to reduce the data by collecting and replacing low-level concepts with higher-level concepts. In the multidimensional model, data are organized into multiple dimensions, and each dimension contains multiple levels of abstraction defined by concept hierarchies. This organization provides users with the flexibility to view data from different perspectives. Data mining on a reduced data set means fewer input and output operations and is more efficient than mining on a larger data set. Because of these benefits, discretization techniques and concept hierarchies are typically applied before data mining, rather than during mining.

CHAPTER TWO

DATA WAREHOUSE AND OLAP TECHNOLOGY

2.1 Data Warehouse

To fulfil the needs of transaction processing systems, data warehouse is a relational database management system (RDBMS) design. It can be broadly categorized as any centralized data repository that can be searched for commercial advantages. It is a database that houses data intended to meet decision-making needs. It is a collection of decision-supporting technologies designed to empower knowledge workers (executive, manager, and analyst) to reach higher and better conclusions. Business executives can systematically organize, comprehend, and apply their information by adopting data warehousing, which supports architectures and tools.

The data warehouse environment includes an extraction, transportation, and loading (ETL) solution, an online analytical processing (OLAP) engine, customer analysis tools, and other programmes that manage the process of obtaining information and providing it to business users.

What is a Data Warehouse?

Data warehouse is a type of information system that holds current and historical data from one or more data sources. It streamlines the organization's reporting and analyzing procedures. For every company's decision-making and forecasting, it also represents a single view of reality.

A data warehouse is a collection of information that is unique to the entire company, not just one single user demographic. It is utilized for decision-making rather than routine tasks like processing transactions and daily activities.

A data system having the following characteristics might be thought of as a data warehouse:

- It is a database created for investigative work that uses information from different apps.
- It supports a limited number of clients with prolonged interactions.
- To provide information a historical perspective, it combines current and historical facts.
- It is heavily used for reading.
- It contains a few large tables.

A subject-oriented, integrated, and time-variant information storage that supports management choices is referred to as a "data warehouse."

2.2Characteristics of Data Warehouse

The key characteristics of data warehouse are listed below.

Subject Oriented

A data warehouse is subject-oriented since it provides data on a particular topic rather than a business ongoing operations. These topics may include distributors, marketing, and sales.

Continuous operations are never the main emphasis of a data warehouse. The emphasis was instead placed on data analysis and modelling for decision making. By excluding information that is not essential to the decision-making process, it also offers a clear and concise perspective on the particular subject.

Integrated

Integration in a data warehouse refers to the creation of a standard unit of measurement for all related data from diverse databases. Additionally, the data must be housed in the data warehouse in a way that is generally recognised as acceptable.

Data from different sources, such as a mainframe, relational databases, flat files, etc. are combined to create a data warehouse. Additionally, it needs to maintain a consistent name structure, format, and code. Effective data analysis is made possible using data warehouse. It is necessary to guarantee consistency in name conventions, attribute measures, encoding structure, and other areas.

Time-Variant

As opposed to operational systems, data warehouse has a much wider temporal horizon. The information provided by the data gathered in a data warehouse is historical in nature and is associated with a specific time period. It either overtly or obliquely refers to time. The structure of the record key is one such location where time variance in data from data warehouses is displayed. Each primary key in the DW should contain a time component, either implicitly or explicitly such as day, week, month, etc. Data cannot be modified or changed once it has been added to the warehouse, which is another facet of time variance.

Non-volatile

The fact that a data warehouse is non-volatile means that when new data is entered into it, the prior data is not overwritten. Data is read-only and updated infrequently. This aids in understanding historical data and what happened when and how. Mechanisms for controlling concurrency, recovery, and transaction processes are not necessary for a data warehouse.

In a data warehouse environment, operations like delete, update, and insert that are carried out in an operational application context are omitted. There are only two sorts of data operations carried out in data warehousing:

i. Data loading and
ii. Data Access

2.3 Need for Data Warehouse

A typical database can hold between MB and GB of data, and that too for a specific need. Storage was moved to a data warehouse to accommodate TB-sized data. A transactional database doesn't lend itself to analytics in addition to this. An organization maintains a central Data Warehouse to analyze its business in-depth by organizing, comprehending, and applying its historical data for making strategic decisions and assessing trends.

Traditional organizational practices, have the following disadvantages:

- Does not have a single system of records.
- The multiple database systems used in the organization are not synchronized.
- Organizations need to analyze activities in a balanced way
- Customer relationship management
- Supplier relationship management

Data warehouse provides an integrated, company-wide view of high quality information (from disparate databases). Also it helps to separate the operational systems and data from the informational systems and data which helps in performance improvement.

Operational system is a system used to run a business in real time. It is related to the operations and transactions carried out on current data. Informational system is designed to support decision making based on historical point-in-time and prediction data for complex queries or data-mining applications.

A crucial business intelligence tool, data warehousing enables firms to:

Ensure consistency

It is simpler for corporate decision-makers to study and share data insights with their colleagues throughout the world since data warehouses are programmed to apply a common format to all acquired data. The likelihood of a misinterpretation error is also decreased and overall accuracy is improved by standardizing data from various sources.

Improve Decision Making in Business

Business executives who are successful create data-driven strategies and hardly ever make decisions without considering the available information. The speed and effectiveness of accessing various data sets is increased thanks to data warehousing, which also makes it simpler for corporate decision-makers to glean insights that will direct their business and marketing plans and help them stand out from their rivals.

Increase Revenue Generation

Business leaders can easily access their organization's historical actions through data warehouse platforms and assess earlier projects to see if they were successful or failed. Executives may then see where their strategy has to be adjusted to save expenses, boost productivity, and boost sales in order to enhance their bottom line.

2.4 Multidimensional Data Model

Data are viewed as a data-cube in a multidimensional model. Data cubes are the format used to store data in multidimensional databases. This implies that data can be viewed and understood from a variety of angles.

The combination of various relational databases results in a multidimensional database. The multidimensional databases enable users to pose analytical inquiries about market or company patterns, whereas relational databases just allow users to access data through queries.

The dimensions are the viewpoints or entities that an organisation considers and keeps track of. It is characterized by facts and measurements. Facts are quantified data. The names of the facts or measures of the associated dimensional tables are contained in the fact table. For OLAP (online analytical processing) and data warehousing, multidimensional databases are primarily employed. They can be employed to display to users data in several dimensions. MOLAP (multidimensional online analytical processing), a method of accessing multidimensional databases, is used. By producing and analysing the data rather quickly, they enable the consumers to receive responses to their inquiries quickly.

A primary subject, like sales, serves as the organising principle for a multidimensional data model. A fact table is used to illustrate this theme. To maintain records of the store's sales for the dimensions of time, item, and location, the organisation may build a sales data warehouse.

The organisation can keep track of sales information using these dimensions, including monthly item sales and the places where the items were sold. A table called a dimensional table is associated with each dimension and contains additional information about the dimension. The attributes item name, brand, and kind, for instance, might be present in a dimensional table for an item.

It is only possible to analyse and calculate an organization's revenue on the basis of a number of variables, including raw materials, production, labour, sales, human resources, the amount of time required, infrastructure, etc. The following list includes both the benefits and drawbacks of multidimensional databases.

Advantages

- **Increased performance**: Compared to the relational databases, the performance of multidimensional databases are much superior.
- **Easy maintenance**
- **Better data presentation:** A multidimensional database's data is multifaceted and contains a wide range of elements. As a result, the data presentation is far better than that of traditional databases.

Disadvantages

The fact that multidimensional databases are highly complex and require experts to fully comprehend and analyse the data in the database is one of its drawbacks.

2.4.1 Schemas for Multidimensional Data Model

A building must first be designed and a model made before construction can begin. In a similar manner, before we can develop a data warehouse, it must first be designed using data warehouse modelling tools and techniques. We do this to show the data in the actual world and examine the connections between business principles. Designing the compiled information into a schema is the process of data warehouse modelling.

Schema is a logical description of the entire database. It includes the name and description of records of all record types including all associated data-items and aggregates. A data warehouse uses Star, Snowflake, and Fact Constellation schema.

2.4.1.1 Star Schema

Given that its structure resembles a star, the Star Schema is the most straightforward data warehouse schema. Fact tables and Dimension tables are the two different kinds of tables in this data warehouse model.

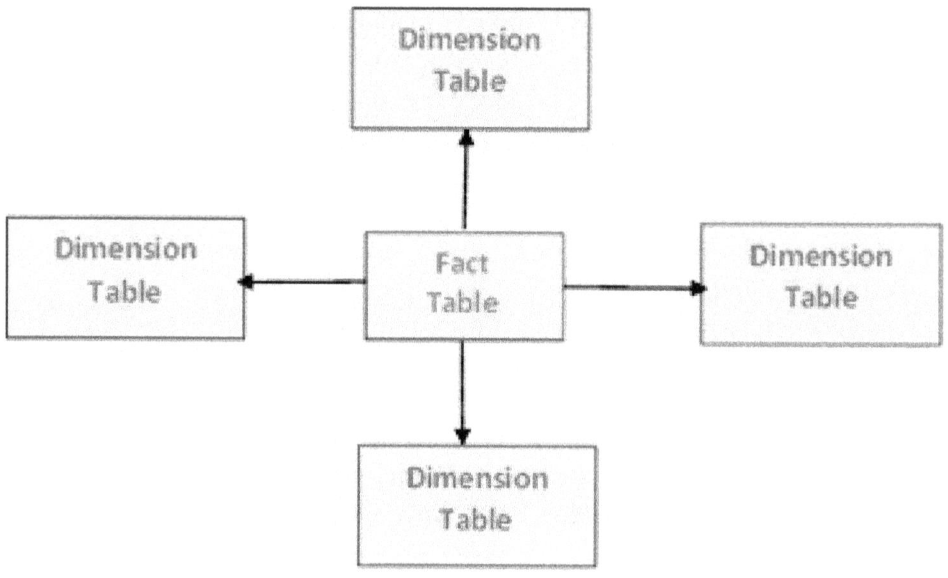

Figure 2.1 Star Schema Model

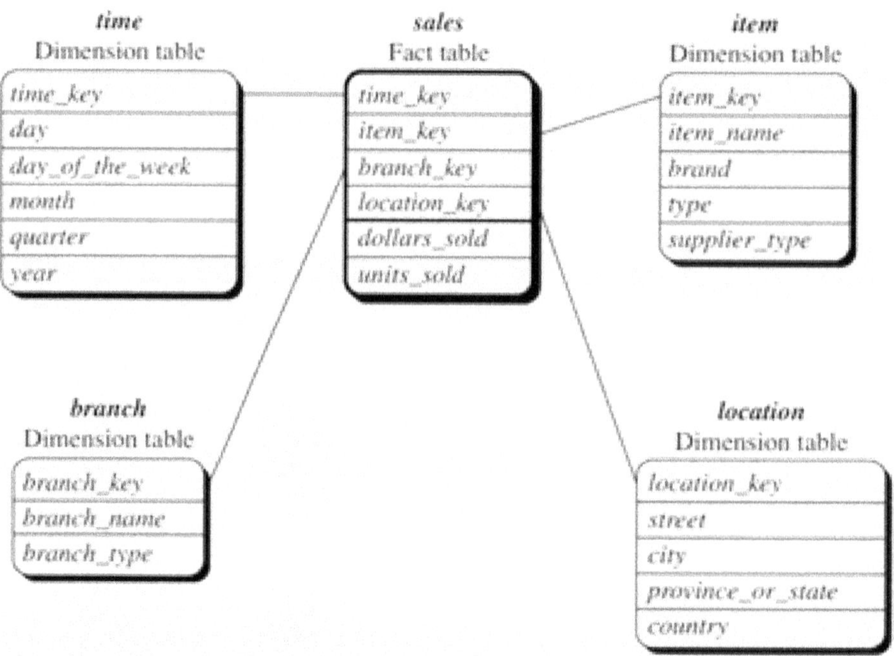

Figure 2.2 Star Schema Example

• **Fact Tables:** A fact table normally contains two types of columns: measurements columns that carry numeric facts and foreign keys to dimension tables. A fact table may include facts at the aggregate or detail level.

• **Dimension tables:** Compared to fact tables, dimension tables typically have fewer records, but each record may have a very high number of characteristics that characterize the fact data.

Fact Table lies at the center point and dimension tables are connected with fact table such that star share is formed as shown in the figure 2.1.

There is just one dimension table per dimension in the star schema, and each table contains a collection of characteristics. Data redundancy may result from this restriction. The next diagram displays sales information for a business in relation to the four dimensions of time, item, branch, and location.

De-normalized dimension tables in the star schema enable simpler queries with fewer join operations, as well as improved system efficiency. On the other hand, star schema's de-normalized tables make it challenging to maintain data integrity. It is the most popular data warehouse schema, and Oracle also suggests using it.

2.4.1.2 Snowflake Schema

The star schema is expanded into the shape of a snowflake, where each star's point multiplies into additional points. The diagram of snowflake schema is what gives it its name; it looks like a snowflake. A technique for standardising the dimension tables in STAR schemas is called snowflaking. When all of the dimension tables are completely normalised, the resulting structure looks like a snowflake with the fact table in the centre. To improve the efficiency of particular queries, snowflaking is employed. Each fact in the schema is surrounded by the corresponding dimensions, which are connected to other dimensions and branch out in a snowflake pattern. In the snowflake schema, one fact table is connected to numerous dimension tables, each of which is connected to another dimension table via a many-to-one relationship. The third normal form is typically used to normalise tables in a snowflake schema. A hierarchy is performed by each dimension table at exactly one level.

The star schema model is modified to create the snowflake schema, which further divides the data into new tables by normalising some of the dimension tables. Because the snowflake's dimension tables are normalised, it is more complex than the star schema. A core fact table coupled to various dimension tables that can be normalised into further dimension tables serves as the representation of the snowflake schema.

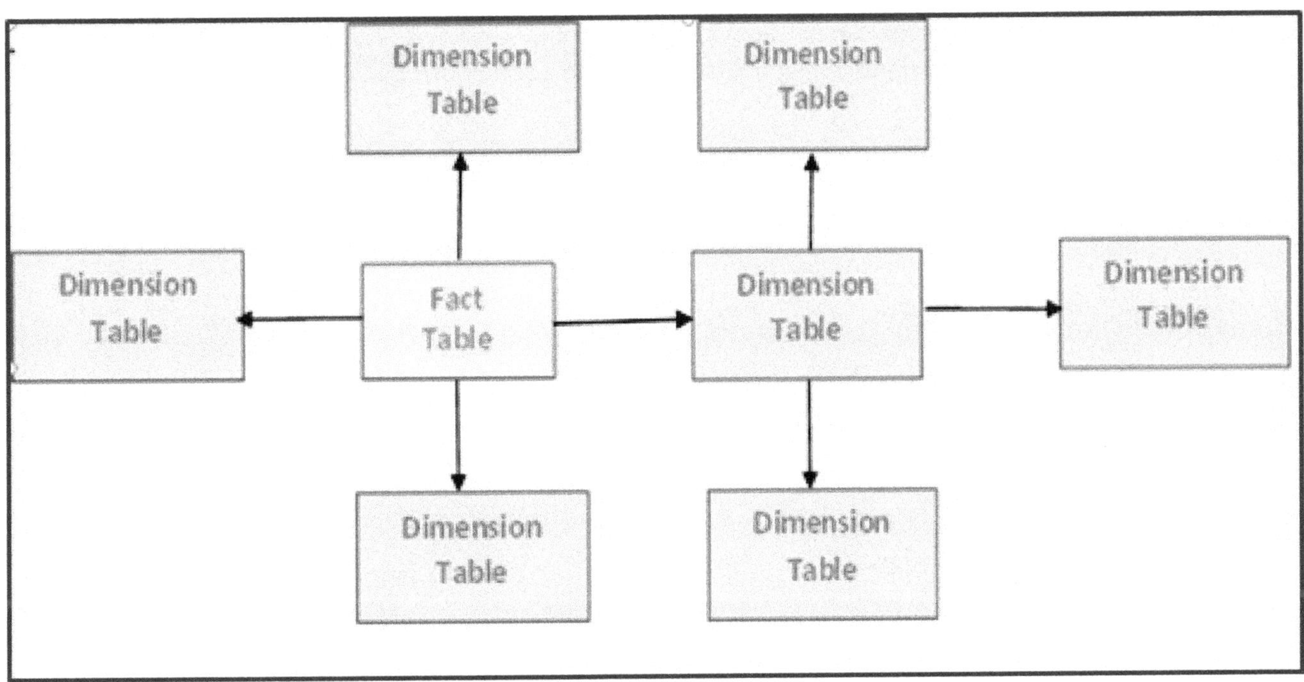

Figure 2.3 Snow Flake Schema Model

The resulting schema graph has a snowflake-like shape. For instance, the item and supplier dimension tables in the star schema are segregated from the item dimension table and normalized.

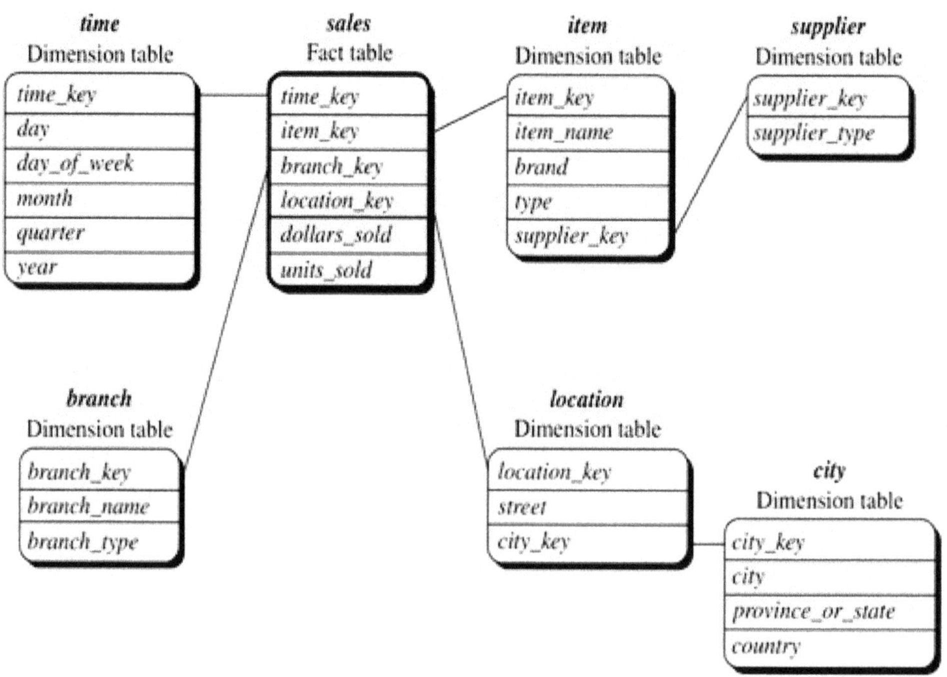

Figure 2.4 Snow Flake Schema Model

2.4.1.3 FactConstellation Schema

Since the Fact Constellation schema can be thought of as a group of stars, it is also known as a galaxy schema or fact constellation. Fact tables can share dimension tables thanks to a fact constellation schema.

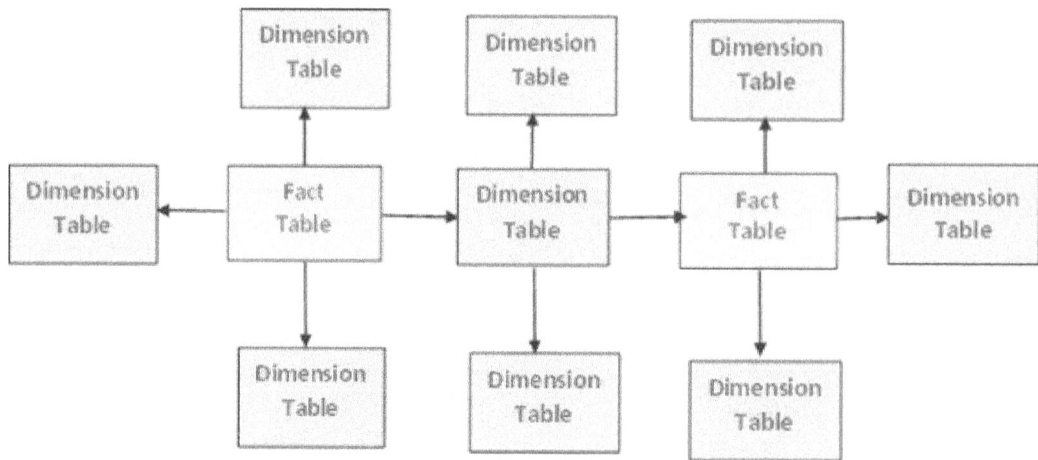

Figure 2.5 Fact Constellation Schema Model

The following schema, for instance, lists two fact tables: sales and shipping. The definition of the sales table and the star schema are both the same. The shipping table has two measures, dollars cost and units transported, as well as five dimensions, or keys: item key, time key, shipper key, from location, and to location.

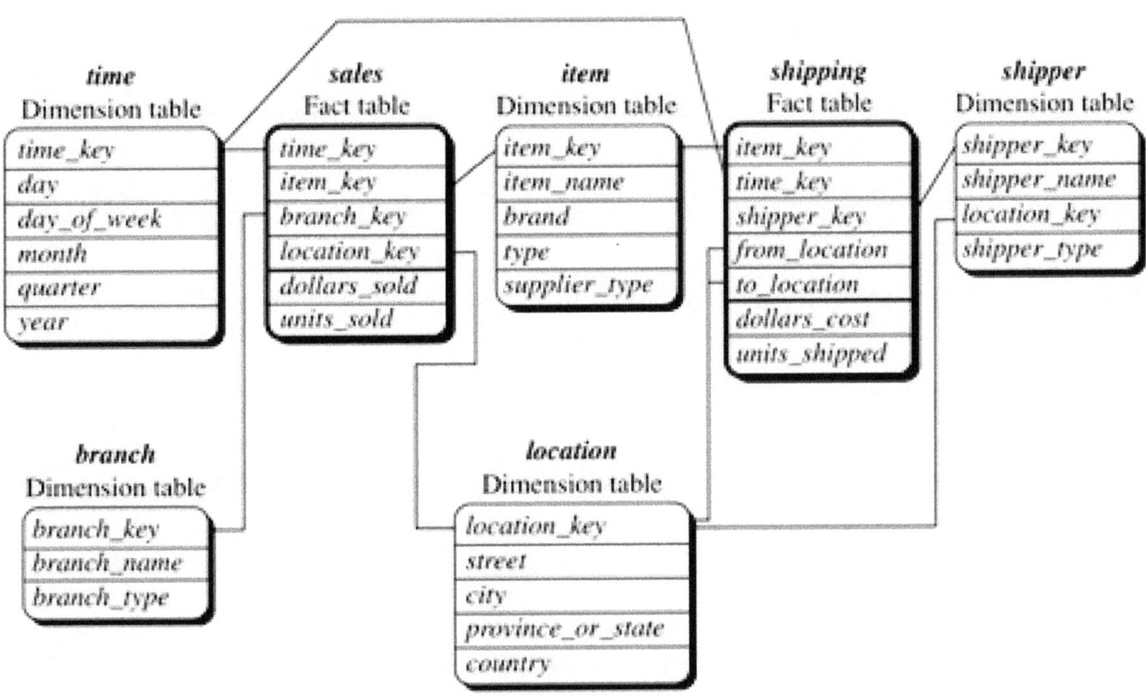

Figure 2.6 Fact Constellation Schema Example

2.5 How is the Data Warehouse different from Operational Database Systems

Dataware collect the data from multiple sources and transform the data using ETL process then load it to the Data Warehouse for business purpose. Operational Database are those databases where data changes frequently. They are mainly designed for high volume of data transaction

Comparing the well-known commercial relational database systems and data warehouse will give a better understanding of data warehouse.

Online transaction and query processing is the primary function of operational database systems. Online transaction processing (OLTP) systems are the name given to these systems. The majority of an organization's daily operations, including purchasing, inventories, production, banking, payroll, registration, and accounting, are covered by them. On the other side, data warehouse solutions assist users or knowledge workers with data analysis and decision-making. To meet the unique demands of many users, such systems can arrange and present data in a variety of forms. Online analytical processing (OLAP) systems are the name given to these systems.

The following is a summary of the key differences between OLTP and OLAP:

• ***Users and system orientation***

Clerks, clients, and IT specialists use an OLTP system, which is customer-oriented, to execute transactions and queries. Knowledge workers, like as managers, executives, and analysts, use an OLAP system, which is market-oriented, to analyse data.

• ***Data contents***

An OLTP system handles up-to-date information that is frequently too complex to be effectively used for decision-making. An OLAP system stores and manages data at various levels of granularity, offers options for summarization and aggregation, and manages vast amounts of historical data. The data is now simpler to use for making educated decisions thanks to these improvements.

• ***Database design***

An entity-relationship (ER) data model and an application-oriented database design are typically used in OLTP systems. A star or snowflake model and a subject-oriented database design are frequently used in an OLAP system.

• ***View***

An OLTP system ignores historical data or data from other organisations in favour of concentrating on the most recent data within a company or department. In contrast, an OLAP system frequently uses numerous database schema versions because of the organisational growth. By combining data from numerous data sources, OLAP systems also cope with information coming from various businesses. Data from OLAP are kept over a variety of storage mediums due to their enormous volume.

• ***Access Patterns***

Short, atomic transactions make up the majority of an OLTP system's access patterns. Concurrency control and recovery techniques are necessary for such a system. However, because most data warehouses store historical rather than current information, accesses to OLAP systems are typically read-only processes, even if many may be sophisticated queries.

2.6 Need for a Separate Data Warehouse

One might wonder, "Why not run online analytical processing directly on such databases instead of spending additional time and resources to establish a separate data warehouse," given how much data operational databases store. To support the excellent performance of both systems is one of the main justifications for such a separation.

An operational database is created and configured based on well-known workloads and tasks, such as primary key hashing and indexing, searching for specific records, and optimizing "canned" queries. On the other hand, data warehouse queries are frequently complex. They may call for the usage of unique data organization, access, and implementation approaches based on multidimensional perspectives and include the computation of massive data groupings at summary levels.

Operational tasks would perform significantly worse if OLAP queries were processed in operational databases. Additionally, a functional database allows for the simultaneous processing of numerous transactions. To guarantee the consistency and robustness of transactions, concurrency control and recovery techniques (such locking and logging) are necessary. In order to summarize and aggregate data records for an OLAP query, read-only access is frequently required. If used for these OLAP processes, concurrency control and recovery techniques may risk the execution of concurrent transactions and significantly lower an OLTP system's throughput. Last but not least, the distinction between operational databases and data warehouses is made on the basis of the various data structures, contents, and uses in these two systems. Operational databases often do not store historic data, whereas decision support applications do. Although operational databases include a lot of data in this regard, it is typically far from sufficient for making decisions.

Data from many sources must be combined for decision support (e.g., aggregated and summarized), producing high-quality, clear, integrated data. Operational databases, on the other hand, only hold specific raw data—such as transactions—that must be combined before examination.

Currently, separate databases must be maintained because the two systems offer very distinct functionality and require various types of data. To accommodate OLAP queries, many providers of operational relational database management systems are starting to enhance their products. The distance between OLTP and OLAP systems is anticipated to narrow as this trend keeps on.

Data Warehouse Systems serve users or knowledge workers for data analysis and decision-making. Such systems can construct and present data in a specific structure to accommodate the diverse requirement of several users. These systems are known as Online-Analytical Processing (OLAP) Systems.

OLTP and OLAP: The two terms look similar but refer to different kinds of systems. Online transaction processing (OLTP) captures, stores, and processes data from transactions in real time. Online analytical processing (OLAP) uses complex queries to analyze aggregated historical data from OLTP systems.

comparison of OLTP and OLAP is given in Table 2.1

Table 2.1 Comparison of OLTP and OLAP

Feature	OLTP	OLAP
Characteristic	*Operational Processing*	*Informational Processing*
Orientation	*Transaction*	*Analysis*
Users	*Clerk, DBA, Database professionals*	*Knowledge workers such as managers, executives, analysts*
Periodicity	*Day to day operations*	*Long-term informational requirements and decision support*
DB Design	*ER based, application-oriented*	*Star/Snowflake, subject-oriented*
Data	*Current, guaranteed up-to-date*	*Historic, accuracy maintained over time*
Summarization	*Primitive, highly detailed*	*Summarized, consolidated*
Metric	*Transaction throughput*	*Query throughput and response time*
Priority	*High performance, high availability*	*High flexibility, end-user autonomy*
DB Size	*GB to high order GB*	*=TB*
Number of Users	*Thousands*	*Hundreds*
Number of Records Accessed	*Tens*	*Millions*
Operations	*Index/Hash on primary key*	*Lots of scans*
Focus	*Data in*	*Information out*
Access	*Read/write*	*Mostly read*
Unit of Work	*Short, simple transaction*	*Complex query*
View	*Detailed, flat relational*	*Summarized, multidimensional*

2.7 Data Warehouse Architectures

The complete design of data processing, communication, and presentation for end-user computing within the organisation can be specified using a data warehouse architecture. Each data warehouse has its own unique characteristics, but they all have a few key things in common.

Every day, every business conducts business related to its goods or services, necessitating the processing of online transactions (OLTP). These programmes use routine processes to gather specific data.

User-specific data requirements, or what is now referred to as "online analytical processing," are accommodated via applications for data warehouses (OLAP). This group of applications includes forecasting, profiling, summary reporting, and trend analysis.

Daily operations/transaction-related databases are routinely updated either manually or by OLTP software. A warehouse database, in contrast, gets regular updates from operating systems, usually after business hours. As OLTP data accumulates in production databases, it is frequently collected, filtered, and placed into a dedicated warehouse server that is accessible to users. Data must be cleaned of errors and duplicates as the warehouse fills with data, and new fields and keys must be added to represent the user's requirements for sorting, combining, and averaging data.

The basic types of data warehouse architectures used are listed below:

i. ***Single-tier architecture***

The objective of a single layer architecture is to minimize the amount of data stored. The goal is to remove data redundancy. This architecture is not frequently used in practice.

i. ***Two-tier architecture***

Physically accessible sources and the data warehouse are separated in a two-layer design. This architecture can't be expanded and can't accommodate a lot of end users. It also has connectivity problems because of network limitations.

iii. ***Three-tier architecture***

This is the most widely used architecture. The Top, Middle, and Bottom Tiers make up this hierarchy. A brief discussion of these tiers are given below.

Bottom Tier

The servers hosting the data warehouse's database act as the bottom tier. Usually, a relational database system is used. Using back-end technologies, data is purified, altered, and put into this layer.

Middle-Tier

An OLAP server that is implemented using the ROLAP or MOLAP model serves as the data warehouse's middle tier. This application layer displays an abstracted view of the database to the user. Additionally, this layer serves as a liaison between the database and the end user.

Top-Tier

A front-end client layer makes up the top tier. It consists of the tools and API that is used to connect to, in order to extract data from the data warehouse.

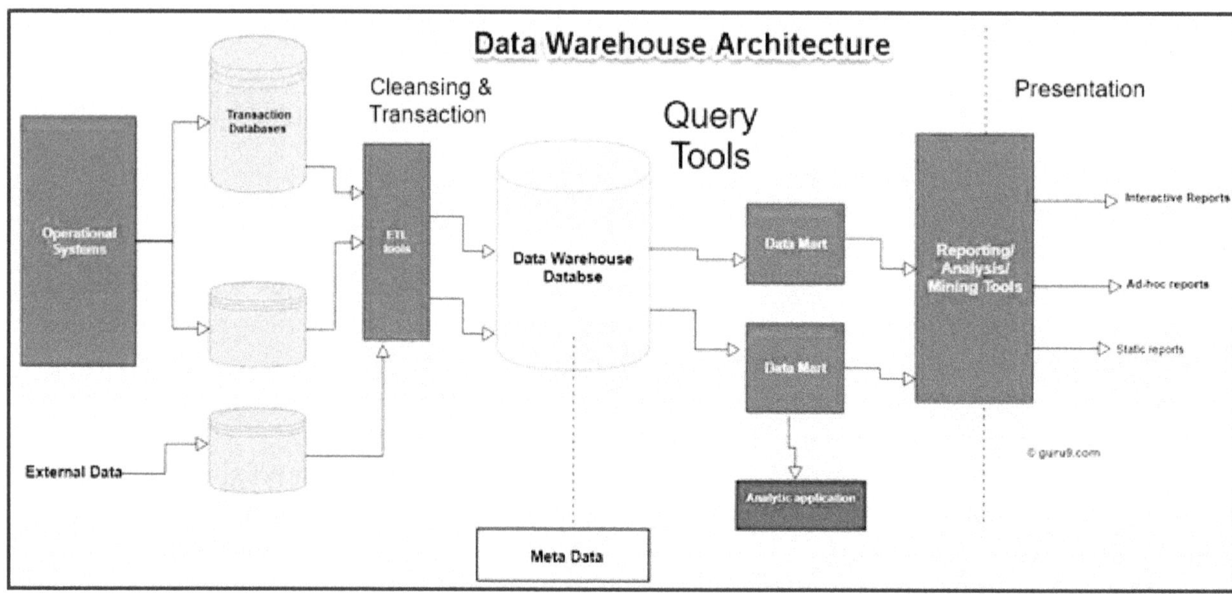

Figure 2.7 Data warehouse Components

From the architecture point of view, there are three data warehouse models:

- the enterprise warehouse
- the data mart
- the virtual warehouse

Enterprise warehouse

Throughout the whole organisation, all of the data is gathered in an enterprise warehouse. Cross-functional in nature, it offers corporate-wide data integration, typically from one or more operational systems or external information suppliers.

It typically contains both extensive and summary information, and its size can range from a few gigabytes to hundreds of gigabytes, terabytes, or even more.

Data mart

A subset of corporate-wide data that is useful to a particular user base is contained in a data mart. The focus is on particular, hand-picked topics. A marketing data mart, for instance, might link its subjects to customers, products, and sales. In data marts, the data is typically summarised.

Data marts can be divided into the following two kinds according to the data source:

(i) Independent data marts draw their data from a variety of operating systems, outside information sources, locally created information within a given department or region, or both.

(ii) Enterprise data warehouses serve as the direct source of dependent data marts.

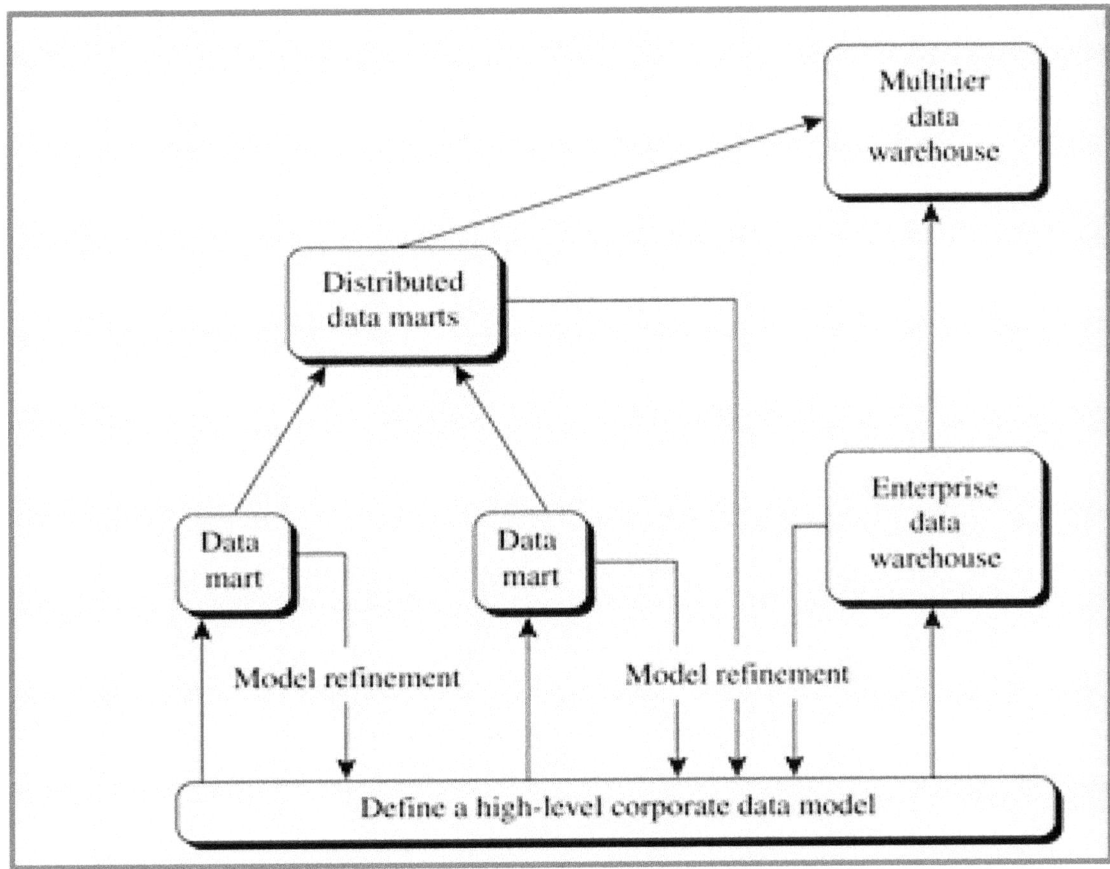

Figure 2.8 A recommended approach for Data warehouse Development

Virtual Warehouse

Virtual warehouses are collections of views over live databases. Only a few of the potential summary views may materialize in order to handle queries efficiently. It is simple to create a virtual warehouse, but this requires extra space on active database servers.

As seen in Figure 2.8, implementing the warehouse in an incremental and evolutionary fashion is a suggested approach for the development of data warehouse systems.

In the first step, a high-level corporate data model is created in a reasonable amount of time (say, one or two months), providing a corporate-wide, unified view of data across many themes and prospective applications. Although this high-level model will need to be improved if departmental data marts and enterprise data warehouses are developed further, it will significantly lessen integration issues in the future. Second, independent data marts based on the same corporate data model set mentioned earlier can be deployed concurrently with the enterprise warehouse. Third, hub servers can be used to connect distributed data marts, which can combine various data marts. The enterprise warehouse serves as the only custodian of all warehouse data and distributes it to the many dependent data marts in a multitier data warehouse that has been built.

2.8 Types of OLAP Servers

Multi-dimensional analytical (MDA) queries can be quickly resolved using the OLAP method. OLAP is a subset of the broader field of business intelligence, which also includes data mining, relational databases, and report creation. Users of OLAP systems can interactively and from various angles analyse multidimensional data. Users can remove (slice) a particular group of data using the feature known as "slicing and dicing."

OLAP Servers can be mainly categorized as follows:

- Relational OLAP (ROLAP)
- Multidimensional OLAP (MOLAP)
- Hybrid OLAP (HOLAP)
- Other Types of OLAP Servers

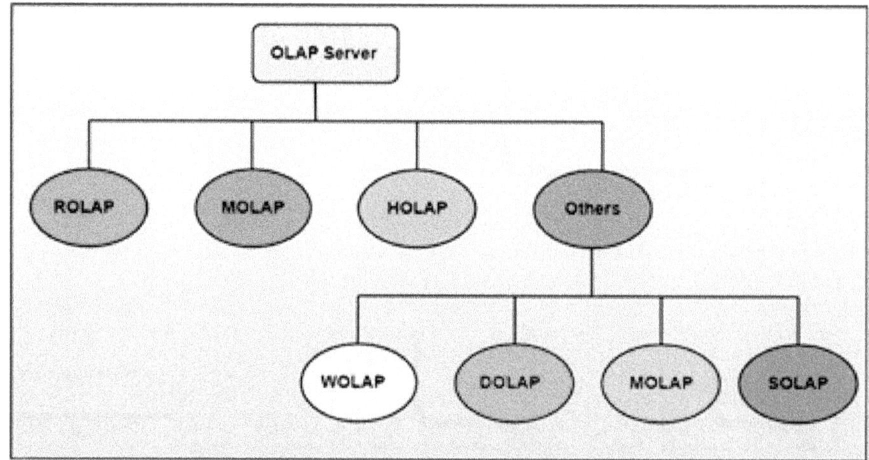

Figure 2.9 Types of OLAP Servers

OLAP consists of three basic analytical operations:

- Consolidation (Roll-Up)
- Drill-Down
- Slicing And Dicing

Aggregating data that can be processed and aggregated in one or more dimensions is what consolidation entails. For instance, to forecast sales trends, all sales offices are rolled up into the sales department or sales division. Users can browse through the details using a method called "drill-down." For example, users can view the sales of certain products that make up a region's sales.

Slicing and dicing is a feature which allows users to remove (slice) a specific set of data of the OLAP cube and view (dicing) the slices from different viewpoints.

2.8.1 Relational OLAP (ROLAP)

Relational databases and ROLAP are directly compatible. New relational tables are constructed to retain the aggregated data when the base data and dimension tables are stored. It is dependent on a unique schema design. To mimic the slicing and dicing capabilities of standard OLAP, ROLAP relies on modifying the data kept in the relational database. Slice and dice operations are essentially identical to adding a "WHERE" clause to a SQL statement. ROLAP tools query the regular relational database and its tables to retrieve the data needed to answer the question rather than using pre-calculated data cubes. Since this technique is not limited to the contents of the cube, ROLAP tools feature the ability to ask any question. ROLAP also has the capacity to delve into the database's most minute degree of information.

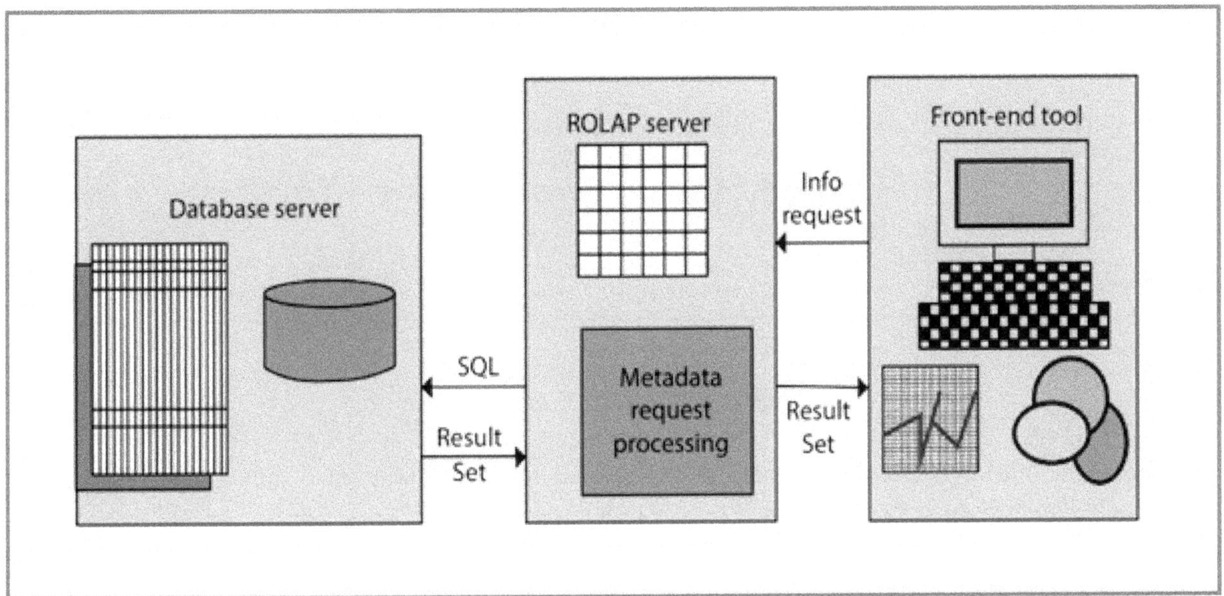

Figure 2.10 ROLAP Architecture

Advantages

- **Ability to Handle Large Volumes of Data:** The ROLAP technology's data size restriction is based on the data capacity of the underlying RDBMS. ROLAP itself does not place a limit on the volume of data.

- **RDBMS already comes with a lot of features.** Therefore, these functionalities are under the control of ROLAP technologies, which sit on top of the RDBMS.

Disadvantages

- **Performance may be Slow**: Each ROLAP report is a SQL query (or a series of SQL queries) in a relational database, and if the underlying data is large, the query time may be prolonged.

- **SQL Functions Limit ROLAP Technology:** SQL statements are used to query a relational database, and SQL statements do not meet all needs.

2.8.2 Multidimensional OLAP (MOLAP)

MOLAP, which is commonly referred to as just OLAP, is the "traditional" variant of OLAP. Instead of storing this data in a relational database, MOLAP saves it in an efficient multi-dimensional array storage. Processing is therefore required, which is the pre-computation and storage of data in the cube. A data cube, which is a pre-calculated data set, is typically used by MOLAP tools.

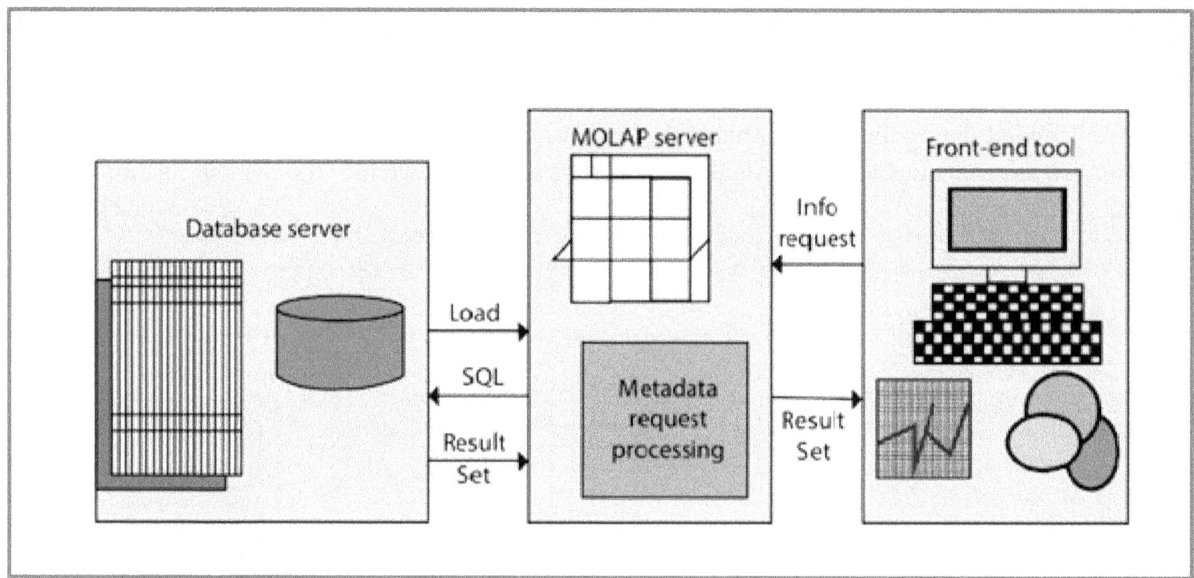

Figure 2.11 MOLAP Architecture

The data cube includes every response that could be given to a particular set of questions. MOLAP tools may swiftly write back data into the data set and have a very quick reaction time.

Advantages

- **Outstanding Performance**: MOLAP cubes are made for speedy data retrieval and are perfect for tasks like slicing and dicing.
- **Capable of Complex Computations:** All evaluations are pre-generated when the cube is built. As a result, complex calculations are not only feasible but also quickly return.

Disadvantages

- **It Can Handle a Limited Amount of Data:** Since all calculations must be completed at the time the cube is generated, a significant amount of data cannot be stored in the cube itself.

- **Why More Capital Is Needed:** Cube technology is typically proprietary and not in use within the organisation. As a result, it is expected that more financial and human resources will be needed to implement MOLAP technology.

2.8.3 Hybrid OLAP (HOLAP)

An application that combines relational and multidimensional techniques is called HOLAP, or Hybrid OLAP Model.

The best features of MOLAP and ROLAP are combined into one architecture called HOLAP. Other than the fact that a database will split data between relational and specialised storage, there is no clear consensus within the industry as to what exactly qualifies as hybrid OLAP. For certain vendors, a HOLAP database might, for the larger amounts of comprehensive data, employ relational tables and, for the lower quantities of more-aggregate or less-detailed data, use specialised storage, at least in part. By integrating the strengths of the two methodologies, HOLAP tackles the drawbacks of MOLAP and ROLAP. Both relational data sources and pre-calculated cubes can be used with HOLAP tools. HOLAP may drill down from the cube to the relational tables for defined data. Microsoft SQL Server 2000 offers an OLAP paradigm that is a combination of the two.

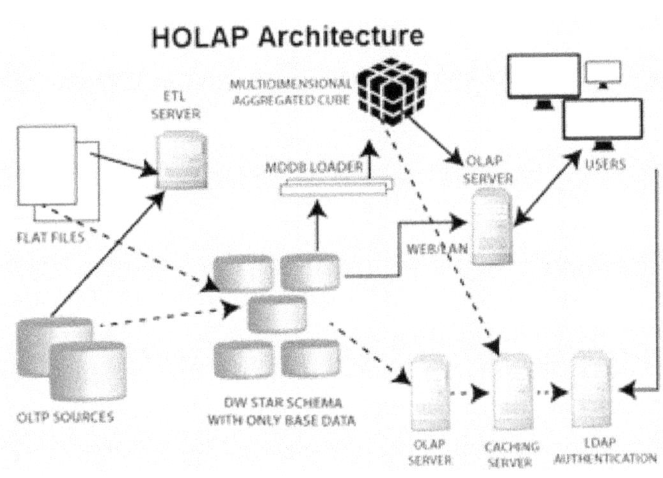

Figure 2.12 HOLAP Architecture

Advantages

- HOLAP combines the benefits of MOLAP and ROLAP.
- It offers quick access at all aggregate levels.
- HOLAP lowers the amount of disc space needed by storing only the aggregate data on the OLAP models and maintaining the detail records in the relational database. As a result, the detail record is not retained in duplicate.

Disadvantages

- The fact that HOLAP architecture supports both MOLAP and ROLAP models adds to its complexity.

2.8.4 Other Types of OLAP Servers

Additionally, there are several OLAP styles that are less common that one could occasionally run into. The following list includes some of the less well-known OLAP server names.

Web-Enabled OLAP (WOLAP) Server

WOLAP relates to OLAP software that is accessed online through a web browser. Contrary to conventional client/server OLAP systems, WOLAP is thought to feature a three-tiered architecture made up of a client, middleware, and database server.

Desktop OLAP (DOLAP) Server

With DOLAP, a user is able to download a subset of the data from the source or database and manipulate it on their desktop or local computer.

Mobile OLAP Server

Mobile OLAP allows users to remotely view and work on OLAP data and applications using their mobile devices.

Spatial OLAP (SOLAP) Server

SOLAP combines OLAP and Geographic Information Systems (GIS) functionality into a single user interface. Both spatial and non-spatial data management are made easier by it.

2.9 Data Warehouse Components

The RDBMS server, which serves as the foundation for the data warehouse, is a primary information repository that is surrounded by a few essential elements that help to keep the environment functioning, managed, and accessible. The Data warehouse primarily consists of the following five components:

- Data Warehouse Database
- Sourcing, Acquisition, Clean-up and Transformation Tools (ETL)
- Metadata
- Query Tools
- Data warehouse Bus Architecture

2.9.1 Data Warehouse Database

The central database serves as the cornerstone of the data warehousing infrastructure. This database uses Relational Data Base Management Systems (RDBMS) technology in its implementation. However, this type of implementation is limited by the fact that standard RDBMS systems are designed for processing transactional databases rather than storing data. Ad hoc queries, multi-table joins, and aggregates, for example, are resource-intensive and affect performance.

As a result, the following different database approaches are employed:

• Relational databases are set up concurrently in a data warehouse to support scalability. On some multiprocessor architectures or massively parallel processors, parallel relational databases also support shared memory or the shared nothing paradigm.

• New index structures are employed to accelerate speed and avoid relational table scan.

• Using multidimensional databases (MDDB) to get beyond any restrictions imposed by the relational data model Essbase from Oracle, for instance.

2.9.2 Sourcing, Acquisition, Clean-up and Transformation Tools (ETL)

To turn data into a consistent format for the data warehouse, all conversions, summarizations, and other changes must be made using the data source, transformation, and migration tools. Alternatively, they are known as Extract, Transform, and Load (ETL) Tools.

These tools are capable of carrying out the following functionalities.

- Anonymize data in accordance with legal requirements.
- Removing unnecessary data from operational databases before it is loaded into the data warehouse.
- For data coming from many sources, look up and replace common names and definitions.
- Generating summary statistics and generated data
- Fill in the blanks if there are any missing data
- Repeating data that has been de-duplicated and is coming from many sources.

These Extract, Transform, and Load tools may produce background jobs, COBOL programmes, shell scripts, cron jobs, and other tasks that routinely update data in the data warehouse. The issues posed by heterogeneous databases and data must be addressed by these ETL tools.

2.9.3 Metadata

Metadata is a moniker that hints to some advanced technological Data Warehousing Concepts. But it's really fairly easy. Data about data, or metadata, is what makes up a data warehouse. It is employed in the creation, upkeep, and administration of the data warehouse.

As it describes the origin, purpose, values, and characteristics of data warehouse data, meta-data is crucial to the Data Warehouse Architecture. Additionally, it describes the alterations and processing of data. It has a strong relationship with the data warehouse.

For example, an entry in the database which has the following details

4201 AB786 199.8

will be meaningless, until we check the metadata that tell us that the above data is related to the Model number, Marketing Agent ID and the Total Sales Amount in $ respectively.

Hence, metadata are essential components in the transformation of data into knowledge. It helps us to find solutions for questions such as listed below.

- What tables, fields, and keys a data warehouse contains?
- Where did the information originate?
- How frequently is data reloaded?
- What adjustments were made with cleansing?

Metadata can be divided into the following two categories:

Technical Metadata

Data warehouse designers and administrators use this type of Metadata to store information about the warehouse.

Business Metadata

This category of Metadata comprises information that enables end users to easily interpret the data warehouse's stored information.

2.9.4 Query Tools

The main objective of data warehouse is to give organizations the information they need to make strategic decisions. Users can communicate with the data warehouse system via query tools. These query tools can be divided into four groups:

i. Query and Reporting Tools
ii. Application Development Tools
iii. Data Mining Tools
iv. OLAP tools

2.9.4.1 Query and Reporting Tools

Reporting tools are a subset of query and reporting tools which can be further classified as follows:

- Reporting tools
- Managed query tools

2.9.4.1.1 Reporting tools

The reporting tools are further classified into Production reporting tools and desktop report writer.

- Report writer are tools which are designed for end-users for analysis.
- Production reporting tools allows organizations in generating regular operational reports. Additionally, it allows large-scale batch tasks like printing and computation. Brio, Business Objects, Oracle, PowerSoft, SAS Institute are some of the popular reporting tools.

2.9.4.1.2 Managed Query Tools

By adding a meta-layer between users and the database, these access tools assist end users in resolving SQL and database structure issues. Managed query tools place a metalayer between users and the database to protect end users from the complexity of SQL and database structures. The metalayer is the software that provides subject-oriented views of a database and supports point-and-click creation of SQL.

2.9.4.2 Application development tools

Integrated graphical and analytical tools may occasionally fall short of an organization's analytical requirements. In these situations, application development tools are used to create custom reports.

2.9.4.3 Data mining tools

Data mining is the process of looking through a vast amount of data to find new correlations, patterns, and trends that are significant. This process is automated using data mining techniques.

2.9.4.4 OLAP tools

Multidimensional databases serve as the foundation for these tools. Users can use extensive and intricate multidimensional perspectives to analyse the data.

2.9.5 Data warehouse Bus Architecture

The data flow in a warehouse is controlled by the data warehouse bus. Inflow, Upflow, Downflow, Outflow, and Meta flow are different types of data flow that can occur in a data warehouse.

The shared dimensions and facts between data marts must be taken into account while creating a data bus.

Data Marts

An access layer called a data mart is used to distribute data to users. It is suggested as a choice for large data warehouses because it is less expensive and time-consuming to construct. The definition of a data mart, however, varies from person to person and is not universal.

A data mart is, to put it simply, a division of a data warehouse. The data mart is utilised to partition the created data among a specific group of users. Data marts could be created in the same database as the Data warehouse or a physically separate Database.

2.10 Data Warehouse Architecture Best Practices

To design Data Warehouse Architecture, the following best practices need to be followed.

- Utilize data warehouse models that are dimensional, denormalized, or hybrid and are designed for information retrieval.
- Select the suitable top-down or bottom-up designing strategy for the data warehouse.
- Data processing speed and accuracy must be ensured. A strategy that compiles data into a single version of the truth at the same time should be used.
- Create the data warehouse's data collecting and cleansing process with care.
- Create a metadata architecture that enables metadata sharing across Data Warehouse components.
- When the demand for information retrieval is towards the base of the data abstraction pyramid or when several operational sources must be accessed, think about developing an Operational Data Store (ODS) model.

2.11 OLAP Operations

The data in the multidimensional model are divided into different dimensions, and each dimension has numerous levels of abstraction that are described by idea hierarchies. This organisation offers people the freedom to see data from a wide range of views. There are several OLAP data cube operations available to illustrate these various views, enabling interactive queries and search of the relevant record. As a result, OLAP enables an environment that is user-friendly for interactive data analysis. Consider about the OLAP operations that need to be run on the multidimensional data. Data cubes for a shop's sales are shown in the figure. The dimensions, location, time, and object are all represented in the cube.

Online Analytical Processing is based on the multidimensional data model that allow user to extract and view data from different points of view. OLAP data stored in multidimensional data. Since OLAP servers are based on multidimensional view of data, a discussion of OLAP operations is done with respect to multidimensional data. The list of OLAP Operations are given below.

- Roll-up
- Drill-down

- Slice and dice
- Pivot (rotate)

Let us recall the definition of Concept Hierarchy to have a better understanding of the OLAP operations.

Concept hierarchy defines a sequence of mappings from a set of low level Concepts to higher level, more general Concepts. Concept hierarchies allow data to be handled at varying levels of abstraction

2.11.1 Roll-up

Roll-up performs aggregation on a data cube in any of the following ways.

- By climbing up a concept hierarchy for a dimension
- By dimension reduction

The figure 2.13 illustrates how roll-up works.

- Roll-up is performed by climbing up a concept hierarchy for the dimension location.
- Initially the concept hierarchy was "street < city < province < country".
- On rolling up, the data is aggregated by ascending the location hierarchy from the level of city to the level of country.
- The data is grouped into cities rather than countries.

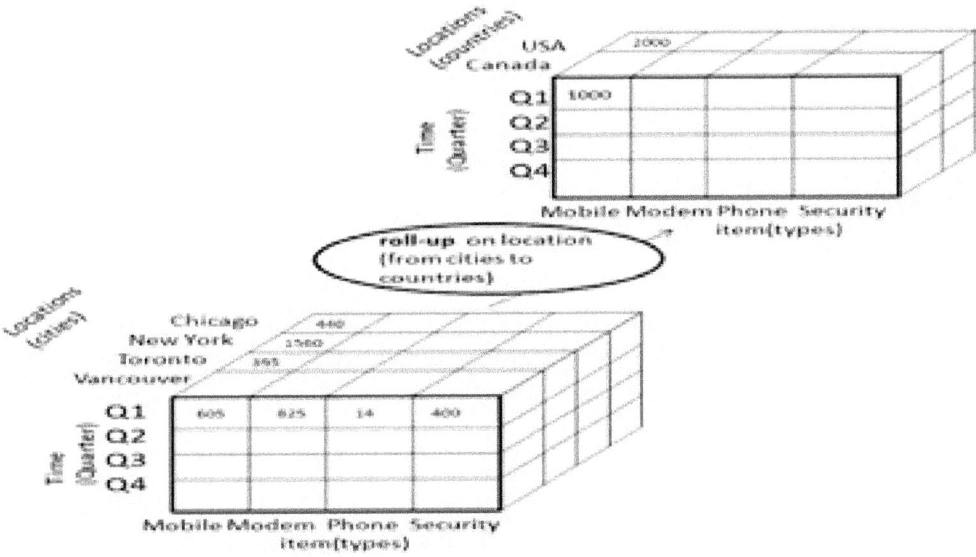

Figure 2.13 Roll-up Operation on Multidimensional data

When roll-up is performed, one or more dimensions from the data cube are removed.

2.11.2 Drill-down

The drill-down operation (also called roll-down) is the reverse operation of roll-up. Drill-down is like zooming-in on the data cube. It navigates from less detailed record to more detailed data. Drill-down can be performed by either stepping down a concept hierarchy for a dimension or adding additional dimensions.

It is performed by either of the following ways:

- By stepping down a concept hierarchy for a dimension
- By introducing a new dimension.

Drill-down is performed by stepping down a concept hierarchy for the dimension time. The figure 2.14 illustrates how drill-down works.

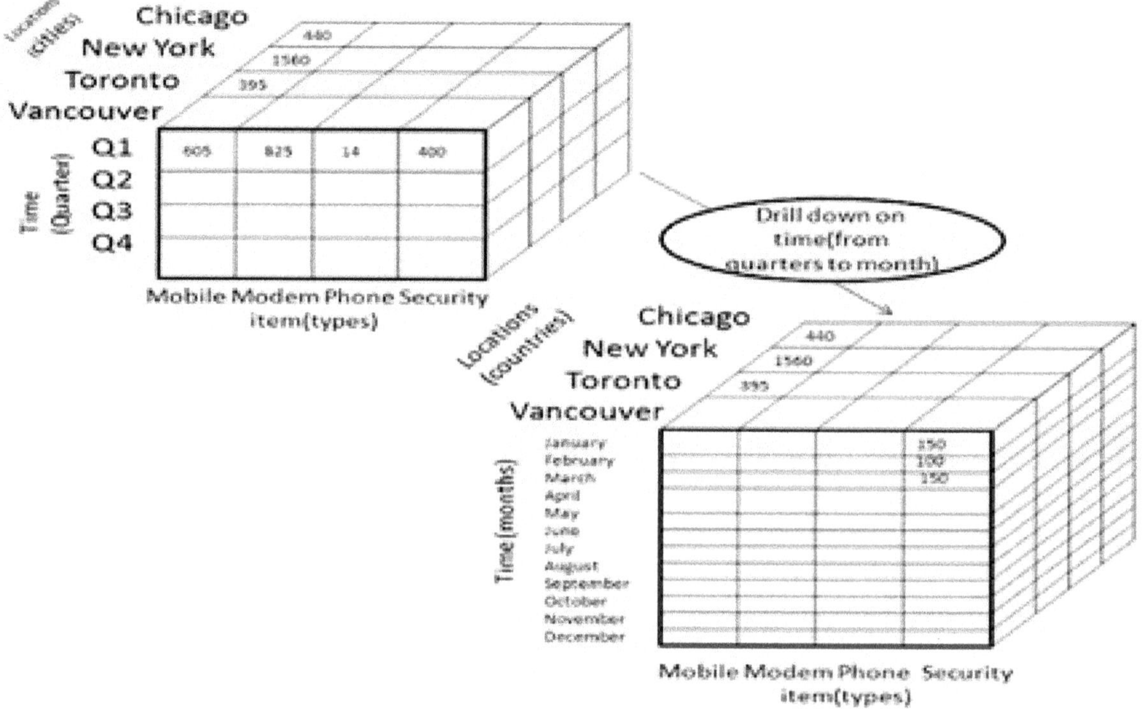

Figure 2.14 Drill-Down Operation on Multidimensional data

- Initially the concept hierarchy was "day < month < quarter < year."
- On drilling down, the time dimension is descended from the level of quarter to the level of month.
- When drill-down is performed, one or more dimensions from the data cube are added.
- It navigates the data from less detailed data to highly detailed data.

2.11.3 Slice

The slice operation selects one particular dimension from a given cube and provides a new sub-cube.

A slice is a subset of the cubes that represent one particular value for one or more dimension members. For instance, a slice operation is used to create a two-dimensional site when a consumer wants to select only one side of a three-dimensional cube. In order to create a subcube, the Slice procedures make a pick on one dimension of the provided cube. Consider the figure 2.15 that shows how slice works.

- Here Slice is performed for the dimension "time" using the criterion time
- It will form a new sub-cube by selecting one or more dimensions.

2.11.4 Dice

Dice selects two or more dimensions from a given cube and provides a new sub- cube. It selects a sub-cube from the OLAP cube by selecting two or more dimensions.

Consider the figure 2.16 that shows the dice operation.

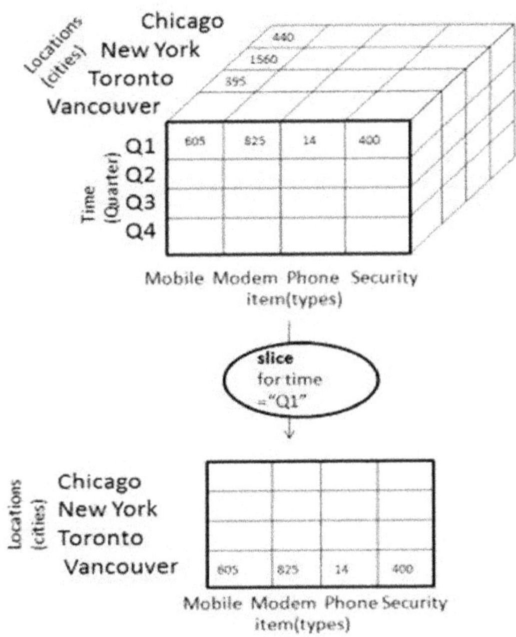

Figure 2.15 Slice Operation on Multidimensional data

The dice operation on the cubes based on the following selection criteria involves three dimensions.
(location = "Toronto" or "Vancouver")
(time = "Q1" or "Q2")
(item =" Mobile" or "Modem")

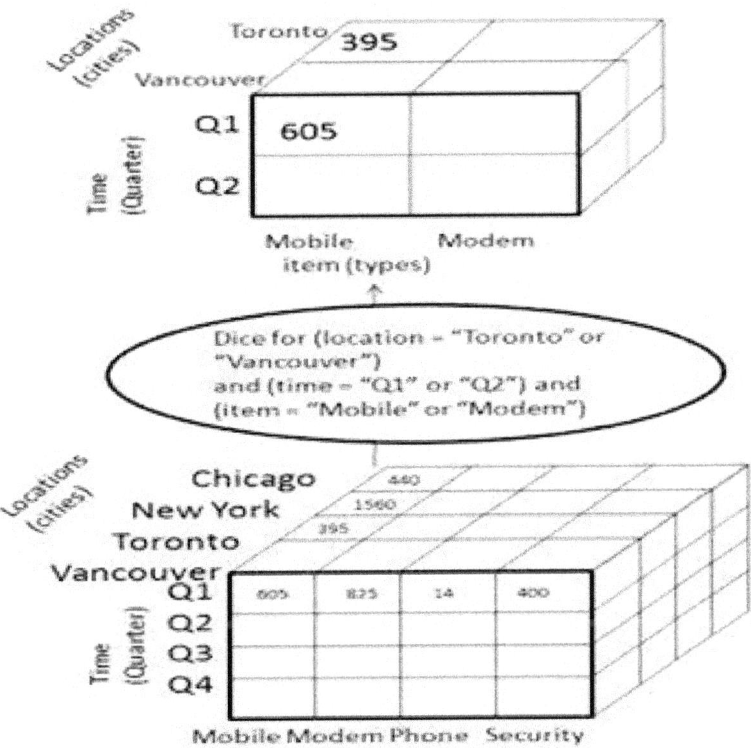

Figure 2.16 Dice Operation on Multidimensional data

2.11.5 Pivot

The pivot operation is also known as rotation. It rotates the data axes in view in order to provide an alternative presentation of data. Consider the figure 2.17 that shows the pivot operation.

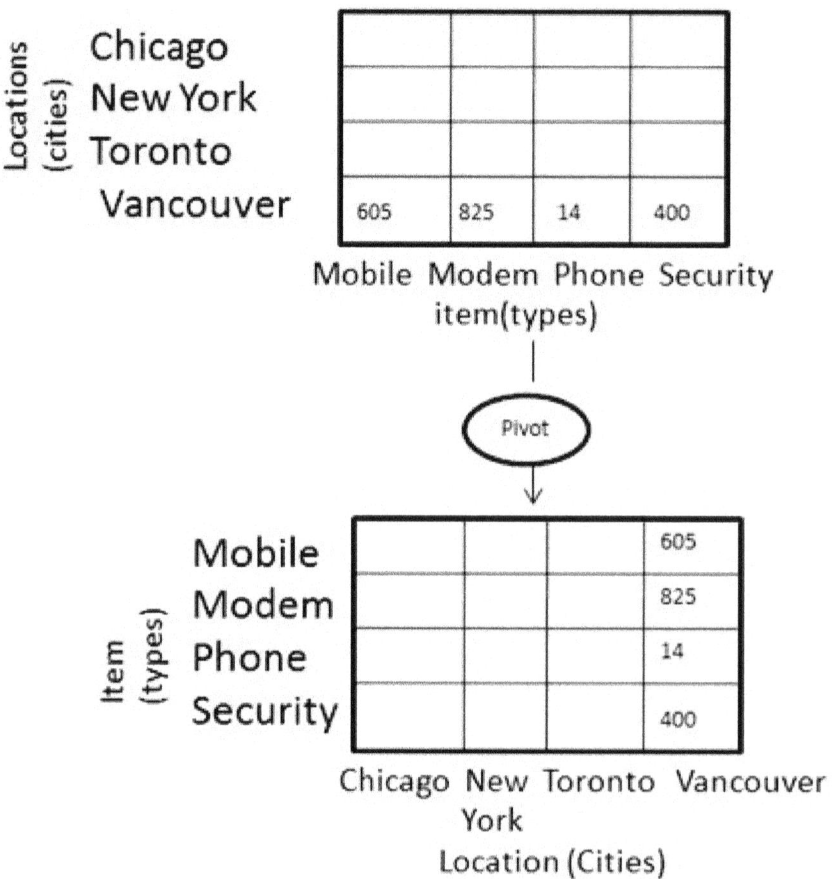

Figure 2.17 Pivot Operation on Multidimensional data

2.12 Data Warehouse Architecture Implementation

The data warehouse stores data from a variety of systems in one centralized location. There are several mission-critical systems in a typical business. The system might include a CRM, ERP, e-commerce system, or marketing automation platform. Data from all of these systems is stored in a relational database. The data warehouse stores data from a variety of systems in one centralized location.

Data is one of an organization's most precious resources, thus it is essential to know how to preserve it and get insightful information from it. Organizations must now develop a strategy for effectively storing, processing, and analysing the data due to a sharp rise in the volume of data being produced. In order to use data cubes for business intelligence and reporting, organisations frequently battle with the choice of building a data warehouse (or even a cloud data warehouse, which gives even more benefits).

Data warehouses will host the enormous data that needs to be handled, processed, and gleaned for insights.

A multidimensional structure used to store data is called a "data cube" in a data warehouse. OLAP technologies, which could quickly access the multidimensional data, were originally intended to use the data cube. However, data mining can also make advantage of the data cube. These warehouses are operated by OLAP servers, which demand quick query processing. Therefore, extremely effective cube computation algorithms, access methods, and query processing techniques should be required for a data warehouse.

The effective computing of aggregations across numerous sets of dimensions is the basis of multidimensional data analysis.

The implementation of a data warehouse must include the efficient computation of data cubes. A lattice of cuboids can be used to visualize a data cube. Aggregations are known as group-in by's SQL. A cuboid can be used to symbolize each group-by. A set of group-bys creates a cuboid lattice that defines a data cube.

The compute cube operator performs aggregate computations across all subsets of the provided dimensions. This can need a lot of storage space, especially if there are many different measurements.

A data cube is a lattice of cuboids

Let's say you want to build a data cube for DigitalElectronics sales that includes the data for the city, the item, the year, and the sales in dollars. You want to be able to use queries like the ones below to assess the data:

- *"Compute the sum of sales, grouping by city and item."*
- *"Compute the sum of sales, grouping by city."*
- *"Compute the sum of sales, grouping by item."*

What is the maximum number of group-bys or cuboids that this data cube can support? The total number of cuboids, or group-bys, that can be computed for this data cube is $2^3 = 8$, taking the three characteristics city, item, and year as the dimensions for the data cube and sales in dollars as the measure. The following group-by combinations are feasible: (city, item, year), (city, year), (item, year), (city), (item), (year), () where () denotes an empty group-by (i.e., the dimensions are not grouped). As seen in Figure 2.7, these group-bys create a lattice of cuboids for the data cube.

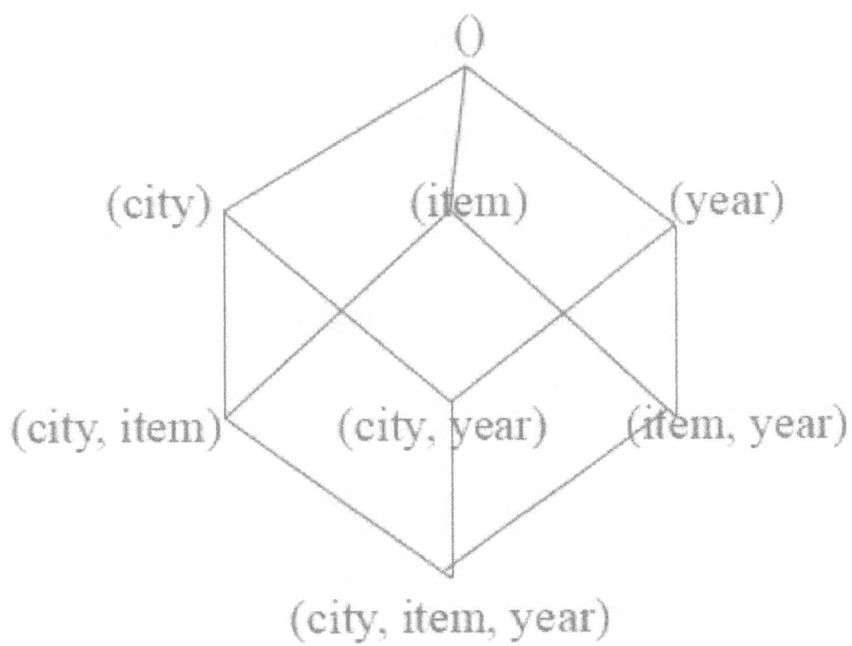

Figure 2.18 Lattice of cuboids, making up a 3-D data cube.

City, item, and year are the three dimensions that are present in the base cuboid. Any three-dimensional combination can have the total sales returned. When the group-by is empty, the situation is referred to as the apex cuboid, or 0-D cuboid. The aggregate of all sales is included. Of all the cuboids, the basic cuboid is the least general (yet most specific). The apex cuboid, which is frequently referred to as all, is the most universal (least specialised) of the cuboids. Drilling down into the data cube is accomplished by starting at the apex cuboid and navigating downward through the lattice. Starting at the bottom cuboid and working our way up is similar to rolling up.

The SQL query "calculate the sum of total sales" is an example of a zero-dimensional operation. Compute the sum of sales, group by city, for example, is a one-dimensional action in a SQL query. A group of group-by statements, one for each subset of the n dimensions, is equivalent to a cube operator on n dimensions. As a result, the cube operator is the group-by operator's n-dimensional generalization.

Similar to the SQL syntax, the data cube could be defined as

define cube sales_cube [city, item, year]:

sum(sales_in_dollars)

For a cube with n dimensions, there are a total of 2^n cuboids, including the base cuboid. A statement such as

compute cube sales_cube

would specifically tell the computer to calculate the sales aggregate cuboids for each of the set's eight subsets, city, item, and year, including the empty subset.

For various inquiries, online analytical processing may require to access several cuboids. Therefore, it could seem wise to compute all or at least some of the cuboids in a data cube in advance. Pre calculation speeds up reaction times and reduces the need for certain unnecessary processing. The majority of OLAP products, if not all of them, pre calculate multidimensional aggregates to some extent.

A significant issue with this precomputation, though, is that if all the cuboids in a data cube are precomputed, especially if the cube has several dimensions, the needed storage space may expand. When many of the dimensions have linked concept hierarchies, each with multiple levels, the storage needs become even more prohibitive. The term "curse of dimensionality" is used to describe this issue. This shows how severe the dimensionality curse is.

In an n-dimensional data cube, how many cuboids are there? We have seen that the total number of cuboids for an n-dimensional data cube is 2^n if there are no hierarchies connected to any of the dimensions. In actuality, though, many dimensions actually have hierarchies. For instance, time is typically investigated at numerous conceptual levels, such as "day month quarter year," as opposed to just one mental level (e.g., year). The total number of cuboids for an n-dimensional data cube that can be produced, including the cuboids produced by ascending the hierarchies along each dimension, is where Li is the dimension i's associated level count. To include the fictitious top level, all, one is added to Li in the example presented above. (Remember that applying a generalisation to everyone results in the dimension being removed.)

$$\text{Total number of cuboids} = \prod_{i=1}^{n}(L_i + 1)$$

This formula is based on the observation that a cuboid will have a maximum of one abstraction level in each dimension. For instance, the previously mentioned time dimension has four conceptual levels, or five if we count the virtual level. The total number of cuboids that can be produced if the cube has 10 dimensions and each dimension has 5 levels (including all of them) is $5^{10} \approx 9.8 \times 10^6$.The cardinality, or number of different values, of each dimension affects each cuboid's size.

The amount of storage space needed for many of the group-by operations will significantly surpass the (fixed) size of the input relation as the number of dimensions, conceptual hierarchies, or cardinality increases.

It would have been clearly figured out by now that it's not realistic to precompute and materialise every cuboids that may potentially be produced for a data cube (i.e., from a base cuboid). Partial materialisation, or materialising only some of the various cuboids that can be formed, is a more logical alternative when there are numerous cuboids and these cuboids are huge in size.

You've undoubtedly figured out by now that it's not realistic to precompute and materialise every cuboids that may potentially be produced for a data cube (i.e., from a base cuboid). Partial materialisation, or materialising only some of the various cuboids that can be formed, is a more logical alternative when there are numerous cuboids and these cuboids are huge in size.

Given a base cuboid, there are three options for materialising a data cube.

There are three choices for data cube materialization given a base cuboid:

- **No materialization:** Do not precompute any of the "nonbase" cuboids. This leads to computing expensive multidimensional aggregates on the fly, which can be extremely slow.
- **Full materialization:** Precompute all of the cuboids. The resulting lattice of computed cuboids is referred to as the full cube. This choice typically requires huge amounts of memory space in order to store all of the precomputed cuboids.
- **Partial materialization:** Selectively compute a proper subset of the whole set of possible Cuboids Partial materialization represents an interesting trade-off between storage space and response time.

The following steps are followed in adapting the type of materialization

- Identify the subsets of cuboids or subcubes to materialize.
- Exploit the materialized cuboids or subcubes during query processing.
- Efficiently update the materialized cuboids or subcubes during load and refresh.

The selection of cuboids to materialize is based on the size, queries in the workload, accessing cost, their frequencies, etc.

2.13 Indexing OLAP Data: Bitmap and Join Index

To facilitate efficient data accessing, most data warehouse systems support index structures and materialized views (using cuboids).

2.13.1 Bitmap Indexing

The bitmap indexing method is popular in OLAP products because it allows quick searching in data cubes. The bitmap index is an alternative representation of the record ID (RID) list.

- In the bitmap index for a given attribute, there is a distinct bit vector, Bv, for each value v in the domain of the attribute. If the domain of a given attribute consists of n values, then n bits are needed for each entry in the bitmap index
- (i.e., there are n bit vectors). If the attribute has the value v for a given row in the data table, then the bit representing that value is set to 1 in the corresponding row of the bitmap index. All other bits for that row are set to 0.

Bitmap indexing is advantageous compared to hash and tree indices. It is especially useful for low cardinality domains because comparison, join, and aggregation operations are then reduced to bit arithmetic, which substantially reduces the processing time. Bitmap indexing leads to significant reductions in space and input/output (I/O) since a string of characters can be represented by a single bit. For higher-cardinality domains, the method can be adapted using compression techniques.

Consider the following example for Bitmap indexing.

Assume that the dimension item at the top level of the DigitalElectronics data warehouse has the following four values (indicating item types): "home entertainment," "computing," "phone," and "security." In the item bitmap index table, each value (like "computer") is represented by a bit vector. Assume that a relation table with 100,000 rows is used to hold the cube. The bitmap index table needs four 100,000-bit bit vectors (or lists) because the item's domain consists of four values. The mapping of a base (data) table with the dimensions item and city to bitmap index tables for each dimension is shown in Figure 2.8.

Base table

RID	*item*	*city*
R1	H	V
R2	C	V
R3	P	V
R4	S	V
R5	H	T
R6	C	T
R7	P	T
R8	S	T

item bitmap index table

RID	H	C	P	S
R1	1	0	0	0
R2	0	1	0	0
R3	0	0	1	0
R4	0	0	0	1
R5	1	0	0	0
R6	0	1	0	0
R7	0	0	1	0
R8	0	0	0	1

city bitmap index table

RID	V	T
R1	1	0
R2	1	0
R3	1	0
R4	1	0
R5	0	1
R6	0	1
R7	0	1
R8	0	1

Figure 2.19 Indexing OLAP using bipmap indices

The abbreviations H for "home entertainment," C for "computer," P for "phone," S for "security,"V for "Vancouver," and T for "Toronto" is used in the figure 2.8.

2.13.2 Join Indexing

Because it is used to process queries for relational databases, the join indexing technique has grown in popularity. Traditional indexing converts a given column's value to a list of rows that also contain that value. The joinable rows of two relations from a relational database are registered instead through join indexing.

Let us now consider an example for join index.

We established a star schema with the notation "sales star [time, item, branch, location]: dollars sold = sum (sales in dollars)" for DigitalElectronics in section 2.4.1.1. Figure 2.9 illustrates an example of a join index link between the location and item dimension tables and the sales fact database.

For instance, the "Main Street" value from the location dimension table combines with the sales fact table's tuples T57, T238, and T884. Similar to this, tuples T57 and T459 of the sales fact table join with the value "Sony-TV" in the item dimension table. Figure 2.10 depicts the associated join index tables.

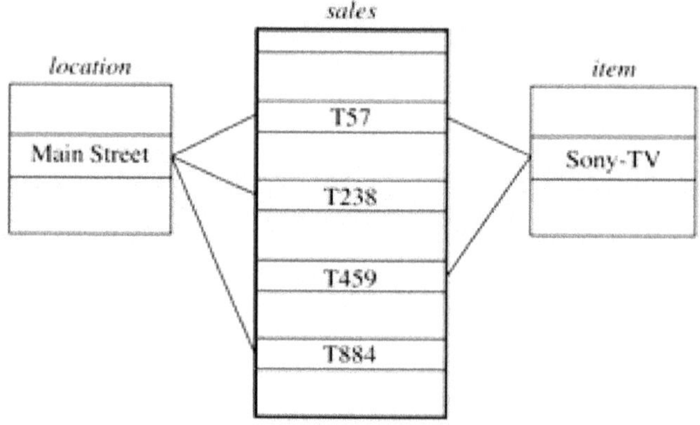

Figure 2.20 Linkages between a sales fact table and location and item dimension tables

For instance, if two relations R.RID, A/ and S.B, SID/ join on the attributes A and B, the pair is present in the join index record. RID, SID/, where RID and SID are, respectively, record identifiers from the R and S relations. As a result, join index records can find joinable tuples without needing to run pricey join operations. For keeping the connection between a foreign key and the primary keys that match it, from the joinable relation, join indexing is particularly helpful. In order to create composite join indices, join indices may span many dimensions. To find interesting sub cubes, we can use join indices.

Because the connectivity between a fact table and the associated dimension tables consists of both the fact table's foreign key and the dimension table's primary key, the star schema architecture of data warehouses makes join indexing appealing for cross-table search.

Join indexing preserves connections between rows in the fact table and attribute values of a dimension (for instance, within a dimension table). In order to create composite join indices, join indices may span many dimensions. Join indices can be used to find interesting subcubes.

Join index table for *location/sales*

location	*sales_key*
. . .	. . .
Main Street	T57
Main Street	T238
Main Street	T884
. . .	. . .

Join index table for *item/sales*

item	*sales_key*
. . .	. . .
Sony-TV	T57
Sony-TV	T459
. . .	. . .

Join index table linking *location* and *item* to *sales*

location	*item*	*sales_key*
. . .	. . .	. . .
Main Street	Sony-TV	T57
. . .	. . .	. . .

Figure 2.21 Join index tables based on the linkages between the sales fact table and the location and item dimension tables shown in Figure 2.20

Most people believe that an organization should only implement a data warehouse when it reaches a particular volume of data. Companies of all sizes delay this step until later in their development process because they do not see the benefits of a centralized repository.

A data repository is essential for most businesses, and for one specific reason: **analytics**. Data warehouses gives the analytics team of an organization, a 360° view of its customers and operations by consolidating data from multiple systems. In addition, centralized repositories can be useful for disaster recovery and system integration. Getting started is easy if it has the right data warehouse implementation plan. A data pipeline powered by ETL can consolidate all of this information. In a data warehouse, the data is extracted from all the organization's essential systems, integrated, cleansed, and then stored in one big relational database.

Decision support questions must be responded to quickly on OLAP servers. Therefore, extremely effective cube computation algorithms, access methods, and query processing techniques are essential for data warehouse systems. An overview of approaches for the effective installation of data warehouse systems is provided in this section.

Once the need for data warehouse is identified, the following steps for implementation of data warehouse is planned.

i. *Requirements Gathering*
ii. *Create Warehouse Environments*
iii. *Choose a Data Model*
iv. *Connect to Sources*
v. *Transform Incoming Data*
vi. *Create Data Marts*
vii. *Configure BI and Analytics*
viii. *viii. Audit and Review*

i. ***Requirements Gathering***

An organization wide data project involves multiple stakeholders related to functionalities such as decision making, information technology, analytics, security and compliance.

Decision Makers are stake holders such as leaders and strategist, who helps to stay aligned with the company's strategic objectives.

The information technology team plays a practical role in the data project in connecting sources to the data pipeline. This team deals with errors and supports the data warehouse if the organization plans to go for an on premise solution.

The analytics team defines the scope of the project by defining the project outcomes which helps in identifying the data sources.

The security and compliance team deals with the handling of sensitive information in the data warehouse.

ii. ***Create Warehouse Environments***

There are several options for choosing the warehouse environment.

- On premise : entails hosting on local hardware
- Public Cloud : an organization can use a hosted cloud service like AWS or Azure for public clouds.
- Private cloud: Private clouds can be hosted on one's own hardware or by a dependable third party.
- Hybrid cloud: Either combine on-premises storage with the cloud, or store data locally and leverage the cloud's processing and analytics capabilities.

A public cloud is mostly the least expensive and most convenient choice because the organization's host does the majority of the labor-intensive tasks for the organization. A hybrid or on-premises solution may appeal if the organization is more concerned about latency and security.

Whichever option is selected, the following three distinct environments must be constructed.

Development

The development team tests new features and integrations in this setting. Sensitive data has been obscured in this environment, which contains test data.

Testing

This warehouse is meant for QA and testing development environment.

Production

The analytics team of an organization and users can use this live data warehouse. It cannot be changed until the modifications have been tested in the other environments.

If necessary, an organization can have more than three environments. For QA and testing, for instance, it might require distinct warehouses. However, since an organization's development team cannot test out new features using production data, it will need at least three since the development team can't update the features on the production data.

iii. *Choose a Data Model*

The hardest element of implementing a data warehouse is probably the data modelling. There is a unique schema for each source database. All incoming data must match the single schema that your warehouse has. Therefore, you need a model that works with all of the current data and can grow in the future.

Among the most common kinds of schemas are:

Star schema

Dimensional tables connected to fact tables.

Snowflake Schema

Improves the star schema by introducing a additional level of dimensional tables.

Galaxy Schema

Multiple fact tables are linked by a common set of dimensions tables.

Constellation Schema

Galaxy schema with an additional structure of dimensions tables is known as the Constellation schema.

Typically, a data scientist will create a schema from scratch. Many commercial cloud and on-premises platforms will assist in customising a schema model for the organization needs.

iv. *Connect to Sources*

It is a two step process. The data from the target source is extracted and then it is uploaded to the data warehouse. There are several ways in extracting the data. API Call, File Transfer and Direct Query are some of the ways by which data can be extracted.

An automated Extract, Transform, Load (ETL) system is used to handle the entire process due to the complexity of the task involved. A library of integrations is included with Integrate.io so that data can be automatically extracted from the target and loaded into the destination. A data pipeline is what an organization have when an automated procedure is transporting data in this manner.

v. *Transform Incoming Data*

Between extract and load, ETL contains an important phase. Transformation is a stage in the ETL process when data is transformed from its original schema to the target schema. Data can't be inserted into the target tables without transformation.

Transformation also includes the other functionalities listed below.

Validation

Ensure that all data adheres to logical restrictions, such as the validity of dates or the correspondence of ZIP codes to addresses.

Cleaning

Eliminate any duplicate or faulty data. Alternately, leave the data alone while highlighting any potential issues.

Harmonization

Consolidate all data into a single format, such changing all temperature units to Fahrenheit or all date formats to MM/DD.

Enrichment

Enriching data involves combining records with information from additional sources.

Schema mappings can be made without coding if a programme like Integrate.io is used. Additionally, rules for data sanitization procedures like cleansing and validation can also be defined.

vi. *Create Data Marts*

Everything is kept in data warehouses, but most people don't require access to everything. Teams in operations and sales need only operational data. Hence the solution is to have the remaining data in the data warehouse. The warehouse is logically divided into marts, which provide a constrained view that only displays pertinent results. Often, an organization can control this with the appropriate information. For instance, some records may be labelled, "Sales" and others "Finance." Records with each matching tag can be displayed in marts. Both tags may be present on a document that is pertinent to both teams, such as a sales invoice. After that, it will show up in both data marts.

Data Marts are an excellent approach to offer focused outcomes. They're also a great approach to increase data security because they prevent people from seeing pertinent data.

vii. ***Configure BI and Analytics***

A data warehouse can be easily integrated with the majority of commercial business intelligence (BI) and analytics products. These tools can also be directly connected to your ETL platform, providing even quicker insights and visualisations.

Analytics and BI tools rely on:

Volume: The analytics insights become more detailed the more data you have.

Velocity: Real-time dashboards require a stream of data that moves quickly.

Veracity: The information you provide must be reliable and provide a complete picture of your situation.

The ability to provide the data your analytics team requires should be possible if your data warehouse installation plan has been followed.

viii. Audit and Review

An organization can start implementing measures to guarantee data quality after the data warehouse is functioning and the analytics team has all they need.

To assess the calibre of the materials in the organization's warehouse, this can entail applying automated data quality testing methods. In order to ensure that there are no glaring differences between raw and stored data, an organisation can also conduct sense checks.

2.14 Efficient OLAP Query Processing

To hasten query processing in data cubes, cuboids are materialised, and OLAP index structures are built. Given materialised views, the following is how query processing should go:

a. Select the procedures to carry out on the available cuboids: Any selection, projection, roll-up (group-by), and drill-down procedures that are given in the query are converted into the appropriate SQL and/or OLAP operations. Cutting and dicing a data cube, for instance, might be equivalent to projection and/or selection operations on a materialised cuboid.
b. Select the realised cuboid(s) to which the pertinent actions should be carried out: This entails locating all materialised cuboids that may be used to address the question, reducing the number of cuboids in the set using knowledge of their "dominance" relationships, calculating the costs of using the remaining materialised cuboids, and choosing the cuboid with the lowest cost.

2.15 From Data Warehousing To Data Mining

Data warehousing and OLAP are very much useful for data mining. On-Line Analytical Mining (OLAM) is a powerful paradigm that integrates OLAP with data mining technology.

2.15.1 **Data Warehousing Applications**

The three major applications of data warehouse are listed below.

- Information processing
    - supports querying, basic statistical analysis, and reporting

- using crosstabs, tables, charts and graphs

- Analytical processing
  - multidimensional analysis of data warehouse data
  - supports basic OLAP operations, slice-dice, drilling, pivoting

- Data mining
  - knowledge discovery from hidden patterns
  - supports associations, constructing analytical models, performing classification and prediction, and presenting the mining results using visualization tools.

2.15.2 From OLAP to OLAM

From On-Line Analytical Processing to On Line Analytical Mining (OLAM)is called from data warehousing to data mining From on-line analytical processing to on-line analytical mining.

On-Line Analytical Mining (OLAM) (also called OLAP mining), which integrates online analytical processing (OLAP) with data mining and mining knowledge in multidimensional databases, is particularly important for the following reasons.

- **High quality of data in data warehouses**

The majority of data mining technologies need to work with integrated, consistent, and cleaned data, which necessitates pricey preparation operations for data cleaning, data transformation, and data integration. Such preprocessing creates a data warehouse that is a great source of high quality data for OLAP and data mining.

- **Available information processing infrastructure surrounding data warehouses**

Around data warehouses, extensive information processing and data analysis infrastructures have been or will be systematically built. These infrastructures include ODBC/OLEDB connections, reporting and OLAP analysis tools, as well as facilities for accessing, integrating, consolidating, and transforming numerous, heterogeneous databases.

- **OLAP-based exploratory data analysis**

Exploratory data analysis is necessary for effective data mining. It is common for a user to wish to browse through a database, pick out relevant data chunks, analyse them at various granularities, and present knowledge and results in various ways. By drilling, pivoting, filtering, dicing, and slicing on a data cube and on some intermediate data mining outputs, online analytical mining offers tools for data mining on various subsets of data and at various levels of abstraction.

- **On-line selection of data mining functions**

Online analytical mining gives users the freedom to select preferred data mining functions and switch data mining tasks on-the-fly by integrating OLAP with a variety of data mining functions.

2.15.2.1 OLAM Architecture

An OLAM engine performs analytical mining in data cubes in a similar manner as an OLAP engine performs on-line analytical processing.

- An integrated OLAM and OLAP architecture is shown in Figure, where the OLAM and OLAP engines both accept users' on-line queries via a User GUI API and work with the data cube in the data analysis via a Cube API.

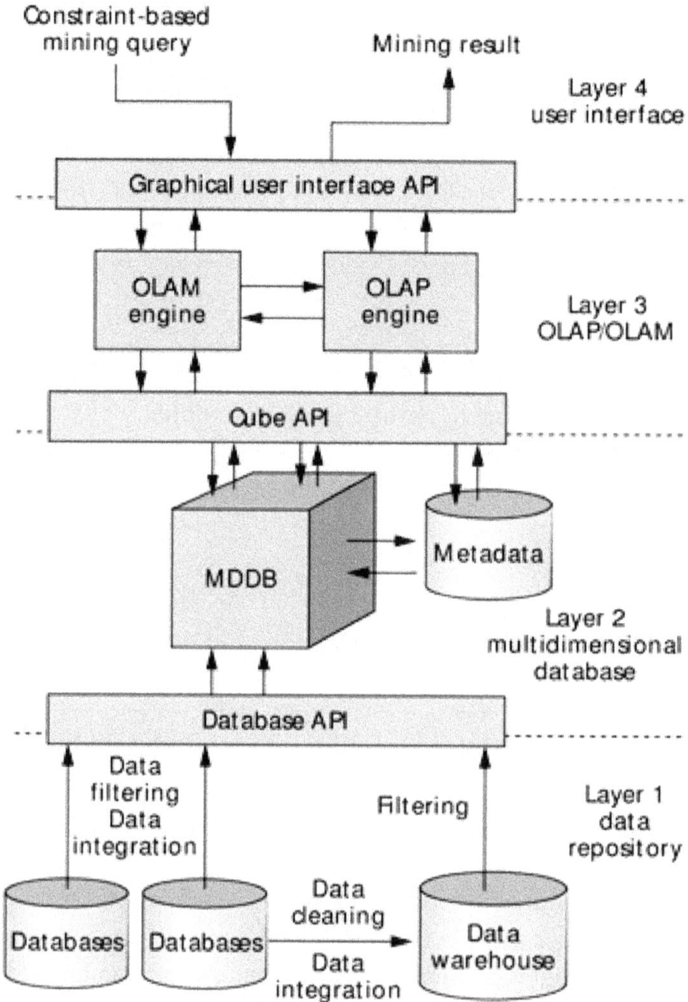

Figure 2.22 An Integrated OLAM and OLAP Architecture

- A metadata directory is used to guide the access of the data cube. The data cube can be constructed by accessing and/or integrating multiple databases and/or by filtering a data warehouse via a Database API which may support OLEDB or ODBC connections.
- Since an OLAM engine may perform multiple data mining tasks, such as concept description, association, classification, prediction, clustering, time-series analysis,etc., it usually consists of multiple, integrated data mining modules and is more sophisticated than an OLAP engine.

2.16 Mining Frequent Patterns, Associations and Correlations

2.16.1 Mining Frequent Patterns

Frequent Pattern Mining is an analytical process that finds frequent patterns, associations, or causal structures from data sets found in various kinds of databases such as relational databases, transactional databases, and other data repositories.

Frequent Pattern are patterns (e.g., itemsets, sub-sequences, or substructures) which appears frequently in a data set. By identifying frequent patterns we can observe strongly correlated items together and easily identify similar characteristics, associations among them. By doing frequent pattern mining, it leads to further analysis like clustering, classification and other data mining tasks.

Examples:

- A set of items, such as milk and bread that appear frequently together in a transaction data set is a frequent itemset.
- A subsequence, such as buying first a PC, then a digital camera, and then a memory card, if it occurs frequently in a shopping history database, is a (frequent) sequential pattern.
- A substructure can refer to different structural forms, such as subgraphs, subtrees, or sub-lattices, which may be combined with itemsets or sub-sequences. If a substructure occurs frequently, it is called a (frequent) structured pattern

2.16.1.1 Market Basket Analysis

A market basket is a collection of items an individual customer purchases in a single transaction, which is a clearly defined business activity. These include a customer's trips to the grocery store or an online purchase from a virtual business on the Internet. By keeping track of their daily business operations, retailers amass enormous collections of transactions.

The search for groups of items, or itemsets, that frequently appear together in transactions is a common study performed on a transactions database. The placement of these items in the store as well as the design of mail-order catalogue pages and website pages can all be improved with the help of a business's understanding of these patterns.

An itemset containing i items is called an i- itemset. The percentage of transactions that contain an itemset is called the itemset's support. An itemset's support must be greater than a user-specified minimum in order for it to be interesting. Such itemsets are said to be frequent.

By identifying relationships between the many items that the customers place in their "shopping baskets," market basket analysis evaluates the purchasing behaviours of those customers as shown in the figure 2.23.

By collecting knowledge on which items customers usually buy together, the identification of these associations can assist businesses in creating marketing strategies. How likely is it, that shoppers will also purchase bread on the same trip to the store if they are purchasing milk, for instance? By assisting merchants with targeted marketing and shelf planning, this information can result in an increase in sales.

The retail data of consumer transactions in a store may be used for market basket analysis to address the queries of the owner of the store. The results can then be used to develop marketing or advertising plans or to design a new catalogue.

Other applications of Frequent Pattern mining are listed below.

- Telecommunication
- Credit Cards
- Banking Services
- Medical Treatments
- Basketball-Game Analysis
- Catalog Design

Figure 2.23 Market basket analysis

2.16.1.2 Frequent Pattern Mining Classification

Frequent pattern mining can be classified into various types based on the following criteria.

- Completeness of Patterns to be mined
- Abstraction
- Dimension
- Types of values handled
- Kinds of Rules to be Mined
- Kinds of Patterns Mined

2.16.1.2.1 Completeness of Patterns to be mined

Based on the completeness of patterns to be mined frequent pattern mining can be done as follows.

- For instance, if a minimal support criterion is met, it can mine the entire collection of frequent itemsets, closed frequent itemsets, and maximal frequent itemsets.
- It can also extract constrained frequent itemsets (It can satisfy a collection of user-defined constraints), approximate frequent itemsets (It can change only approximate support counts for the mined frequent itemsets), near-match frequent itemsets (It can count the support count of the relatively matching itemsets), top-k frequent itemsets (i.e., the k most frequent itemsets for a user-specified value, k), etc.

The integrity of the patterns to be mined is a requirement for a number of applications, and these requirements can influence the computations and optimization techniques used.

2.16.1.2.2 Abstraction

Association rule mining uses a variety of techniques to find rules at various abstraction levels. For instance, consider that a group of association rules mined involves the following rules where X is a variable defining a customer –

buys(X, "computer") ⇒ buys(X, "HP printer")
buys(X, "laptop computer") ⇒ buys(X, "HP printer")

In the above rules, items bought are referenced at different abstraction levels. That is computer is a higher level abstraction of laptop computer.

2.16.1.2.3 Dimensions

If the items or attributes in an association rule reference only one dimension, thus it is a single-dimensional association rule. The following rule is an example of a single dimensional rule.

buys(X, "computer"))=>buys(X, "antivirus software")

If one or two dimensions such as age, income, buys are referenced in a rule, then it is a multidimensional association rule. The following rule is an example of a multidimensional rule.

age(X, "30,31...39") ^ income(X, "42K,...48K"))=>buys(X, "high resolution TV")

2.16.1.2.4 Types of values

Different types of values can be used in an association rule. A rule is a Boolean association rule if it contains associations between items' presence and absence. A rule is considered to be a quantitative association rule if it establishes relationships between quantitative objects or qualities. Quantitative values for objects or attributes are divided into intervals in these rules.

2.16.1.2.5 Kinds of rules to be mined

Regular pattern analysis can produce a variety of intriguing relationships and rules. The well-known class of rules derived from frequent patterns are association rules.

A lot of the rules that can be produced through association rule mining are repetitive or do not show a correlation between item sets.

It is possible to further examine the identified links to find statistical correlations and develop correlation rules.

2.16.1.2.6 Kinds of Patterns to be Mined

A number of regular patterns can be seen in data sets of various types. Frequent itemset mining, or the extraction of collections of items that appear frequently in relational or transactional data sets, is the main area of concentration.

Sequential pattern mining, for example, can be used to evaluate the order in which frequently purchased items are acquired. Customers frequently buy a PC, a digital camera, and then a memory card in that order.

Structured pattern mining looks for recurrent substructures in a set of structured data. A single piece makes up the most basic kind of structure.

Each component of an itemset may include a subsequence, a subtree, or something else entirely. So, it can be claimed that structured pattern mining is the most general sort of frequent pattern mining.

2.16.2 Association Rule Mining

Mining association rules in large databases is a popular and well researched method for discovering interesting relationships between variables. It is designed to identify strong rules in databases based on different measures of interest. Rakesh Agrawal et al. introduced association rules on the basis of strong rules.

Problem Definition:

The problem of association rule mining is defined as:

Let I = $\{i_1, i_2, ..., i_n\}$ be a set of binary attributes called items.

Let D = $\{t_1, t_2, ..., t_m\}$ be a set of transactions called the database.

Each transaction in **D** has a unique transaction ID and contains a subset of the items in **I**.

A rule is defined as an implication of the form X Þ Y where X,Y Í I and X∩Y=Φ .

The sets of items (for short itemsets) **X** and **Y** are called antecedent (left-hand-side or LHS) and consequent (right-hand-side or RHS) of the rule respectively.

For example, to illustrate these concepts, we use a small example from the supermarket domain. The set of items is I = {milk, bread, butter, beer} and a small database containing the items (1 codes presence and 0 absence of an item in a transaction) is shown in the table. An example rule for the supermarket could be {butter, bread} Þ {milk} meaning that if butter and bread are bought, customers also buy milk. This example has 5 transactions and 4 items per transaction. The transaction table is given below.

Table 2.2 Transaction Table

Transaction ID	Milk	Bread	Butter	Beer
T001	1	1	0	0
T002	0	0	1	0
T003	0	0	0	1
T004	1	1	1	0
T005	0	1	0	0

2.16.2.1 Association Rule Mining Concepts

The support, **supp(X)** of an itemset **X** is defined as the proportion of transactions in the data set which contain the itemset. In the example database, the itemset, {milk, bread, butter} has a support of 1/5 = 0.2 since, it occurs in 20% of all transactions (1 out of 5 transactions).

$$Supp(X) = \frac{Freq(X)}{T}$$

The confidence of a rule is defined as

$$Confidence = \frac{Freq(X,Y)}{Freq(X)}$$

That is,

$$Confidence_{(A \rightarrow B)} = P(B|A) = \frac{support\_count(AUB)}{support\_count(A)}$$

For example, the rule {butter, bread}Þ{milk} has a confidence of 0.2/0.2 = 1.0 in the database, which means that for 100% of the transactions containing butter and bread the rule is correct (100% of the times a customer buys butter and bread, milk is bought as well). The confidence of an association rule is a percentage value that shows how frequently the rule head occurs among all the groups containing the rule body. The confidence value indicates how reliable this rule is. The higher the value, the more likely the head items occur in a group if it is known that all body items are contained in that group. Confidence can be interpreted as an estimate of the probability P(Y|X), the probability of finding the RHS of the rule in transactions under the condition that these transactions also contain the LHS.

The lift of a rule is defined as follows

$$Lift = \frac{Supp\ (X, Y)}{Supp(X) \times Supp(Y)}$$

or the ratio of the observed support to that expected if X and Y were independent. The rule {milk, bread} Þ {butter} has a lift of 0.2/(0.4*0.4) = 1.25.

The conviction of a rule is defined as

$$Conviction\ (X \rightarrow Y) = \frac{1\text{-}Supp(Y)}{1\text{-}Confidence\,(X \rightarrow Y)} = \frac{P(X)*P(^\wedge Y)}{P(X \cup ^\wedge Y)}$$

The rule {milk, bread} Þ {butter} has a conviction of (1-0.4)/(1-0.5) = 1.2 , and can be interpreted as the ratio of the expected frequency that X occurs without Y (that is to say, the frequency that the rule makes an incorrect prediction) if X and Y were independent divided by the observed frequency of incorrect predictions.

2.16.3 Apriori Algorithm

The Apriori Algorithm is one of the most effective methods for mining frequent itemsets, finding them through candidate generation.

The ground breaking method Apriori was developed by R. Agrawal and R. Srikant in 1994 to mine frequent item sets for Boolean association rules. The name of the method comes from the fact that it uses previously learned information about typical properties of an itemset.

Candidate generation, used by Apriori, is a "bottom-up" mechanism that involves extending frequent subgroups one item at a time and testing groups of candidates against the data. The algorithm is complete after no further successful extensions can be made.

Using a hash tree structure and breadth-first search, Apriori effectively counts candidate item sets. It produces candidate items from item sets having a length of k-1 and creates candidate item sets of length k.

The candidates having an uncommon sub-pattern are then disqualified. The downward closure lemma states that the candidate set contains all typical k-length item sets. The next step is to locate the most frequent item sets for candidate candidates by searching the transaction database.

Apriori Property

1. It makes use of “Upward Closure property” (Any superset of infrequent itemset is also an infrequent set). It follows Bottom-up search, moving upward level-wise in the lattice.

2. It makes use of “downward closure property”(any subset of a frequent itemset is a frequent itemset).

3. If Support of an itemset exceeds the support of its subsets, then it is known as the anti_monotone property of support.

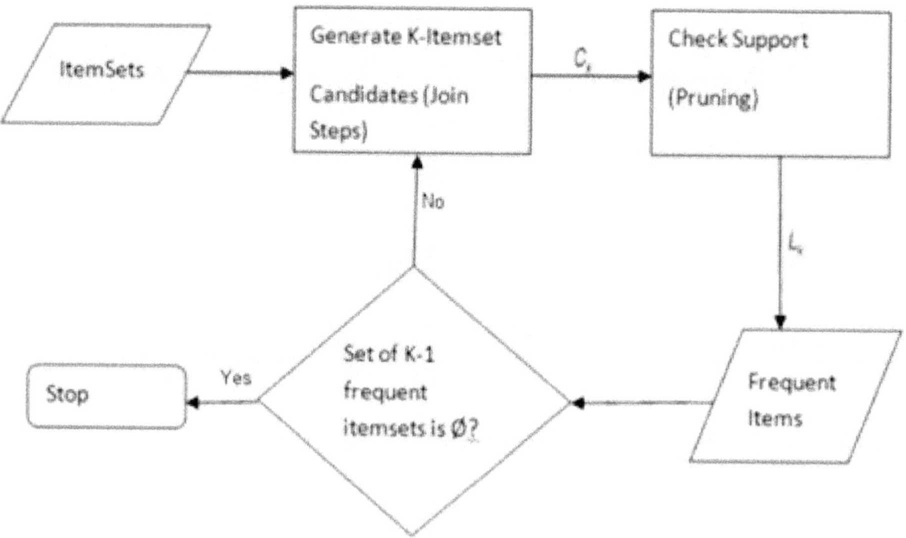

Figure 2.24 Apriori Algorithm

The Apriori algorithm for discovering frequent itemsets for mining Boolean association rules is given below.
Algorithm: Apriori. Find frequent itemsets using an iterative level-wise approach based on candidate generation.
Input:

- D, a database of transactions;
- min_sup, the minimum support count threshold.

Output: L, frequent itemsets in D.

Method:

```
(1) L1 = find_frequent_1-itemsets(D);
(2) for (k = 2;Lk-1 ?φ;k++) {
(3)       Ck = apriori_gen(Lk-1);
(4)       for each transaction t ? D { // scan D for counts
(5)            Ct= subset(Ck, t); // get the subsets of t that are candidates
(6)            for each candidate c ? Ct
(7)                 c.count++;
(8)       }
(9)       Lk = {c ? Ck|c.count = min sup}
(10)   }
(11) return L = ? kLk;
```

```
procedure apriori_gen(Lk-1:frequent (k - 1)-itemsets)
(1) for each itemset l1 ? Lk-1
(2)     for each itemset l2 ? Lk-1
(3)         if (l1[1] = l2[1]) ? (l1[2] = l2[2])
                ?... ? (l1[k - 2] = l2[k - 2]) ? (l1[k - 1] < l2[k - 1]) then {
(4)             c = l1 ⋈ l2; // join step: generate candidates
(5)             if has infrequent subset(c, Lk-1) then
(6)                 delete c; // prune step: remove unfruitful candidate
(7)             else add c to Ck;
(8)         }
(9)     return Ck;
```

```
procedure has_infrequent_subset(c: candidate k-itemset;
            Lk-1: frequent (k - 1)-itemsets); // use prior knowledge
(1) for each (k - 1)-subset s of c
(2) if s ∉ Lk-1 then
(3)         return TRUE;
(4) return FALSE;
```

Figure 6.4 Apriori algorithm for discovering frequent itemsets for mining Boolean association rules.

Example: Consider the following database D, with 9 transactions as given in table 2.3 and the minimum support as 2.

Table 2.3 Transaction Table

TID	List of item IDs
T100	I1, I2, I5
T200	I2, I4
T300	I2, I3
T400	I1, I2, I4
T500	I1, I3
T600	I2, I3
T700	I1, I3
T800	I1, I2, I3, I5
T900	I1, I2, I3

Steps:

1. In the first iteration of the algorithm, each item is a member of the set of candidate1-itemsets, C1. The algorithm simply scans all of the transactions in order to count the number of occurrences of each item.

2. Suppose that the minimum support count required is 2, that is, min sup = 2. The set of frequent 1-itemsets, L1, can then be determined. It consists of the candidate 1-itemsets satisfying minimum support. In our example, all of the candidates in C1 satisfy minimum support.

3. To discover the set of frequent 2-itemsets, L2, the algorithm uses the join L1 on L1

to generate a candidate set of 2-itemsets, C2. No candidates are removed from C2 during the prune step because each subset of the candidates is also frequent.

4. Next, the transactions in D are scanned and the support count of each candidate itemset In C2 is accumulated.

5. The set of frequent 2-itemsets, L2, is then determined, consisting of those candidate2-itemsets in C2 having minimum support.

6. The generation of the set of candidate 3-itemsets, C3, From the join step, we first get C3 =L2x L2 = ({I1, I2, I3}, {I1, I2, I5}, {I1, I3, I5}, {I2, I3, I4},{I2, I3, I5}, {I2, I4, I5}. Based on the Apriori property that all subsets of a frequent itemset must also be frequent, we can determine that the four latter candidates cannot possibly be frequent.

7. The transactions in D are scanned in order to determine L3, consisting of those candidate 3-itemsets in C3 having minimum support.

8. The algorithm uses L3x L3 to generate a candidate set of 4-itemsets, C4

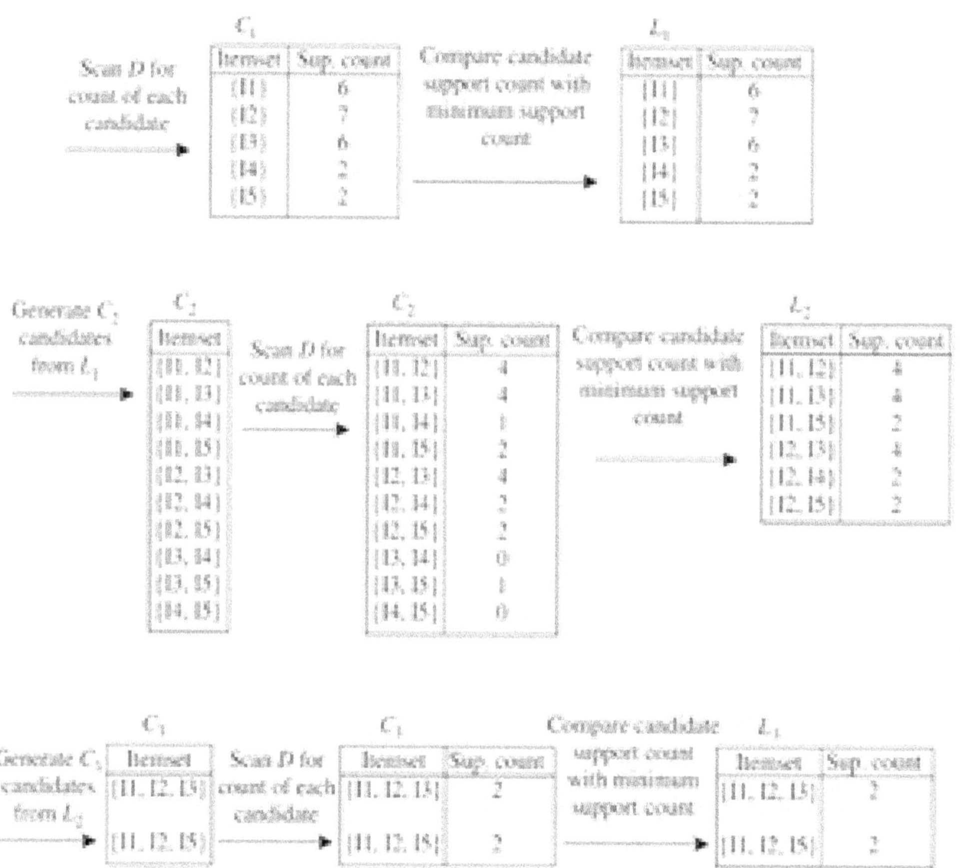

Figure 2.25 Generation of the candidate itemsets and frequent itemsets, for the given example with minimum support count 2

(a) Join: $C_3 = L_2 \bowtie L_2$ = {{I1, I2}, {I1, I3}, {I1, I5}, {I2, I3}, {I2, I4}, {I2, I5}} $\bowtie${{I1, I2}, {I1, I3}, {I1, I5}, {I2, I3}, {I2, I4}, {I2, I5}} = {{I1, I2, I3}, {I1, I2, I5}, {I1, I3, I5}, {I2, I3, I4}, {I2, I3, I5}, {I2, I4, I5}}.

(b) Prune using the Apriori property: All nonempty subsets of a frequent itemset must also be frequent. Do any of the candidates have a subset that is not frequent?

- The 2-item subsets of {I1, I2, I3} are {I1, I2}, {I1, I3}, and {I2, I3}. All 2-item subsets of {I1, I2, I3} are members of L_2. Therefore, keep {I1, I2, I3} in C_3.
- The 2-item subsets of {I1, I2, I5} are {I1, I2}, {I1, I5}, and {I2, I5}. All 2-item subsets of {I1, I2, I5} are members of L_2. Therefore, keep {I1, I2, I5} in C_3.
- The 2-item subsets of {I1, I3, I5} are {I1, I3}, {I1, I5}, and {I3, I5}. {I3, I5} is not a member of L_2, and so it is not frequent. Therefore, remove {I1, I3, I5} from C_3.
- The 2-item subsets of {I2, I3, I4} are {I2, I3}, {I2, I4}, and {I3, I4}. {I3, I4} is not a member of L_2, and so it is not frequent. Therefore, remove {I2, I3, I4} from C_3.
- The 2-item subsets of {I2, I3, I5} are {I2, I3}, {I2, I5}, and {I3, I5}. {I3, I5} is not a member of L_2, and so it is not frequent. Therefore, remove {I2, I3, I5} from C_3.
- The 2-item subsets of {I2, I4, I5} are {I2, I4}, {I2, I5}, and {I4, I5}. {I4, I5} is not a member of L_2, and so it is not frequent. Therefore, remove {I2, I4, I5} from C_3.

(c) Therefore, C_3 = {{I1, I2, I3}, {I1, I2, I5}} after pruning.

Figure 2.26 Generation and pruning of candidate 3-itemsets, C3, from L2 using the Apriori property

2.16.3.1 Generating Association Rules from Frequent Itemsets

Once the frequent itemsets from transactions in a database D have been found, it is straightforward to generate strong association rules from them.

$$Confidence_{(A \rightarrow B)} = P(B|A) = \frac{support\_count(AUB)}{support\_count(A)}$$

Enter Caption

The conditional probability is expressed in terms of itemset support count, where *support_count*(AUB) is the number of transactions containing the itemsets AUB, and *support_count*(A) is the number of transactions containing the itemset A. Based on this equation, association rules can be generated as given below.

- For each frequent itemset l, generate all nonempty subsets of l.
- For every non empty subset s of l, output the rule "sÞ(l-s)" if

min_conf, where min_conf is the minimum confidence threshold.

Each association rule developed automatically satisfies the minimum support because the rules are generated from frequently occurring itemsets. Hash tables can be used to store frequently used itemsets and their counts in advance for easy access.

Let us consider an example for generating association rules. For the transaction table given above, suppose the data contain the frequent itemset l={I1,I2,I5}, what are the association rules that can be generated from l?

Given the frequent itemset l = {I1, I2, I5},

The non empty subsets of l are given below:

{I1}, {I2}, {I5}, {I1, I2}, {I1, I5},{I2, I5}

I1ÞI2∩I5, confidence = 2/6 = 33%

I2Þ I1∩I5, confidence = 2/7 = 29%

I5Þ I1∩I2, confidence = 2/2 = 100%

I1∩I2 ÞI5, confidence = 2/4 = 50%

I1∩I5ÞI2, confidence = 2/2 = 100%

I2∩I5ÞI1, confidence = 2/2 = 100%

2.16.3.2 Advantages

The advantages of the Apriori algorithm are due to the following reasons. Among association rule learning algorithms, this one is the easiest to use and understand.

a. The resulting rules are simple and straightforward to explain to a user.
b. It is completely unsupervised, thus it doesn't require labelled data; as a result, you can apply it in a variety of contexts since unlabeled data is frequently easier to get.
c. Based on this implementation, other extensions have been proposed for various use situations. For instance, there are association learning algorithms that take into account the ordering of items, their quantity, and associated timestamps.
d. The algorithm finds all the rules with the appropriate support and confidence because it is exhaustive.

2.16.3.3 Disadvantages

The Apriori Algorithm's slowness is one of its greatest drawbacks. The Apriori approach is inefficient due to the following reasons:

- A large number of itemsets in the Apriori algorithm dataset.
- Low minimum support in the data set
- Time needed to hold a large number of candidate sets with many frequent itemsets.

Hence the Apriori approach is inefficient when applied with big volumes of datasets due to the reasons mentioned above.

Consider a frequent-1 itemset with 10^4 items as an example. The Apriori algorithm code must generate more than 10^7 candidates with a 2-length before testing and compiling the results. In this example, the Apriori approach is used to generate 2^{100} options in search of a size frequent pattern of size 100 (containing v1, v2, and v100).

This results in higher yield costs and lengthy candidate generation for the Apriori algorithm.

Additionally, in an effort to optimise the Apriori algorithm for examining the various candidate itemsets obtained from the numerous sets, it continually scans the database using expensive resources. The algorithm is impacted when the system memory is low and there are many frequent transactions. This causes the method to be slow and inefficient when working with large databases.

2.16.3.4 Methods to Improve Apriori Efficiency

There are several methods for improving the efficiency of the Apriori algorithm. A brief discussion of the same are given below.

i. **Hash-Based Technique:** This technique generates the k-itemsets and their accompanying counts using a hash-based structure known as a hash table. It creates the table using a hash function.
ii. **Transaction Reduction:** This technique lessens the quantity of transactions that must be scanned iteratively. Transactions that don't include frequently used items are flagged or deleted.
iii. **Partitioning:** The frequent itemets can be mined using this strategy with just two database scans. It states that any itemset must be frequent in at least one database partition in order for it to be considered potentially frequent in the database.
iv. **Sampling:** Using this technique, a random sample S is chosen from Database D, and the frequent itemset is then looked for in S. A common itemset that is used globally could perhaps be lost. The min sup value might be decreased to lessen this.
v. **Dynamic Itemset Counting:** During database scanning, this technique can add new candidate itemsets at any designated database start point.

2.16.4 Pattern Growth for Mining Frequent Itemsets

The Apriori candidate generate and test approach greatly decreases the size of the candidate sets, producing good performance and gain, but it can incur two nontrivial costs that are indicated under disadvantages.

Can we develop a technique that mines the entire collection of frequent itemsets without requiring such an expensive candidate generation procedure? Frequent pattern growth, often known as FP-growth, is an intriguing technique used in this endeavour. It uses a divide-and-conquer tactic. In order to preserve the itemset association information, it first compresses the database of often occurring items into a frequent pattern tree, or FP-tree. The compressed database is then divided into a number of conditional databases (a particular type of projected database), each linked to a single frequent item or "pattern fragment," and each database is mined independently. Only the data sets that are related with each "pattern fragment" need to be looked at. As a result, this strategy may significantly reduce both the "development" of the patterns being looked at and the quantity of the data sets to be searched.

2.16.5 Mining Multilevel Association Rules

Due to the sparsity of data at low or primitive levels of abstraction, it can be challenging for many applications to identify strong correlations among data objects at those levels. Strong correlations found at very high abstraction levels might be common sense. Since several levels of abstraction can be easily traversed, data mining systems should have the ability to mine association rules at each level of abstraction.

Multiple-level or multilevel association rules are those produced by data mining operations on data that have been analysed at several levels of abstraction. In a support-confidence paradigm, idea hierarchies can be effectively used to mine multilevel association rules. Typically, a top-down technique is utilised, where counts are added up for the calculation of frequent itemsets at each concept level, starting at concept level 1 and working down the hierarchy toward the more complex concept levels, until no more frequent itemsets can be found.

A concept hierarchy is a table that shows how certain low-level concepts are mapped to higher-level, more general concepts. Data can be generalised by replacing low-level concepts in the data with higher-level concepts from a concept hierarchy, or vice versa.

Table 2.4 Transaction Table

Task-Relevant Data, *D*

TID	*Items Purchased*
T100	Apple 17" MacBook Pro Notebook, HP Photosmart Pro b9180
T200	Microsoft Office Professional 2010, Microsoft Wireless Optical Mouse 5000
T300	Logitech VX Nano Cordless Laser Mouse, Fellowes GEL Wrist Rest
T400	Dell Studio XPS 16 Notebook, Canon PowerShot SD1400
T500	Lenovo ThinkPad X200 Tablet PC, Symantec Norton Antivirus 2010
...	...

Concept hierarchies for nominal characteristics are frequently implicit in the database schema, which is automatically constructed. Concept hierarchy for numeric characteristics is generated using discretization techniques.

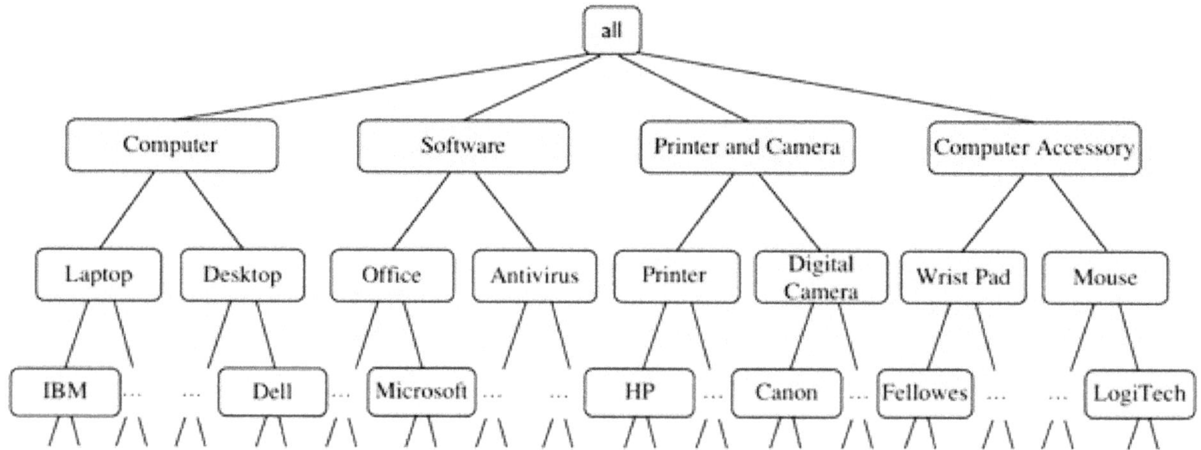

Figure 2.27 Mining Multilevel Association Rules Example

In the example given above, the concept hierarchy has five levels, referred to as 0 to 4, starting with the root node.

- Here, Level 1 includes computer, software, printer & camera, and computer accessory.
- Level 2 includes laptop computer, desktop computer, office software, antivirus software
- Level 3 includes IBM desktop computer, . . . , Microsoft office software, and so on.
- Level 4 is the most specific abstraction level of this hierarchy.

2.16.5.1 Approaches for Mining Multilevel Association Rules

There are several approaches for mining multilevel association rules which are listed below.

- Uniform Minimum Support
- Reduced Minimum Support
- Group Based Minimum Support

Let us have a brief discussion on these approaches.

2.16.5.1.1 Uniform Minimum Support

When mining at each level of abstraction, the same minimal support criterion is applied. The search process is made simpler when a standard minimum support threshold is employed. Users simply need to define one minimum support criterion, making the process easy. The universal support strategy does have certain challenges, though. Items at lower levels of abstraction are not likely to occur as frequently as those at higher levels. Too high of a minimal support criterion may overlook certain significant linkages that occur at low abstraction levels. A threshold that is set too low may produce a large number of uninteresting associations at high abstraction levels.

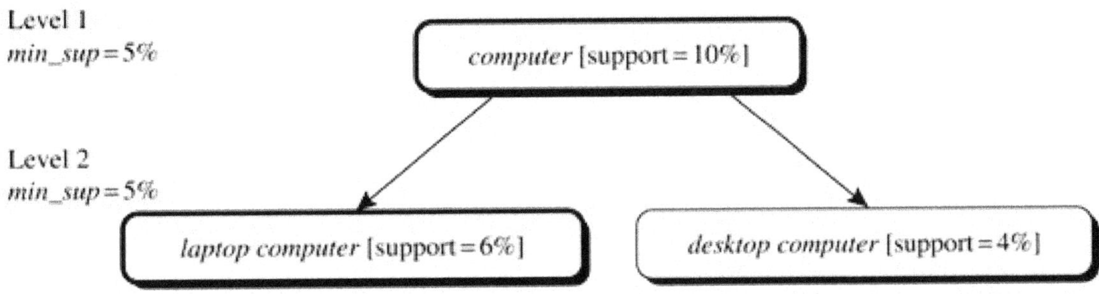

Figure 2.28 Multilevel Mining with Uniform Support

2.16.5.1.2 Reduced Minimum Support

Each abstraction level has a unique minimum support threshold. The matching threshold gets smaller the higher the level of abstraction. For levels 1 and 2, for instance, the minimal support criteria are 5% and 3%, respectively. Therefore, the terms "computer," "laptop computer," and "desktop computer" are all regarded as common.

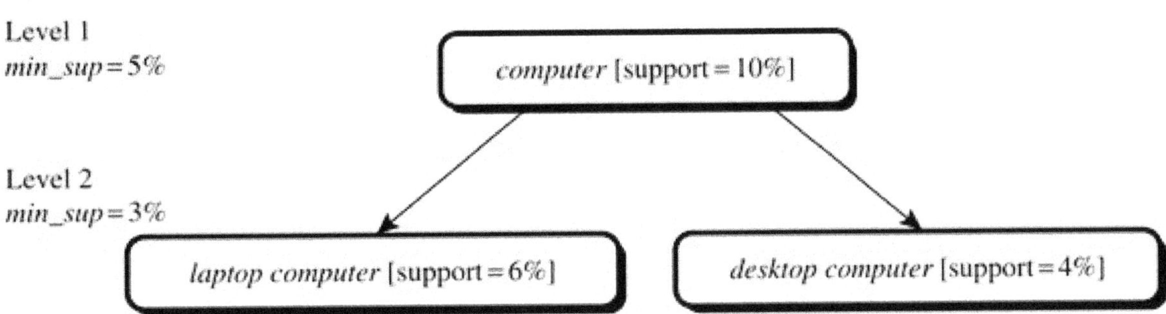

Figure 2.29 Group-Based Minimum Support

When mining multilevel rules, it is sometimes more beneficial to build up user-specific, item- or group-based minimal support criteria because users or experts frequently have knowledge of which groups are more crucial than others. By establishing extremely low support levels for laptop computers and flash drives, for instance, a user might pay close attention to the association patterns involving products from these categories while also setting minimal support thresholds based on product pricing or items of interest.

2.16.6 Mining Multidimensional Association Rules from Relational Databases and Data Warehouses

Single dimensional or intra dimensional association rule contains a single distinct predicate (e.g., buys) with multiple occurrences i.e., the predicate occurs more than once within the rule:

buys (X, “digital camera”)=>buys(X, “HP printer”)

Association rules that involve two or more dimensions or predicates can be referred to as multidimensional association rules. Example:

age(X, “20...29”)^occupation(X, “student”)=>buys(X, “laptop”)

Age, occupation, and purchases are the three predicates that make up the aforementioned rule; each predicate only appears once in the rule. As a result, we declare that it lacks repeated predicates. Interdimensional association rules are multidimensional association rules without repeated predicates. We may also extract repeated predicates from multidimensional association rules, which have numerous instances of some predicates. Hybrid dimensional association rules are the name given to these guidelines. The following is an illustration of such a rule, where the predicate buys is repeated:

age(X, "20...29")^buys(X, "laptop")=>buys(X, "HP printer")

2.16.7 Mining Quantitative Association Rules

In order to meet certain mining objectives, such as maximising the confidence or compactness of the rules mined, quantitative association rules are multidimensional association rules in which the numeric characteristics are dynamically discretized throughout the mining process. This section focuses especially on how to mine quantitative association rules that include two quantitative properties on the rule's left and right sides, respectively. That is,

Aquan1 ^Aquan2 =>Acat

where Aquan1 and Aquan2 are tests on quantitative attribute interval. AcAT analyses data that is pertinent to the task and assesses a categorical attribute. Due to the fact that these rules have two quantitative dimensions, they are known as two-dimensional quantitative association rules. Consider the case where you are interested in the correlation between pairs of quantitative characteristics, such as customer age and wealth, and the preferred television type (such as high-definition TV, or HDTV). Such a 2-D quantitative association rule's illustration is

age(X, "30...39")^income(X, "42K...48K")=>buys(X, "HDTV").

2.16.8 From Association Mining to Correlation Analysis

To improve the support-confidence framework for association rules, a correlation metric can be utilised. As a result, A=>B [support, confidence, correlation] correlation rules are produced. That is, the correlation of itemsets A and B is taken into account while evaluating a correlation rule in addition to its support and confidence. You can pick from a wide variety of correlation metrics. To evaluate which correlation measures would be best for mining massive data sets, we examine various correlation measures in this section.

The lift is a straightforward correlation metric and is given as follows. If P(AUB) = P(A)P(B), then the occurrence of itemset A is independent of the occurrence of itemset B; otherwise, the events of itemsets A and B are dependent and connected. More than two itemsets can be included in this definition with ease. The lift between the occurrence of A and B can be measured by computing

$$lift(A, B) = \frac{P(A \cup B)}{P(A)P(B)}$$

When lift (A,B) is less than 1, there is a negative correlation between the occurrences of A and B. This implies that the occurrence of one will probably result in the absence of the other. When the resultant value exceeds 1, A and B are said to be positively linked, which means that the occurrence of one presupposes the occurrence of the other. If the outcome is 1, A and B are independent of one another and there is no correlation between them.

CHAPTER THREE

WEKA TOOL

3.1 Introduction

Weka is a free and open-source software designed by researchers and scientists at the University of Waikato in New Zealand. Waikato Environment for Knowledge Analysis is referred to as WEKA.

WEKA is a framework for machine learning that consists of numerous tools that enable numerous machine learning operations.

Java is the primary language used to construct WEKA. It offers SQL database integration through Java Database connection. To carry out data mining activities, it offers a variety of machine learning techniques. These algorithms can either be utilised directly with the WEKA tool or indirectly with other Java-programmed software.

There are numerous tools available for feature extraction, classification, clustering, regression analysis, association rule construction, and data visualisation. It is an effective tool that aids in the creation of new algorithms in Machine Learning.

3.2 Why Use WEKA Machine Learning Tool

Weka is a free and open-source programme created by researchers and scientists at the University of Waikato in New Zealand (figure 3.1). WEKA stance Machine learning algorithms are easily accessible to users with WEKA. These techniques can be used by ML experts to extract relevant data from large amounts of data. Here, experts can set up a setting for the creation and application of novel machine learning techniques on actual data.

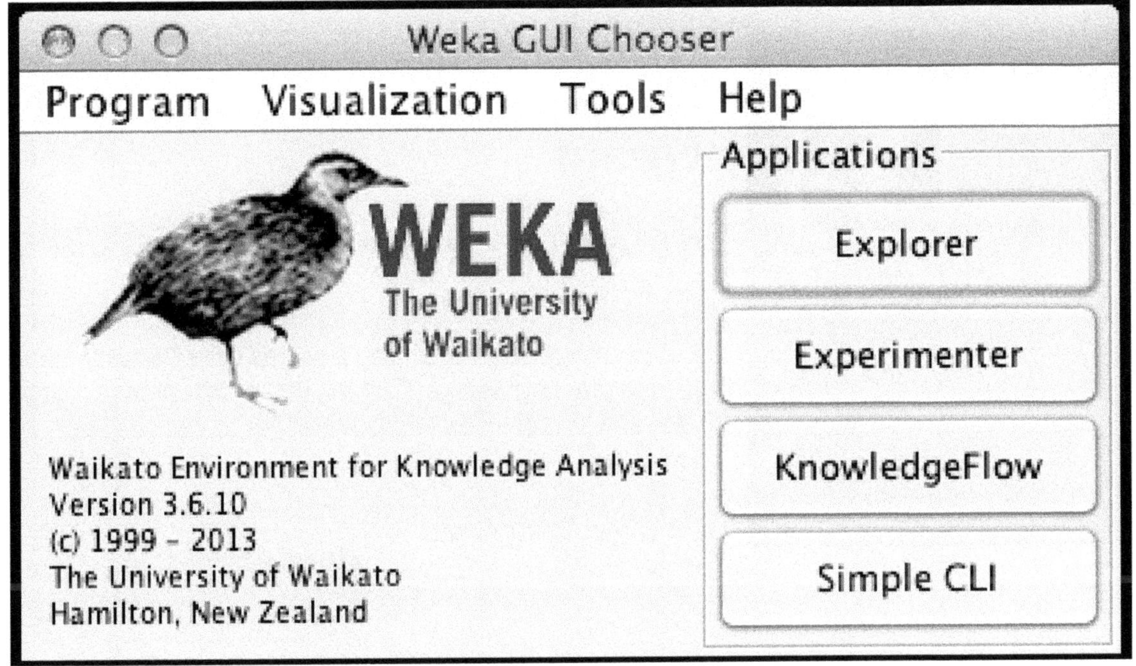

Figure 3.1 WEKA Tool Home Page

Machine learning and applied science researchers use WEKA for learning. It is a useful tool for completing a variety of data mining tasks.

3.3 Installation

3.3.1 WEKA Download And Installation

Steps involved in the download and installation of WEKA tool are given below.

1. Download the software from Downloading and installing Weka - Weka Wiki (waikato.github.io). Check the configuration of the computer system and download the stable version of WEKA (currently 3.8) from the url https://waikato.github.io/weka-wiki/downloading_weka/ highlighted in figure 3.2 .

Figure 3.2 Downloading and Installing WEKA

2. After successful download, open the file location and double-click on the downloaded file. The Step Up wizard will appear. You will get the*WEKA 3.8.3 Setup Wizard* screen as shown in Figure 3.3. Click on Next.

Figure 3.3 WEKA 3.8.3 Setup Wizard

3. On clicking Next, The License Agreement terms will open as seen in figure 3.4. Read it thoroughly and click on "I Agree".

Figure 3.4 WEKA License Agreement

4. The next screen (figure 3.5) shows the list of components to be installed. Select the type of installation and the list of components as per your requirements. Full component installation is recommended. Then, click on Next.

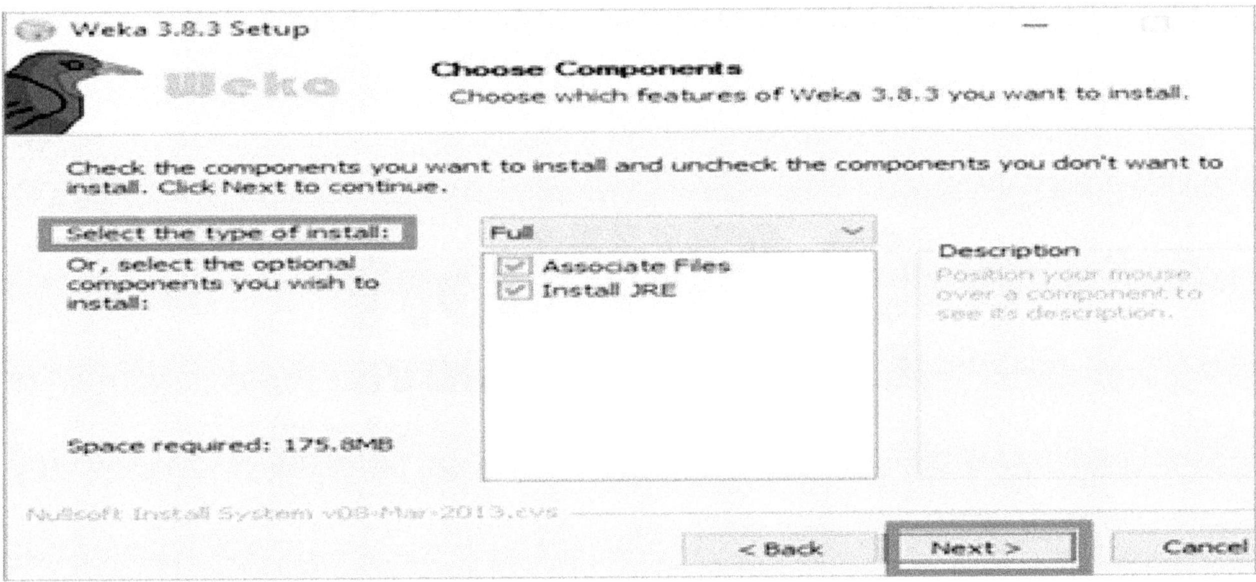

Figure 3.5 WEKA Tool Choose Components Screen

5. With this, the installation will start as shown in figure 3.6.

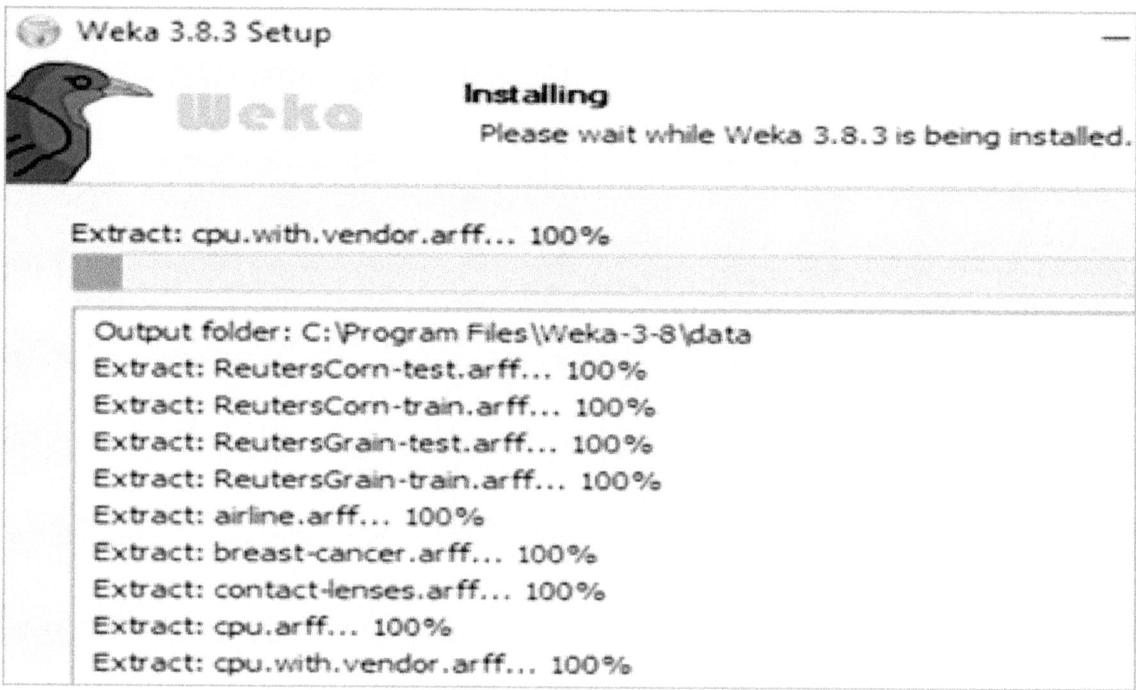

Figure 3.6 WEKA Installation Screen

6. If Java is not installed in the system, Java will be installed first as shown in figure 3.7.

Figure 3.7 Java Installation Screen

7.After the installation is complete, the following window will appear as seen in figure 3.8. Click on Next.

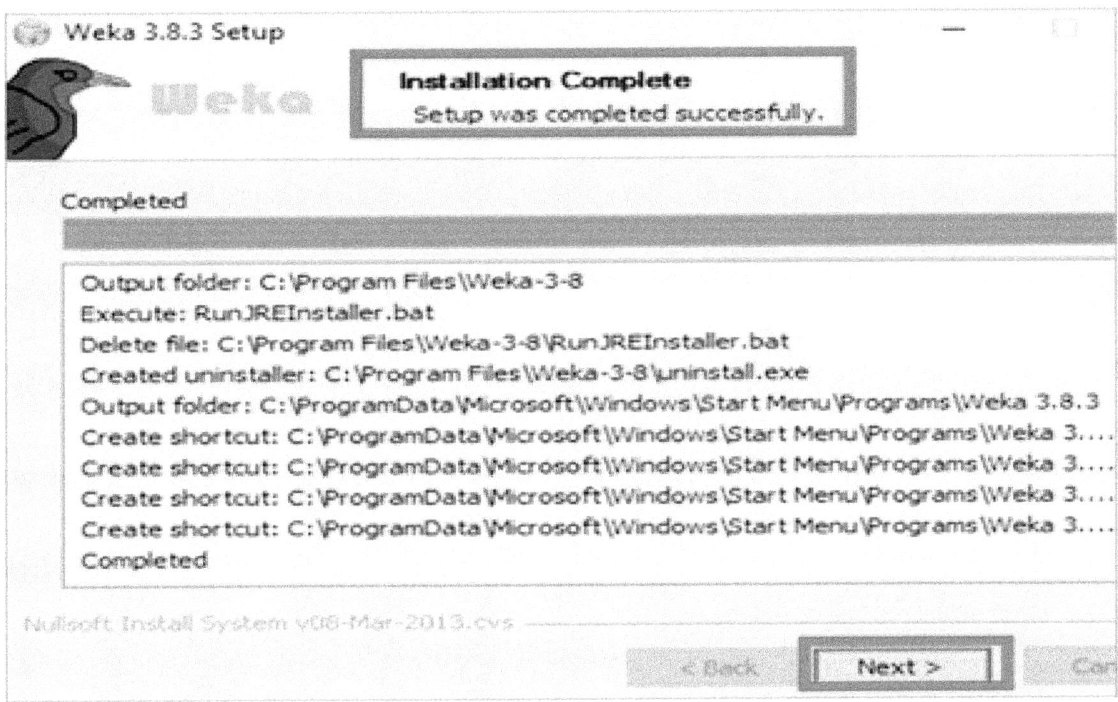

Figure 3.8 WEKA Installation Complete Screen

8. The following screen (figure 3.9) will appear. Now select the Start Weka checkbox. Click on Finish.

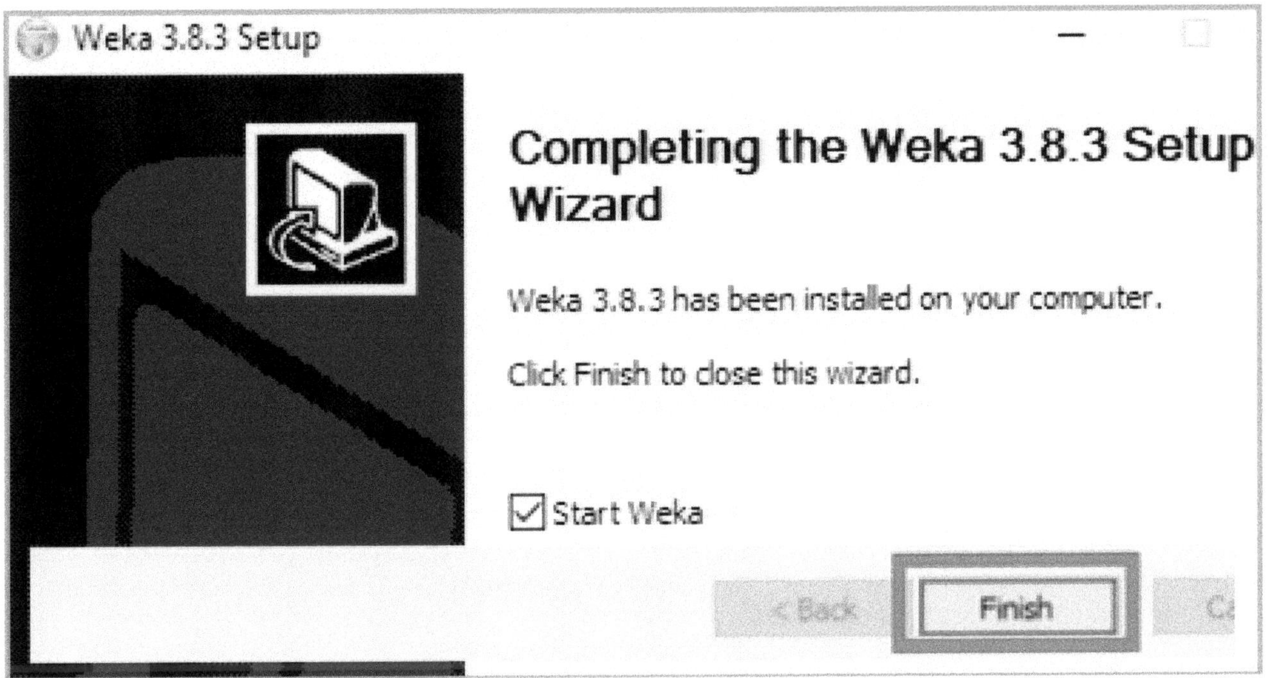

Figure 3.9 WEKA Setup Completion Wizard

9. WEKA Tool and Explorer window opens.

Figure 3.10 WEKA Tool Window

3.4 Graphical User Interface of WEKA

```
java <classname> <args>
          Lists the capabilities of the specified class.
          If the class is a weka.core.OptionHandler then
          trailing options after the classname will be
          set as well.

kill
          Kills the running job, if any.

script <script_file>
          Executes commands from a script file.

set [name=value]
          Sets a variable.
          If no key=value pair is given all current variables are l

unset name
          Removes a variable.


Notes:
- Variables can be used anywhere using '${<name>}' with '<name>'
  being the name of the variable.
- Environment variables can be used with '${env.<name>}',
  e.g., '${env.PATH}' to retrieve the PATH variable.

help
```

Figure 3.11 WEKA, Simple Command Line Interface

The GUI of WEKA gives five options: Explorer, Experimenter, Knowledge flow, Workbench, and Simple Command Line Interface. Let us understand each of these individually.

3.4.1 Simple CLI

Weka Shell is a simple CLI that has a command line and output as shown in figures 3.11 and 3.12. The overview of all the commands can be seen by typing "help." All classes, including classifiers, clusters, filters, etc., are accessible using Simple CLI.

Some of the simple CLI commands are:

- **Break:** To stop the current thread
- **Exit:** Exit the CLI
- **Help[<command>] :** Outputs the help for the specified command
- **-java weka.classifiers.trees.J48 -t c:/temp/iris.arff :** To invoke a WEKA class, prefix it with Java. This command will direct WEKA to load the class and execute it with the given parameters. In this command, J48 classifier is invoked on the IRIS dataset.

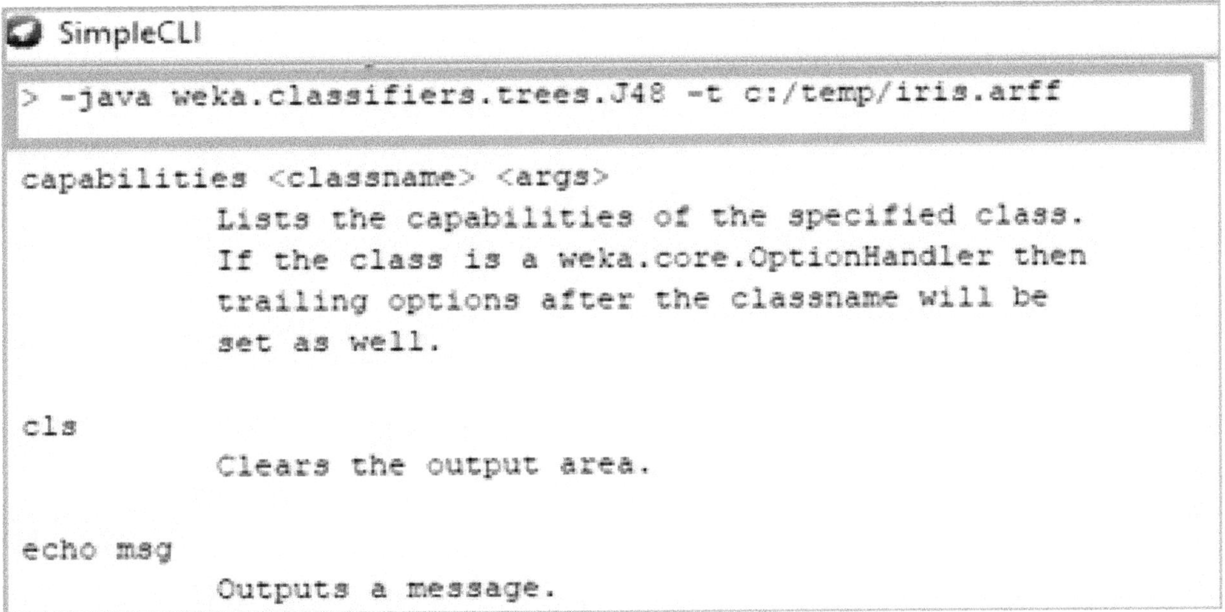

Figure 3.12 WEKA, Simple Command Line Interface

3.4.2 Explorer

The WEKA Explorer windows show different tabs starting with preprocessing as shown in figure 3.13. Initially, the preprocess tab is active, as first the data set is preprocessed before applying algorithms to it and exploring the dataset

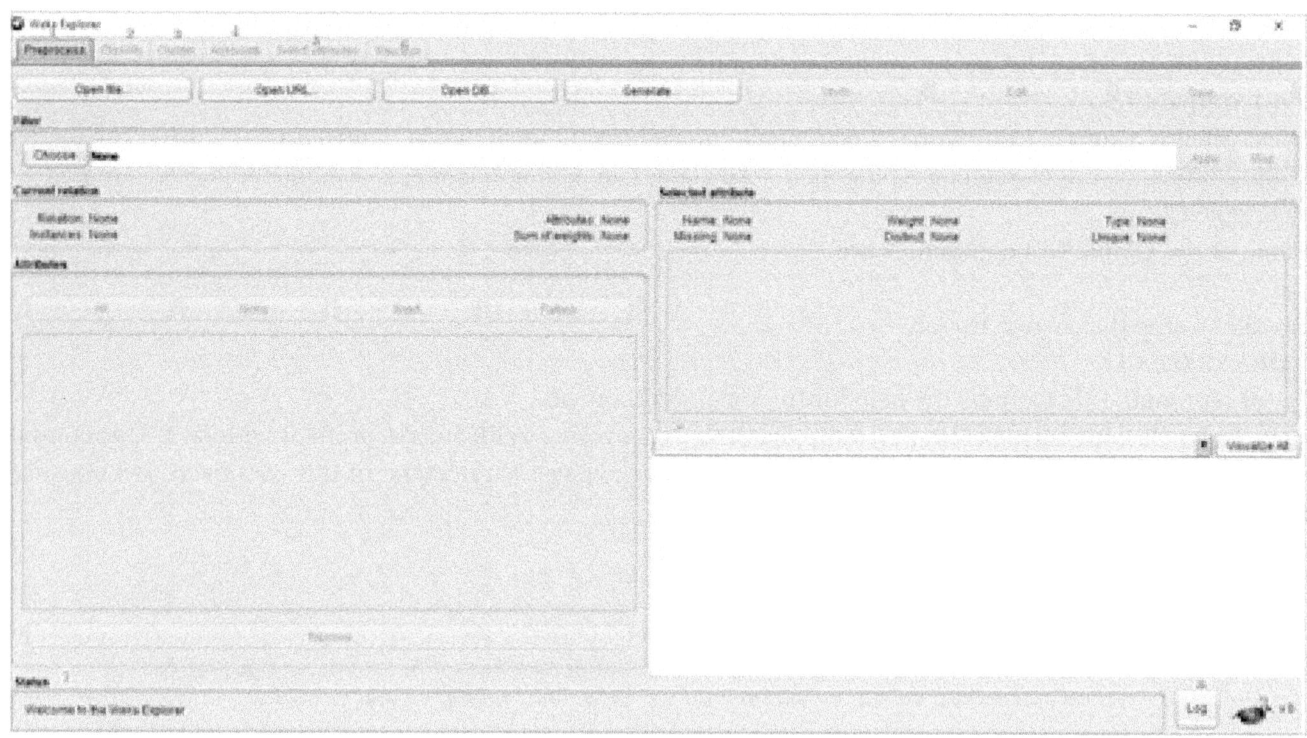

Figure 3.13 WEKA Preprocess Tab

The tabs are as follows:

1. Preprocess: Choose and modify the loaded data.

2. Classify: Apply techniques for training and testing that will classify and regress the data to the data.

3. Cluster: Create groups based on the data.

4. Associate: Find the data's association rule by mining the data.

5. Choose attributes: Measures for attribute selection are used.

6. Visualize: Data is shown in 2D form.

7. Status Bar: The status bar is displayed in the window's bottom-most portion. This section displays messages that describe what is occurring right now, such as a file being loaded. If you perform a right-click on this, memory details are shown. To clear up space, you can run the garbage collector.

8. The Log button: keeps a record of every activity made in Weka, along with the timestamp. When the Log button is clicked, logs are displayed in a separate window.

9. WEKA Bird Icon: The WEKA bird, which denotes the number of concurrent processes, is shown in the bottom right corner (by x.). The bird will move about while the operation is running.

The tabs are as follows:

1. **Log Button:** It stores a log of all actions in Weka with the timestamp. Logs are shown in a separate window when the Log button is clicked.
2. **WEKA Bird Icon:** Present on the bottom right corner shows the WEKA bird with represents the number of processes running concurrently (by x.). When the process is running the bird will move around.

3.4.3 Experimenter

The WEKA experimenter button enables users to build, test, and adjust various schemes within a single experiment on a dataset. Two configuration kinds are available to the experimenter: Simple and Advanced. Users can conduct experiments both locally and remotely using any arrangement.

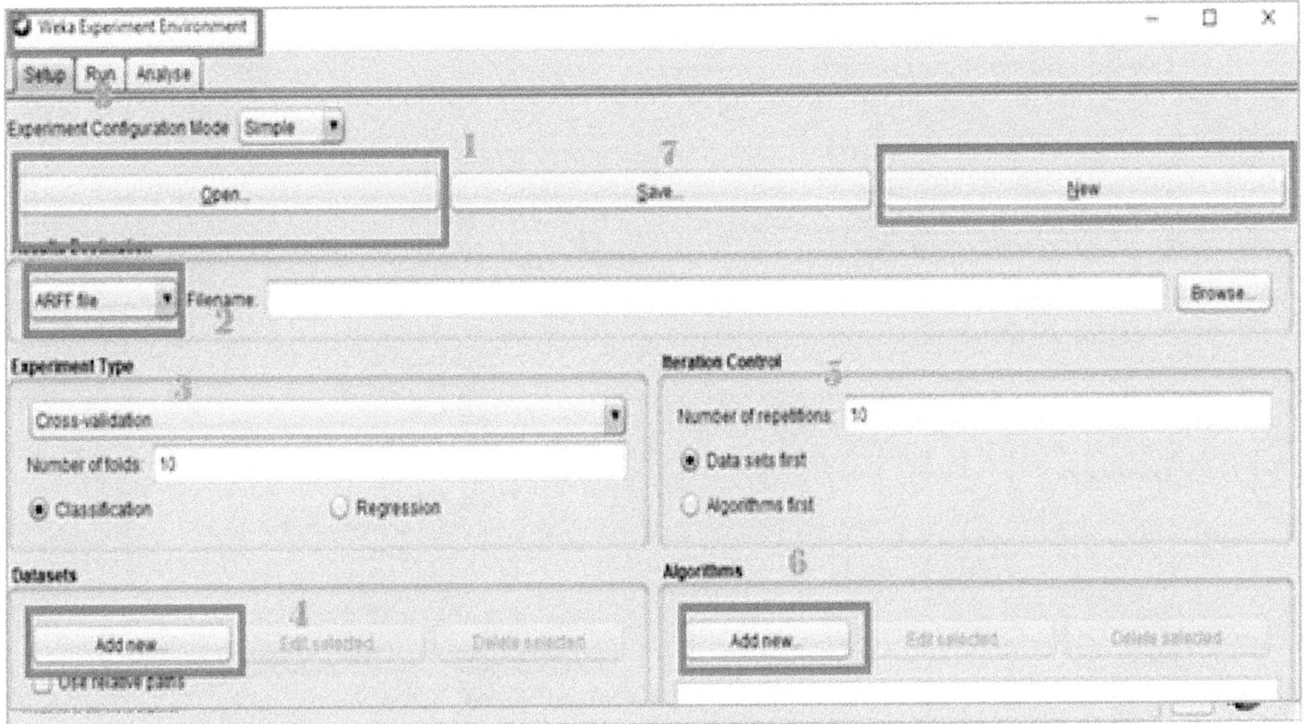

Figure 3.14 WEKA Experiment Environment

1. When users click the "Open" or "New" buttons, a new experiment window will open.
2. **Results:** Choose an ARFF, JDFC, or CSV file as the destination file for the results.
3. The user can select between cross-validation and a train/test percentage split for the experiment type. Depending on the dataset and classifier being used, the user can select between classification and regression.
4. **Datasets:** The user can browse and select datasets from here. The relative path checkbox is clicked if working on different machines. The format of datasets supported is ARFF, C4.5, CSV, libsvm, bsi, and XRFF.
5. **Iteration:** The default iteration number is set to 10. Datasets first and algorithms first help in switching between dataset and algorithms so that algorithms can be run on all datasets.
6. **Algorithms:** New algorithms are added by “New Button”. The user can choose a classifier.
7. Save the experiment using the Save button.
8. Run the experiment using the Run button.

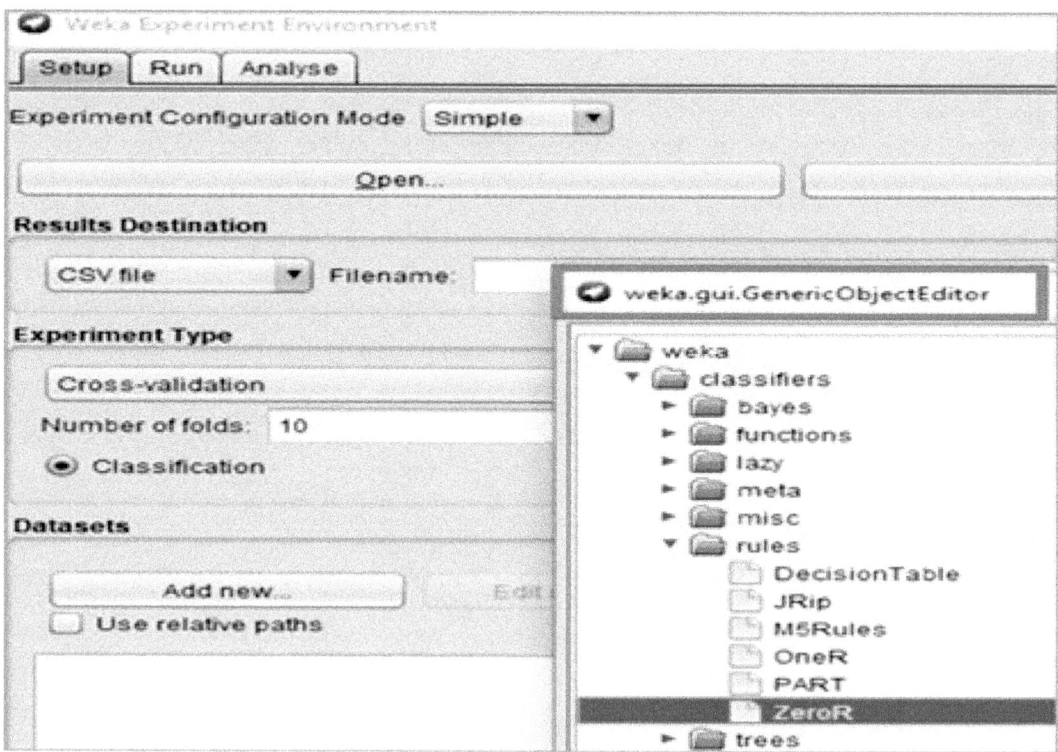

Figure 3.15 WEKA Experiment Environment Setup

3.4.4 Knowledge Flow

Knowledge flow shows a graphical representation of WEKA algorithms. The user can select the components and create a workflow to analyze the datasets. The data can be handled batch-wise or incrementally. Parallel workflows can be designed and each will run in a separate thread.

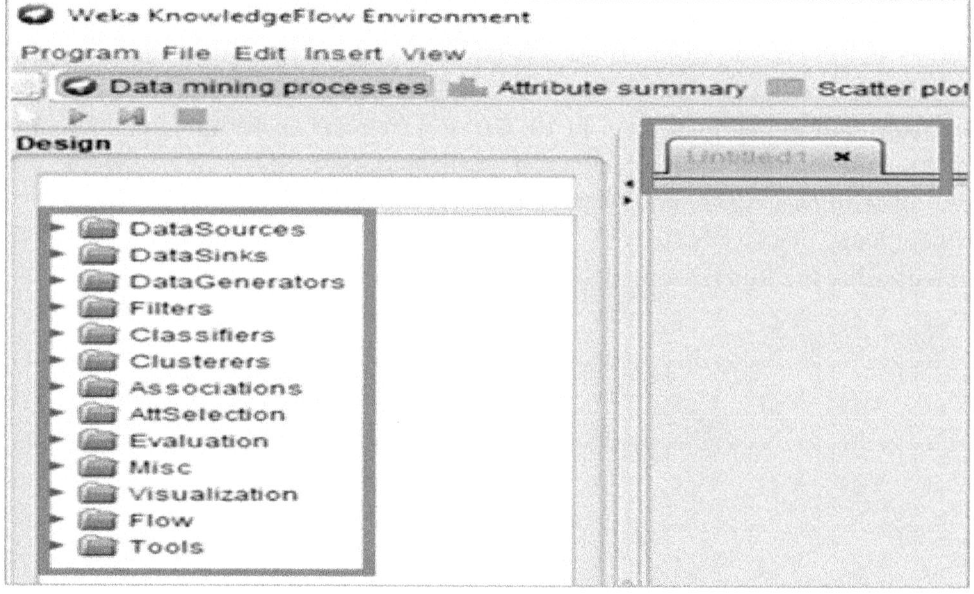

Figure 3.16 WEKA Knowledge Flow

The different components available are Datasources, Datasavers, Filters, Classifiers, Clusters, Evaluation, and Visualization.

3.4.5 Workbench

WEKA has a workbench module which contains all the GUI in a single window.

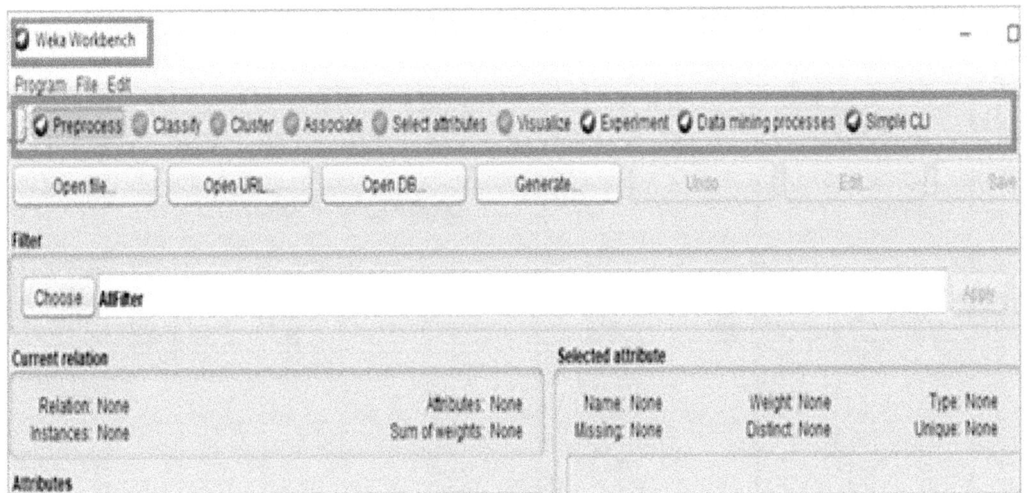

Figure 3.17 WEKA Workbench

3.5 Data Visualization

The method of representing data through graphs and plots with the aim to understand data clearly is data visualization.

There are many ways to represent data. Some of them are as follows:

1) Pixel Oriented Visualization: Here the color of the pixel represents the dimension value. The color of the pixel represents the corresponding values.

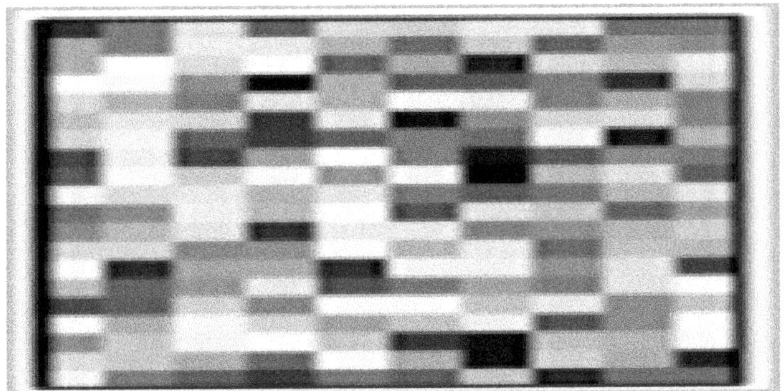

Figure 3.18 WEKA Pixel Oriented Visualization

2) Geometric Representation: The multidimensional datasets are represented in 2D, 3D, and 4D scatter plots.

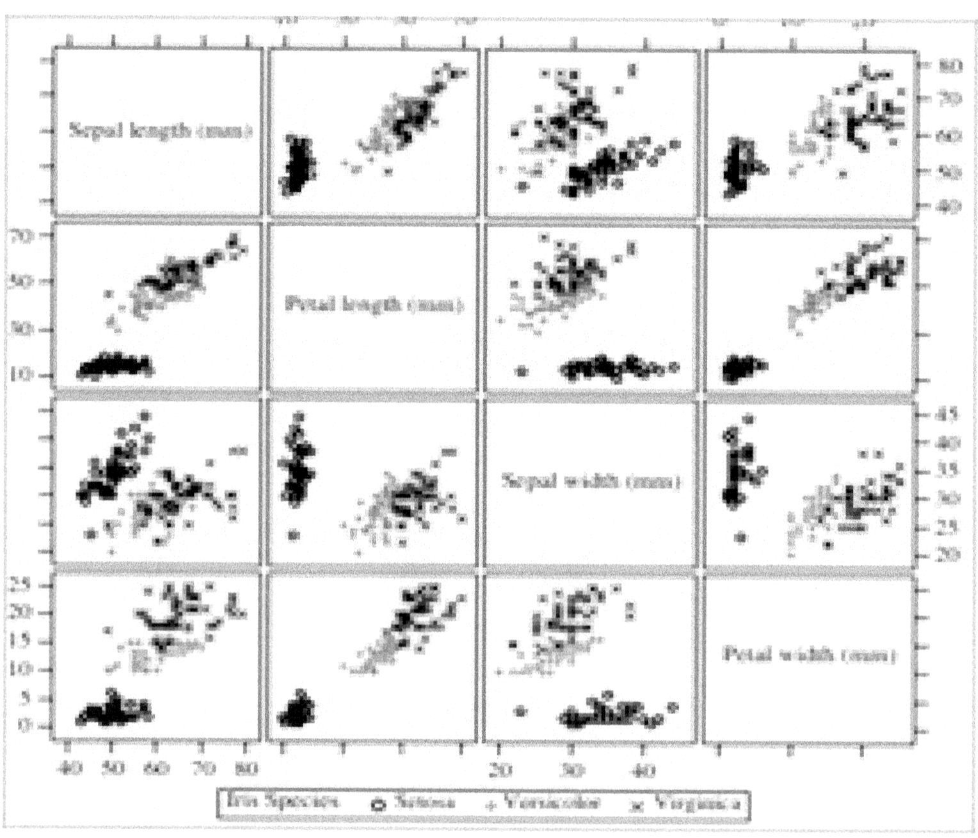

Figure 3.19 WEKA Geometric Representation

3) Icon-Based Visualization: The data is represented using Chernoff's faces and stick figures. Chernoff's faces use the human mind's ability to recognize facial characteristics and differences between them. The stick figure uses 5 stick figures to represent multidimensional data.

Figure 3.20 WEKA Icon-Based Visualization

4) Hierarchical Data Visualization: The datasets are represented using treemaps. It represents hierarchical data as a set of nested triangles.

Figure 3.21 Hierarchical Data Visualization

3.5.1 Data Visualization Using WEKA Explorer

Data Visualization using WEKA is done on the IRIS.arff dataset.

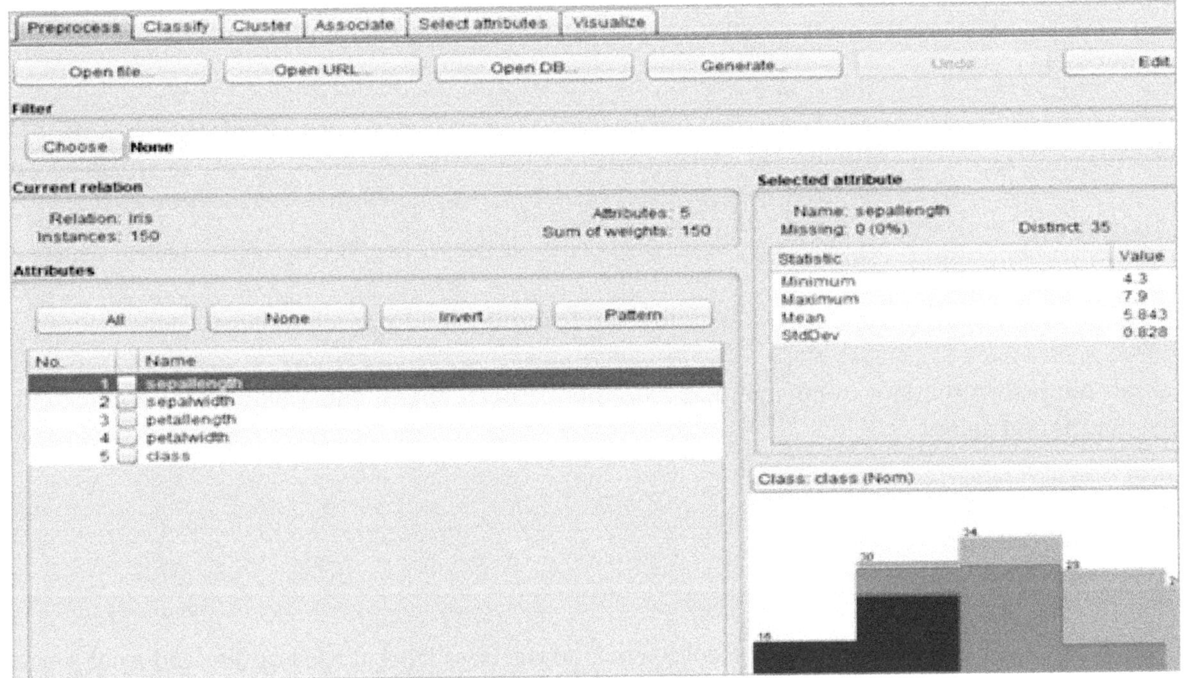

Figure 3.22 Data Visualization Using WEKA Explorer Screen 1

The steps involved are as follows:

1) Go to the Preprocess tab and open IRIS.arff dataset.

2) The dataset has 4 attributes and 1 class label. **The attributes in this dataset are:**

- **Sepallength :** Type -numeric
- **Sepalwidth:** Type- numeric
- **Petalength:** Type-numeric
- **Petalwidth:** Type-numeric
- **Class:** Type-nominal

3) To visualize the dataset, go to the Visualize tab. The tab shows the attributes plot matrix. The dataset attributes are marked on the x-axis and y-axis while the instances are plotted. The box with the x-axis attribute and y-axis attribute can be enlarged.

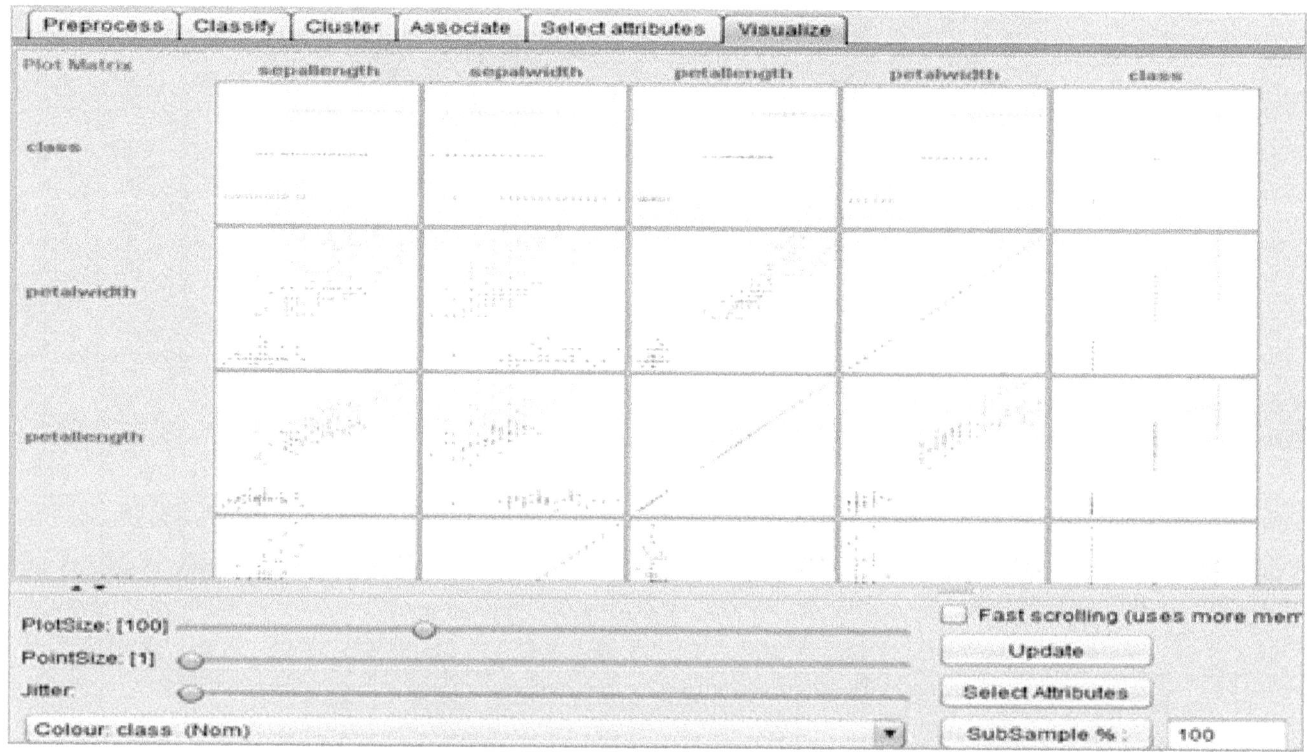

Figure 3.23 Data Visualization Using WEKA Explorer Screen 2

4) Click on the box of the plot to enlarge. **For example,** x: petal length and y:petalwidth. The class labels are represented in different colors.

- Class label- Iris-setosa: blue color
- Class label- Iris-versicolor: red
- Class label-Iris-virginica-green

These colors can be changed. To change the color, click on the class label at the bottom, and a color window will appear

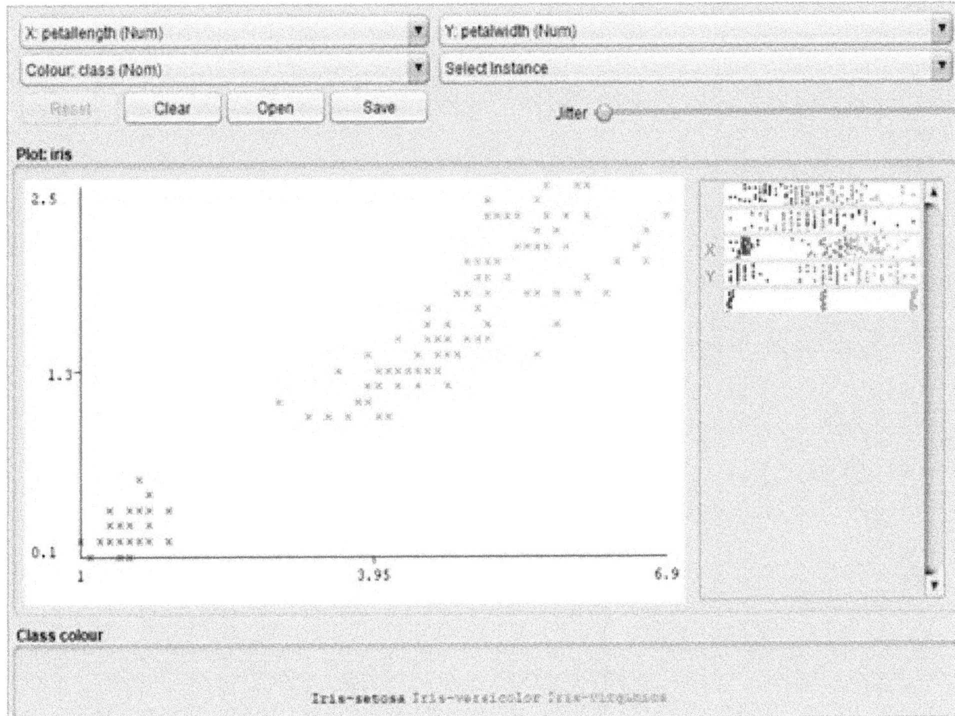

Figure 3.24 color window1

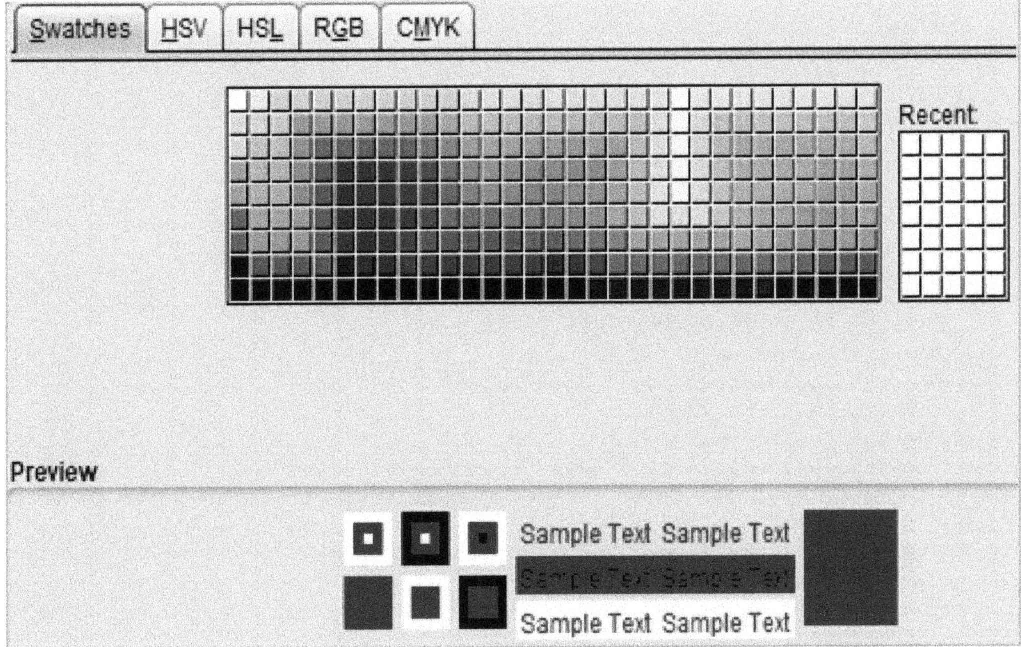

Figure 3.25 color window2

5) Click on the instance represented by 'x' in the plot. It will give the instance details. **For example:**

- **Instance number:** 91

- **Sepalength:** 5.5
- **Sepalwidth:** 2.6
- **Petalength:** 4.4
- **Petalwidth:** 1.2
- **Class:** Iris-versicolor

Some of the points in the plot appear darker than other points. These points represent 2 or more instances with the same class label and the same value of attributes plotted on the graph such as petalwidth and petallength.

The figure below represents a point with 2 instances of information.

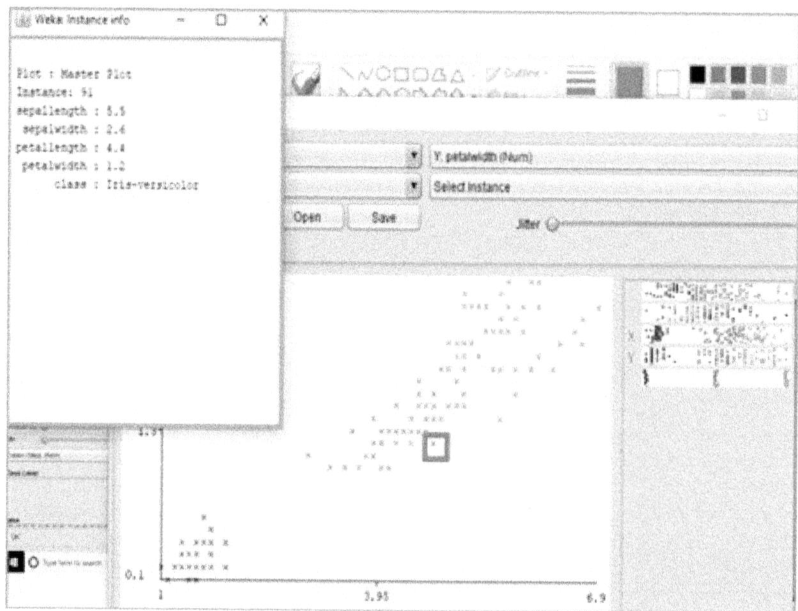

Figure 3.26 weka instance iformation

```
Weka: Instance info

Plot : Master Plot
Instance: 61
sepallength : 5.0
 sepalwidth : 2.0
petallength : 3.5
 petalwidth : 1.0
      class : Iris-versicolor

Plot : Master Plot
Instance: 80
sepallength : 5.7
 sepalwidth : 2.6
petallength : 3.5
 petalwidth : 1.0
      class : Iris-versicolor
```

Figure 3.27 weka instance information

6) The X and Y-axis attributes can be changed from the right panel in Visualize graph. The user can view different plots.

7) The Jitter is used to add randomness to the plot. Sometimes the points overlap. With jitter, the darker spots represent multiple instances.

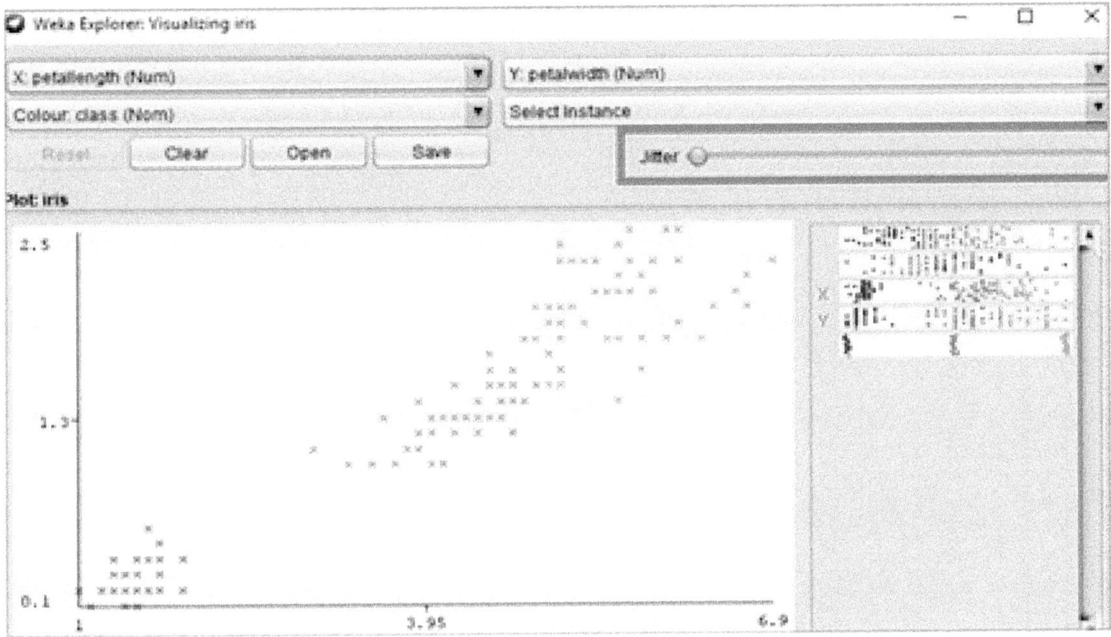

Figure 3.28 Jitter

8) To get a clearer view of the dataset and remove outliers, the user can select an instance from the dropdown. Click on the "select instance" dropdown. Choose "Rectangle". With this, the user will be able to select points in the plot by plotting a rectangle.

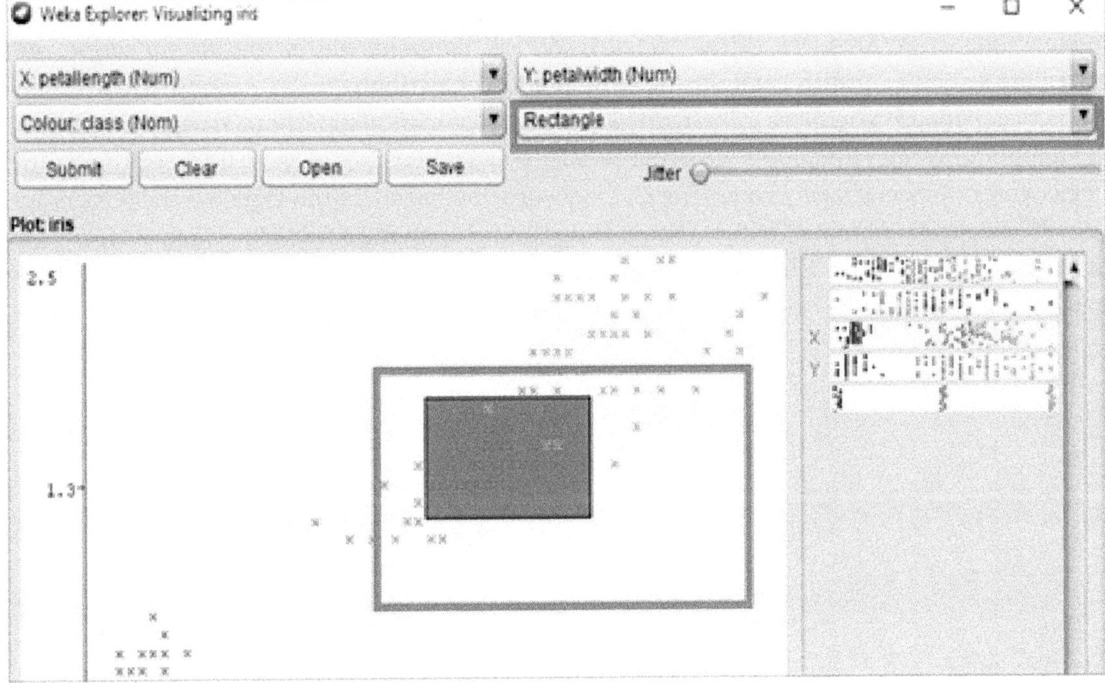

Figure 3.29 Jitter -multiples instances

9) Click on "Submit". Only the selected dataset points will be displayed and the other points will be excluded from the graph.

The figure below shows the points from the selected rectangular shape. The plot represents points with only 3 class labels. The user can click on "Save" to save the dataset or "Reset" to select another instance. The dataset will be saved a separately.ARFF file.

Figure 3.30 Jitter- selected rectangular instances

2. Setting Filters

Pre-processing tools in WEKA are called "filters". WEKA contains filters for discretization, normalization, resampling, attribute selection, transformation and combination of attributes.

. For you practice, suppose you need to perform a test on categorical data. There are two attributes that need to be converted: 'temperature' and 'humidity'. In other words, you will keep all of the values for these attributes in the data. This means you can discretize by removing the keyword "numeric" as the type for the'temperature' attribute and replace it with the set of "nominal" values. You can do this by applying a filter.

In 'Filters' window, click on the 'Choose' button.Click on the Choose button in the Filter sub window and select the following filter – weka→filters→supervised→attribute→Discretize

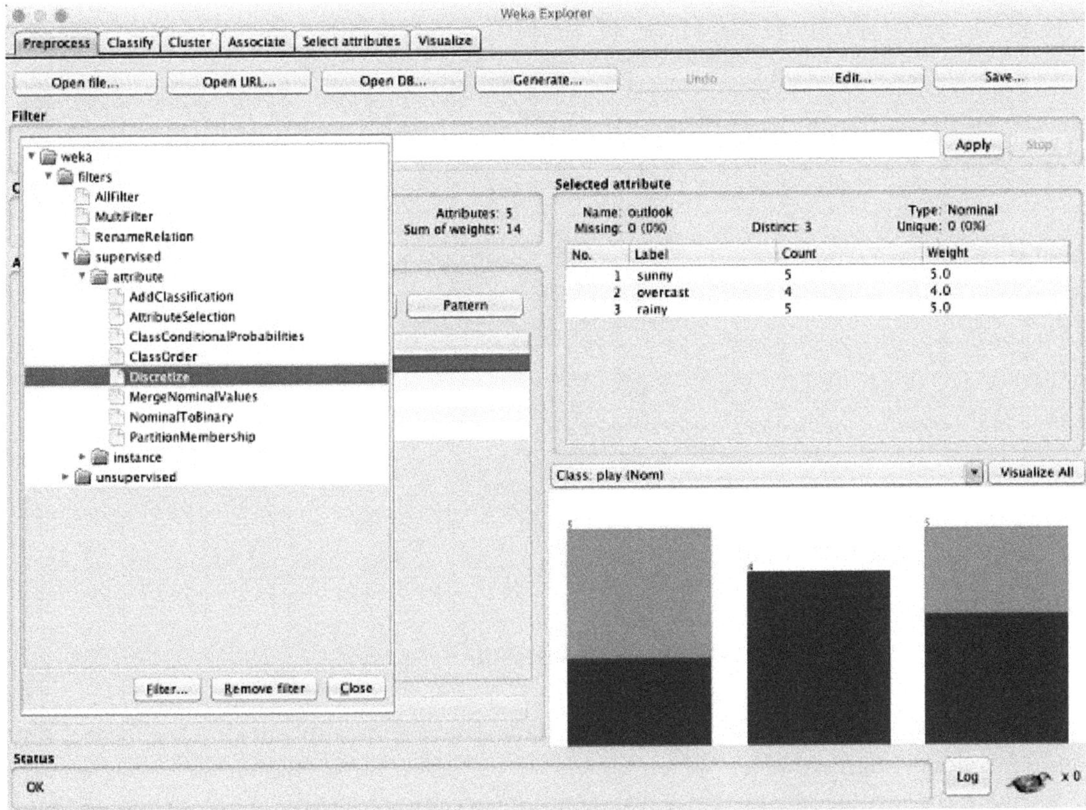

Figure 3.31 Filter

Click on the Apply button and examine the temperature and/or humidity attribute. You will notice that these have changed from numeric to nominal types.

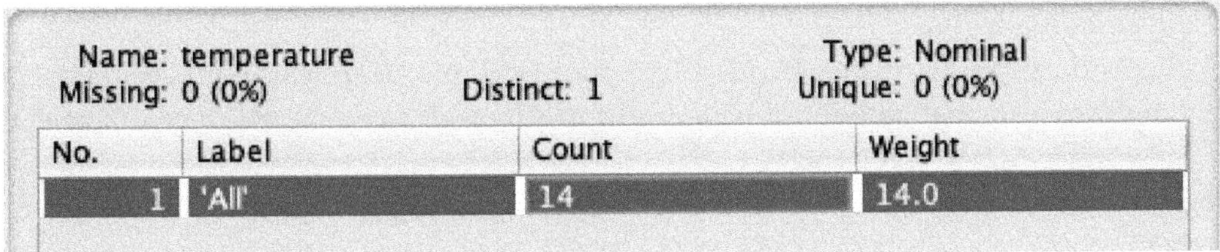

Name: temperature
Missing: 0 (0%)
Distinct: 1
Type: Nominal
Unique: 0 (0%)

No.	Label	Count	Weight
1	'All'	14	14.0

Figure 3.32 Applying FIlter

Suppose you want to select the best attributes for deciding the play. Select and apply the following filter –weka→filters→supervised→attribute→AttributeSelection

This will show pull-down menu with a list of available filters. Select Supervised à Attribute àDiscretize and click on 'Apply' button. The filter will convert Numeric values into Nominal.

When filter is chosen, the fields in the window changes to reflect available options.

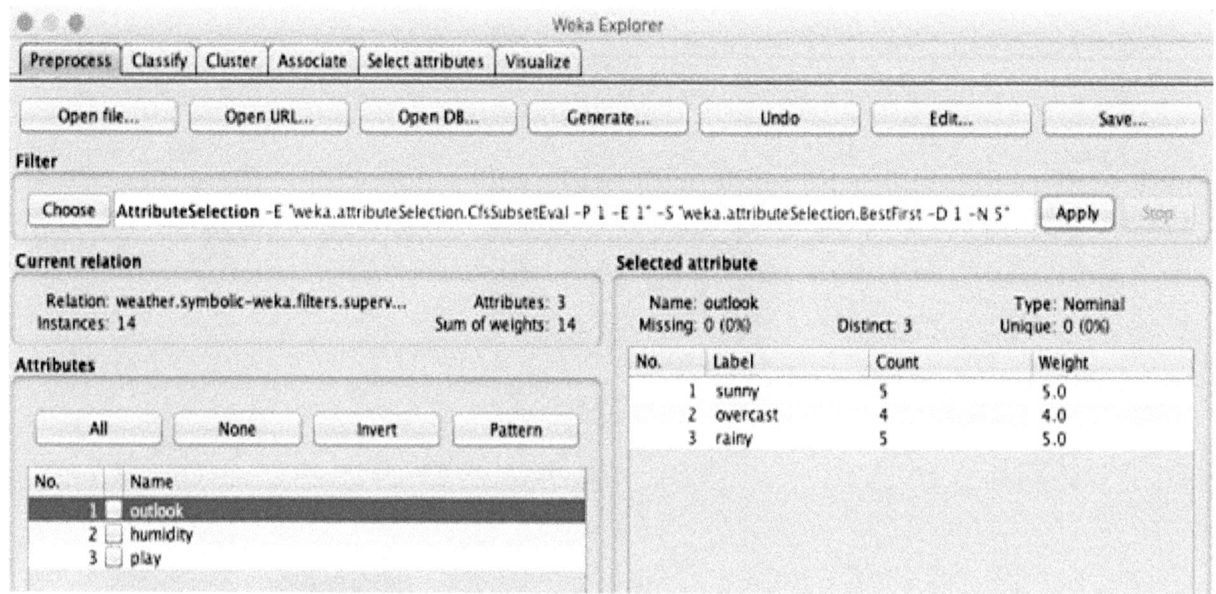

Figure 3.33 Attribute Selection

After you are satisfied with the preprocessing of your data, save the data by clicking the Save ... button. You will use this saved file for model building.

When it is finished, the results of selection are shown on the right part of the window and entry is added to the 'Result list'.

3.5 **Classification Task**

3.5.1 Data Classification

Data Classification involves selecting a label from a predefined set of labels and assigning them to every data point. Classification has numerous applications in all fields of business, including but not limited to marketing, operations, and finance.

Types of Classification Algorithms

Classification Algorithms can be further divided into statistical and deep learning-based algorithms. Statistical learning generally involves a smaller amount of data, fewer features, and a single instance of a specific algorithm at work.

Deep Learning techniques extend statistical learning by creating a deep network of neurons that embed statistical concepts within them.

Statistical learning-based algorithms excel when the amount of data is lesser, and the relationships are not complex. They can be trained quickly without high hardware requirements and provide acceptable results. Let us explore a few of them which are commonly used.

3.5.2 Naive Bayes Algorithm

It is a classification algorithm based on **Bayes's theorem** which gives an assumption of independence among predictors. In simple terms, a Naive Bayes classifier assumes that the presence of a particular feature in a class is unrelated to the presence of any other feature.

Even if the features depend on each other, all of these properties contribute to the probability independently. Naive Bayes model is easy to make and is particularly useful for comparatively large data sets. Even with a simplistic approach, Naive Bayes is known to outperform most of the classification methods in machine learning. Following is the Bayes theorem to implement the Naive Bayes Theorem.

$$P(C_i| x_1, x_2 \ldots, x_n) = \frac{P(x_1, x_2 \ldots, x_n|C_i).P(C_i)}{P(x_1, x_2 \ldots, x_n)} \; for \; 1 < i < k$$

Advantages and Disadvantages

The Naive Bayes classifier requires a small amount of training data to estimate the necessary parameters to get the results. They are extremely fast in nature compared to other classifiers.

The only disadvantage is that they are known to be a bad estimator.

Use Cases

Disease Predictions

Document Classification

Spam Filters

Sentiment Analysis

It is a very effective and simple approach to fit linear models. Stochastic Gradient Descent is particularly useful when the sample data is in a large number. It supports different loss functions and penalties for classification.

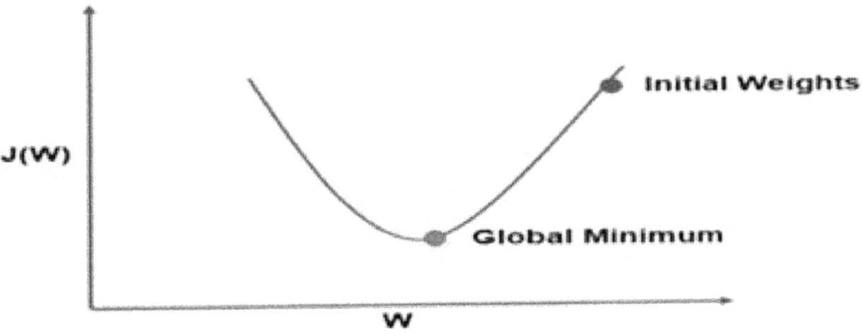

Figure 3.34 Fit linear models

Stochastic gradient descent refers to calculating the derivative from each training data instance and calculating the update immediately.

Advantages and Disadvantages

The only advantage is the ease of implementation and efficiency whereas a major setback with stochastic gradient descent is that it requires a number of hyper-parameters and is sensitive to feature scaling.

Use Cases

Internet Of Things

Updating the parameters such as weights in neural networks or coefficients in linear regression

3.5.3 Logistic Regression

Logistic Regression predicts the probability of a data row belonging to the label as a zero to one value. A threshold is then defined to assert whether the data element belongs to that class or not. The same concept can be extended for multiple classes to implement a multi-class classifier. Logistic regression does not do a good job in a multi-label classification where each row can belong to more than one label.

It is a classification algorithm in machine learning that uses one or more independent variables to determine an outcome. The outcome is measured with a dichotomous variable meaning it will have only two possible outcomes.

The goal of logistic regression is to find a best-fitting relationship between the dependent variable and a set of independent variables. It is better than other binary classification algorithms like nearest neighbor since it quantitatively explains the factors leading to classification.

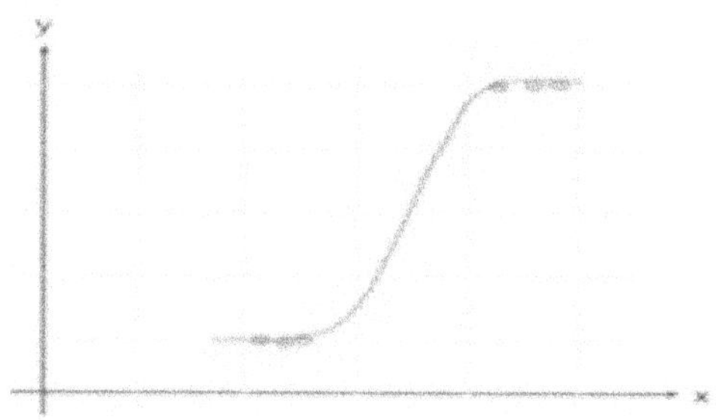

Figure 3.35 Logistic Regression

Advantages and Disadvantages

Logistic regression is specifically meant for classification, it is useful in understanding how a set of independent variables affect the outcome of the dependent variable.

The main disadvantage of the logistic regression algorithm is that it only works when the predicted variable is binary, it assumes that the data is free of missing values and assumes that the predictors are independent of each other.

Use Cases

Identifying risk factors for diseases

Word classification

Weather Prediction

Voting Applications

3.5.6 Support Vector Machine

The support vector machine is a classifier that represents the **training data as points in space** separated into categories by a gap as wide as possible. New points are then added to space by predicting which category they fall into and which space they will belong to.

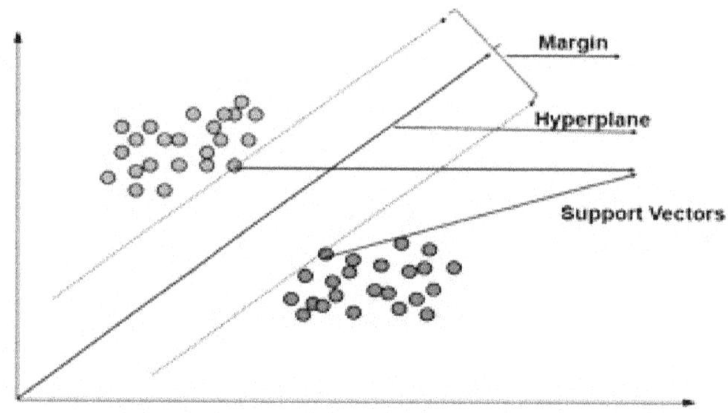

Figure 3.36 Training Data As Points In Space

Advantages and Disadvantages

It uses a subset of training points in the decision function which makes it memory efficient and is highly effective in high dimensional spaces. The only disadvantage with the support vector machine is that the algorithm does not directly provide probability estimates.

Use cases

Business applications for comparing the performance of a stock over a period of time

Investment suggestions

Classification of applications requiring accuracy and efficiency

3.5.7 Decision Tree

The decision tree algorithm builds the classification model in the form of a tree structure. It utilizes the if-then rules which are equally exhaustive and mutually exclusive in classification. The process goes on with breaking down the data into smaller structures and eventually associating it with an incremental decision tree. The final structure looks like a tree with nodes and leaves. The rules are learned sequentially using the training data one at a time. Each time a rule is learned, the tuples covering the rules are removed. The process continues on the training set until the termination point is met.

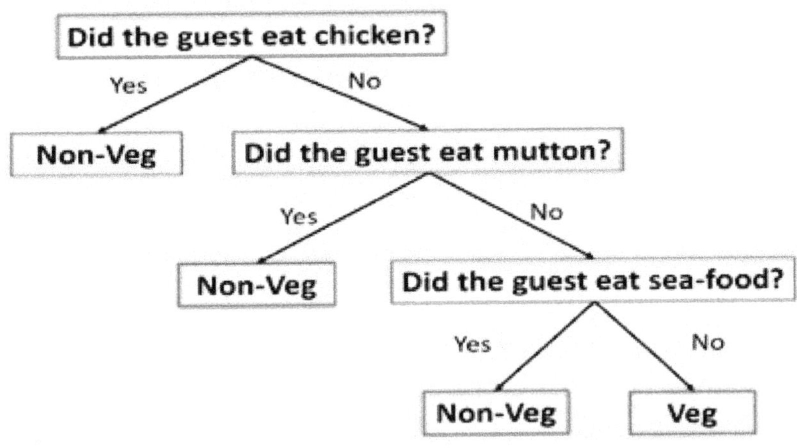

Figure 3.37 Decision Tree

The tree is constructed in a top-down recursive divide and conquer approach. A decision node will have two or more branches and a leaf represents a classification or decision. The topmost node in the decision tree that corresponds to the best predictor is called the root node, and the best thing about a decision tree is that it can handle both categorical and numerical data.

Advantages and Disadvantages

A decision tree gives an advantage of simplicity to understand and visualize, it requires very little data preparation as well. The disadvantage that follows with the decision tree is that it can create complex trees that may bot categorize efficiently. They can be quite unstable because even a simplistic change in the data can hinder the whole structure of the decision tree.

Use Cases

Data exploration

Pattern Recognition

Option pricing in finances

Identifying disease and risk threats

3.5.8 Random Forest

It is an extension of Decision trees. A random forest is a sequential combination of decision trees created on random data splits. They are preferred over decision trees in case data volume is moderate and many features are significant in dividing the data. Random Forest reduces the probability of the decision tree being stuck with a feature that does not scale well in test data but significantly affects training data. In other words, the randomness in random forests prevents overfitting, which is a common complaint with decision trees.

Random decision trees or random forest are an ensemble learning method for classification, regression, etc. It operates by constructing a multitude of decision trees at training time and outputs the class that is the mode of the classes or classification or mean prediction(regression) of the individual trees.

A random forest is a meta-estimator that fits a number of trees on various subsamples of data sets and then uses an average to improve the accuracy in the model's predictive nature. The sub-sample size is always the same as that of the original input size but the samples are often drawn with replacements.

Advantages and Disadvantages

The advantage of the random forest is that it is more accurate than the decision trees due to the reduction in the over-fitting. The only disadvantage with the random forest classifiers is that it is quite complex in implementation and gets pretty slow in real-time prediction.

Use Cases

Industrial applications such as finding if a loan applicant is high-risk or low-risk

For Predicting the failure of mechanical parts in automobile engines

Predicting social media share scores

Performance scores

3.8 Artificial Neural Network

The term "**Artificial Neural Network**" is derived from Biological neural networks that develop the structure of a human brain. Similar to the human brain that has neurons interconnected to one another, artificial neural networks also have neurons that are interconnected to one another in various layers of the networks. These neurons are known as nodes.

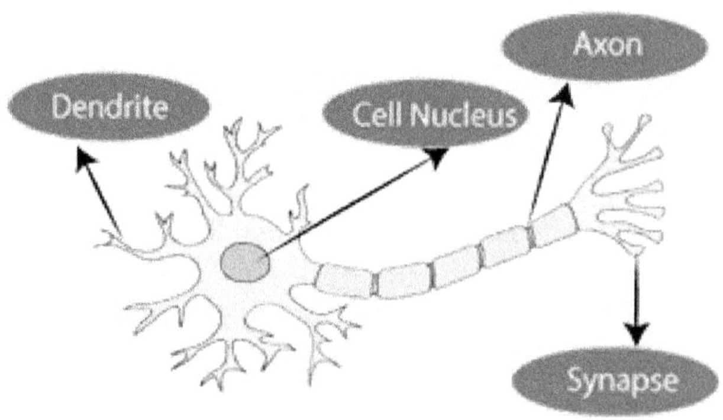

Figure 3.38 Artificial Neural Network

A neural network consists of neurons that are **arranged in layers**, they take some input vector and convert it into an output. The process involves each neuron taking input and applying a function which is often a non-linear function to it and then passes the output to the next layer.

The typical Artificial Neural Network looks something like the given figure.

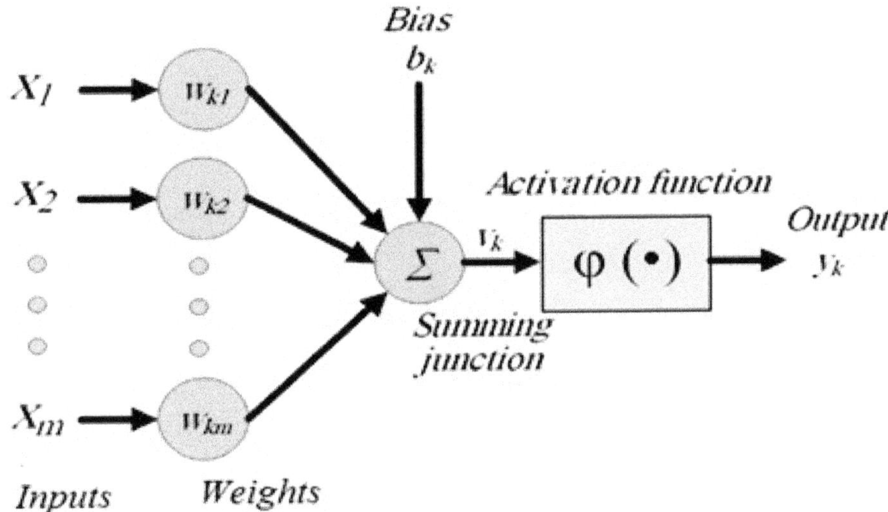

Figure 3.39 Weighings Applied to Artificial Nueral Network

In general, the network is supposed to be feed-forward meaning that the unit or neuron feeds the output to the next layer but there is no involvement of any feedback to the previous layer.

Weighings are applied to the signals passing from one layer to the other, and these are the weighings that are tuned in the training phase to adapt a neural network for any problem statement.

An **Artificial Neural Network** in the field of **Artificial intelligence** where it attempts to mimic the network of neurons makes up a human brain so that computers will have an option to understand things and make decisions in a human-like manner. The artificial neural network is designed by programming computers to behave simply like interconnected brain cells.

There are around 1000 billion neurons in the human brain. Each neuron has an association point somewhere in the range of 1,000 and 100,000. In the human brain, data is stored in such a manner as to be distributed, and we can extract more than one piece of this data when necessary from our memory parallelly. We can say that the human brain is made up of incredibly amazing parallel processors.

3.8.1 Architecture of an artificial neural network:

To understand the concept of the architecture of an artificial neural network, we have to understand what a neural network consists of. In order to define a neural network that consists of a large number of artificial neurons, which are termed units arranged in a sequence of layers. Lets us look at various types of layers available in an artificial neural network.

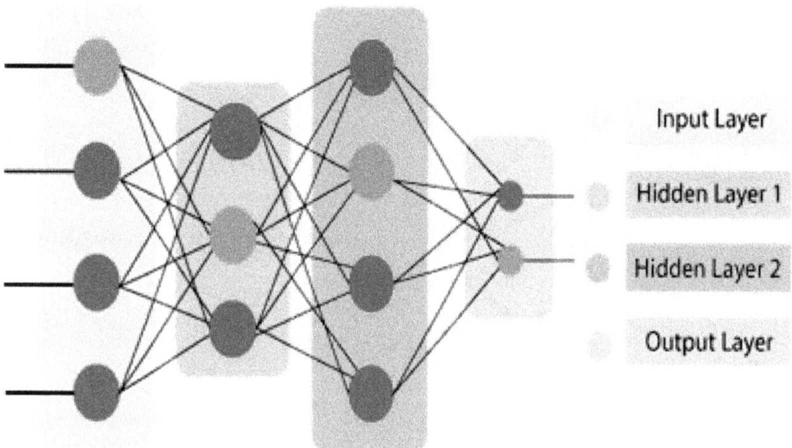

Figure 3.40 Architecture of Artificial Neural Network

Input Layer:

As the name suggests, it accepts inputs in several different formats provided by the programmer.

Hidden Layer:

The hidden layer presents in-between input and output layers. It performs all the calculations to find hidden features and patterns.

Output Layer:

The input goes through a series of transformations using the hidden layer, which finally results in output that is conveyed using this layer.

The artificial neural network takes input and computes the weighted sum of the inputs and includes a bias. This computation is represented in the form of a transfer function.

$$\sum_{i=1}^{n} Wi * Xi + b$$

It determines weighted total is passed as an input to an activation function to produce the output. Activation functions choose whether a node should fire or not. Only those who are fired make it to the output layer. There are distinctive activation functions available that can be applied upon the sort of task we are performing.

3.8.2 Advantages and Disadvantages

Parallel processing capability:

Artificial neural networks have a numerical value that can perform more than one task simultaneously.

Storing data on the entire network:

Data that is used in traditional programming is stored on the whole network, not on a database. The disappearance of a couple of pieces of data in one place doesn't prevent the network from working.

Capability to work with incomplete knowledge:

After ANN training, the information may produce output even with inadequate data. The loss of performance here relies upon the significance of missing data.

Having a memory distribution:

For ANN is to be able to adapt, it is important to determine the examples and to encourage the network according to the desired output by demonstrating these examples to the network. The succession of the network is directly proportional to the chosen instances, and if the event can't appear to the network in all its aspects, it can produce false output.

Use Cases

Handwriting analysis

Colorization of black and white images

Computer vision processes

Captioning photos based on facial features

3.8.3 How do artificial neural networks work?

Artificial Neural Network can be best represented as a weighted directed graph, where the artificial neurons form the nodes. The association between the neurons outputs and neuron inputs can be viewed as the directed edges with weights. The Artificial Neural Network receives the input signal from the external source in the form of a pattern and image in the form of a vector. These inputs are then mathematically assigned by the notations x(n) for every n number of inputs.

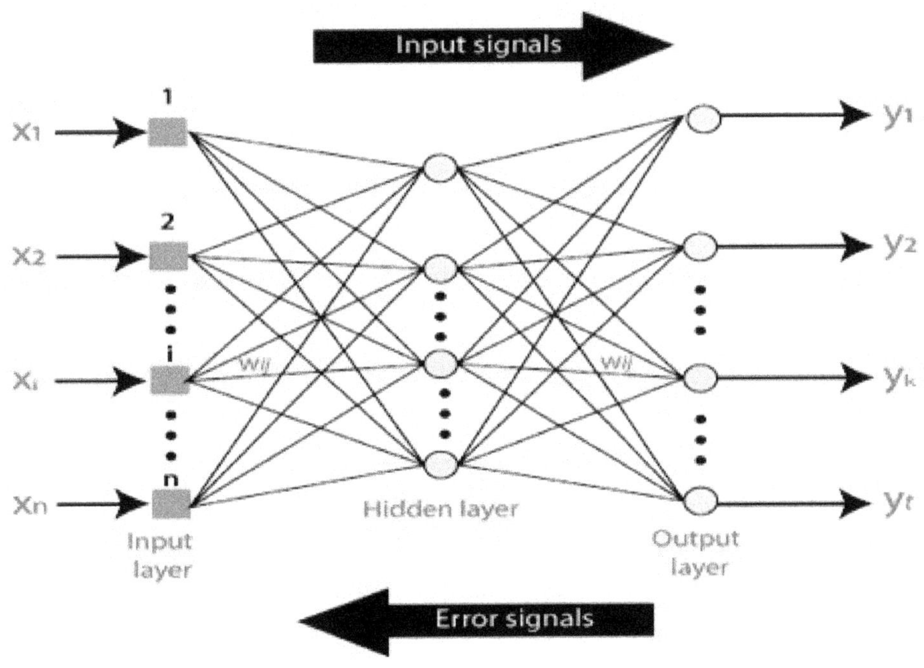

Figure 3.41 Working of Artificial Neural Network

Afterward, each of the input is multiplied by its corresponding weights (these weights are the details utilized by the artificial neural networks to solve a specific problem). In general terms, these weights normally represent the strength of the interconnection between neurons inside the artificial neural network. All the weighted inputs are summarized inside the computing unit.

If the weighted sum is equal to zero, then bias is added to make the output non-zero or something else to scale up to the system's response. Bias has the same input, and weight equals to 1. Here the total of weighted inputs can be in the range of 0 to positive infinity. Here, to keep the response in the limits of the desired value, a certain maximum value is benchmarked, and the total of weighted inputs is passed through the activation function.

The activation function refers to the set of transfer functions used to achieve the desired output. There is a different kind of the activation function, but primarily either linear or non-linear sets of functions. Some of the commonly used sets of activation functions are the Binary, linear, and Tan hyperbolic sigmoidal activation functions.

Let us take a look at each of them in details:

Binary:

In binary activation function, the output is either a one or a 0. Here, to accomplish this, there is a threshold value set up. If the net weighted input of neurons is more than 1, then the final output of the activation function is returned as one or else the output is returned as 0.

Sigmoidal Hyperbolic:

The Sigmoidal Hyperbola function is generally seen as an "S" shaped curve. Here the tan hyperbolic function is used to approximate output from the actual net input. The function is defined as:

F(x) = (1/1 + exp(-????x))

Where ???? is considered the Steepness parameter.

CHAPTER FOUR

CLUSTERING AND ESTIMATION

4.1 Classification andPrediction

To extract models representing significant data classes or to forecast future data trends, two types of data analysis can be used: classification and prediction. Classification forecasts categorical (discrete, unordered) labels, while prediction simulates continuously valued functions.

We can create a classification model to classify bank loan applications as safe or unsafe, for instance, or a prediction model to forecast how much a potential consumer will spend on computer equipment based on their work and income. Figure 4.1 depicts the classification and prediction process.

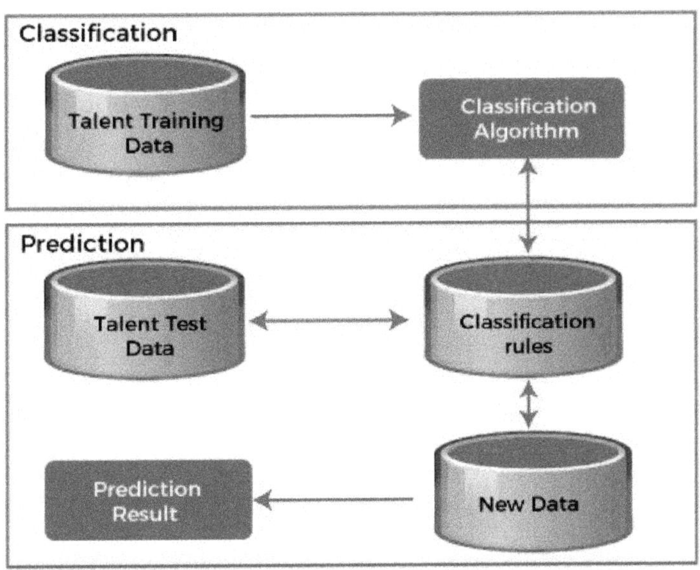

Figure 4.1 Classification and Prediction Process

4.2 Preparing data for classification and prediction

The data may go through the following preparation procedures to help increase the classification or prediction process's accuracy, efficacy, and scalability.

1. Data Cleaning
2. Relevance Analysis
3. Data Transformation

Data Cleaning

Data cleaning is the preprocessing of data to eliminate or decrease noise (for example, by using smoothing techniques) and to handle missing values (for example,

by substituting a missing value with the most frequent value for that attribute or the most likely value based on statistics).

Relevance Analysis

A large number of the data's properties may not be useful for classification or prediction tasks. Any duplicate or irrelevant qualities from the learning process can be eliminated by performing a relevance analysis on the data. This action is known as feature selection in machine learning. When learning from the "reduced" feature subset that results from relevance analysis, the learning time should be shorter than when learning from the original set of features.

Data Transformation

The information can be applied to higher-level concepts. Concept hierarchies may be employed in this situation. For continuous-valued characteristics, this is especially helpful. For instance, discrete ranges of low, medium, and high numeric values for the attribute income are possible. There may be fewer input/output operations required during learning because generalisation compresses the initial training data.

The information may also be normalised, particularly for neural networks or other techniques.

4.2 Comparison of Classification Methods

The following criteria can be used to compare and assess classification and prediction techniques.

- Accuracy
- Speed
- Robustness
- Scalability
- Interpretability

Accuracy

A classifier's accuracy refers to its capacity to properly predict the class label of brand-new or previously unobserved data (i.e., tuples without class label information).

Speed

This is the amount of computing required to create and use the specified classifier or predictor.

Robustness

This is the capacity of the classifier or predictor to generate accurate predictions in the presence of noisy data or data with missing values.

Scalability

The capacity to efficiently build a classifier or predictor in the face of a vast amount of data

Interpretability

This describes the degree of knowledge and perception that the classifier or predictor offers. Since interpretability is subjective, evaluating it might be more challenging.

4.3 Classification by Decision Tree Induction:

The process of learning decision trees from class-labeled training tuples is known as decision tree induction. A decision tree is a tree structure that resembles a flowchart. In a decision tree, there is a test on an attribute for each internal node. The results of the test are represented by each branch. Each leaf node is equipped with a class label. In a tree, the root node is the node at the top. An Example for decision tree is given in figure 4.2.

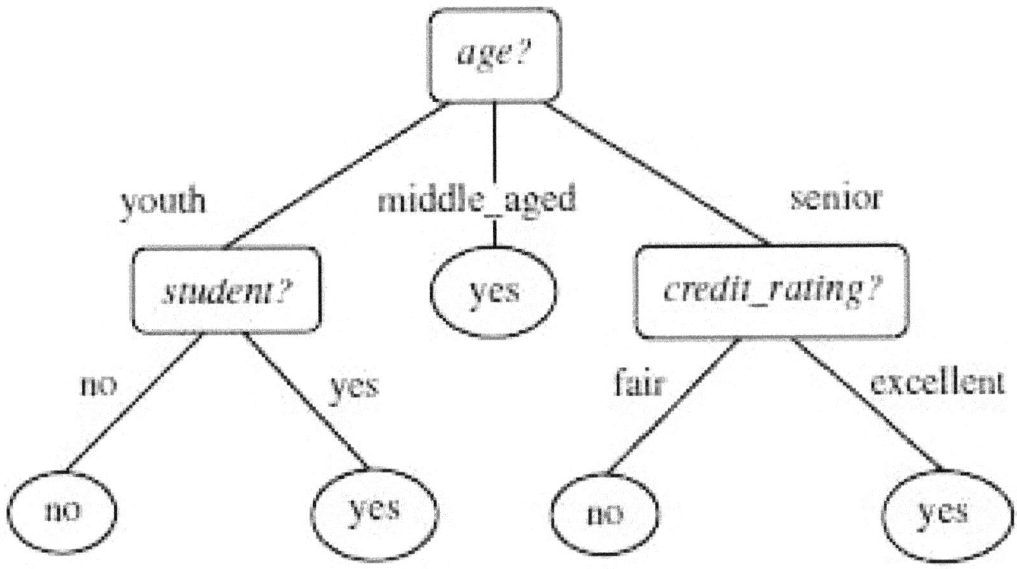

Figure 4.2 Decision Tree

Decision tree classifiers are ideal for exploratory knowledge discovery since they may be built without the need for parameter setting or domain knowledge. High- dimensional data can be handled via decision trees. Their use of a tree-like representation of learned information is intuitive and generally simple for humans to comprehend. The decision tree induction process involves simple and quick learning and categorization phases. Decision tree classifiers typically have high accuracy. Numerous application domains, including medical, industry, financial analysis, astronomy, and molecular biology, have used decision tree induction methods for classification.

4.3.1 Decision Tree Induction Algorithm:

The decision tree induction algorithm is given in figure 4.3.

Algorithm: Generate_decision_tree. Generate a decision tree from the training tuples of data partition *D*.

Input:

- Data partition, *D*, which is a set of training tuples and their associated class labels;
- *attribute_list*, the set of candidate attributes;
- *Attribute_selection_method*, a procedure to determine the splitting criterion that "best" partitions the data tuples into individual classes. This criterion consists of a *splitting_attribute* and, possibly, either a *split point* or *splitting subset*.

Output: A decision tree.

Method:

```
(1)  create a node N;
(2)  if tuples in D are all of the same class, C then
(3)       return N as a leaf node labeled with the class C;
(4)  if attribute_list is empty then
(5)       return N as a leaf node labeled with the majority class in D; // majority voting
(6)  apply Attribute_selection_method(D, attribute_list) to find the "best" splitting_criterion;
(7)  label node N with splitting_criterion;
(8)  if splitting_attribute is discrete-valued and
          multiway splits allowed then // not restricted to binary trees
(9)       attribute_list ← attribute_list − splitting_attribute; // remove splitting_attribute
(10) for each outcome j of splitting_criterion
     // partition the tuples and grow subtrees for each partition
(11)      let D_j be the set of data tuples in D satisfying outcome j; // a partition
(12)      if D_j is empty then
(13)           attach a leaf labeled with the majority class in D to node N;
(14)      else attach the node returned by Generate_decision_tree(D_j, attribute_list) to node N;
     endfor
(15) return N;
```

Figure 4.3 Decision Tree Induction Algorithm

Three parameters are used to invoke the algorithm:

- Data partition S
- Attribute list
- Attribute selection method

A collection of attributes that describe the tuples is contained in the parameter attribute list. The attribute selection technique outlines a heuristic method for choosing the attribute that "best" separates the provided tuples into their respective classes. The training tuples in D are represented by a single node, N, at the beginning of the tree. The node N becomes a leaf and is labelled with the class if the tuples in D are all of the same class. The algorithm's conclusion explains each of the termination circumstances. If not, the splitting criterion is determined by calling the Attribute Selection Method in the algorithm. The splitting criterion determines the "optimal" way to divide or partition the tuples in D into distinct classes, hence indicating which attribute to test at node N.

There are three potential outcomes. The splitting attribute will be A. Based on the training data, A has v different values (a1, a2,...,av).

A has discrete values:

In this instance, the results of the test at node N are identical to the known values of A. For each known value of A, aj, a branch is made and labelled with that value. Any upcoming partitioning of the tuples will not take aneed into account.

A has continuous value:

In this instance, the split-point supplied by the attribute selection method as part of the splitting criterion corresponds to the conditions A =sp1it point and A

>sp1it point, respectively.

A is discrete-valued, hence one must create a binary tree:

"ACSA?" is the format of the test at node N.

The attribute selection method's return value for A's splitting subset, SA, is a component of the splitting criterion. It is a subset of A's recognised values.

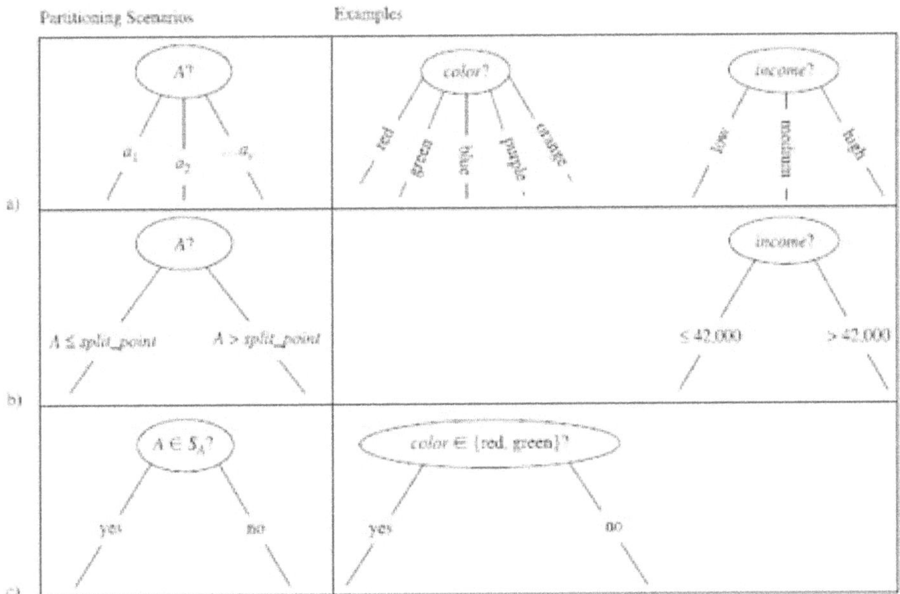

Figure 4.4 (a) If A is Discrete valued (b)If A is continuous valued (c) IfA is discrete-valuedand a binary tree must be produced

4.4 Bayesian Classification

Bayesian classifiers are statistical classifiers. They have the capacity to forecast class membership probabilities, such as the likelihood that a given tuple belongs to a specific class. The foundation of Bayesian classification is the Bayes theorem.

4.4.1 Bayes' Theorem

Let X be a data tuple. In Bayesian semantics, X is "evidence" and is described by measurements taken on a set of n qualities.

Let H be a hypothesis, such as that the data tuple X belongs to a specific class C. In classification problems, the probability that the hypothesis H is true given the "evidence" or observed data tuple X is known as P(H|X). The posterior probability, or a posteriori probability, of H given X is denoted by the symbol P(H|X). In that it offers a method for determining the posterior probability, Bayes' theorem is useful.

P{IfX), Rom P{11), P{ H), and P{X).

$$P(H|\mathbf{X}) = \frac{P(\mathbf{X}|H)P(H)}{P(\mathbf{X})}$$

4.4.2 Naive Bayesian Classification

The basic Bayesian classifier, also known as the Naive Bayesian classifier, functions as follows:

1. Assume that D is a training set of tuples and the class labels that go with them. Every tuple is represented as per usual by an n-dimensional attribute vector, X = (x1, x2,...,xn), which shows n measurements performed on the tuple from n attributes, correspondingly, A1, A2,..., An
2. Assume there are m classes, including Cl, C2,..., and Cm. When given a tuple, X, the classifier will assert, conditionally on X, that X belongs to the class with the highest posterior probability. That is, the naive Bayesian classifier predicts that tuple X belongs to the class Ci if and only if

$$P(C_i|\mathbf{X}) > P(C_j|\mathbf{X}) \quad \text{for } 1 \le j \le m, j \ne i$$

Thus, we maximize P(Ci |X). The class Ci for which P(Ci |X) is maximized is called the maximum posteriori hypothesis.
By Bayes' theorem

$$P(C_i|\mathbf{X}) = \frac{P(\mathbf{X}|C_i)P(C_i)}{P(\mathbf{X})}$$

3. As P(X) is constant for all classes, only P(X|Ci)P(Ci) needs to be maximized. If the class prior probabilities are not known, then it is commonly assumed that the classes are equally likely, that is, P(C1) = P(C2) = ··· = P(Cm), and we would therefore maximize P(X|Ci). Otherwise, we maximize P(X|Ci)P(Ci). Note that the class prior probabilities may be estimated by P(Ci) = |Ci,D|/|D|, where |Ci,D| is the number of training tuples of class Ci in D.

4. Given data sets with many attributes, it would be extremely computationally expensive to compute P(X|Ci). To reduce computation in evaluating P(X|Ci), the Naive assumption of class- conditional independence is made. This presumes that the attributes values are conditionally independent of one another, given the class label of the tuple (i.e., that there are no dependence relationships among the attributes). Thus,

$$P(\boldsymbol{X}|C_i) = \prod_{k=1}^{n} P(x_k|C_i)$$
$$= P(x_1|C_i) \times P(x_2|C_i) \times \cdots \times P(x_n|C_i)$$

We can easily estimate the probabilities P(x1|Ci), P(x2|Ci),..., P(xn|Ci) from the training tuples. Recall that here xk refers to the value of attribute Ak for tuple X. For each attribute, we look at whether the attribute is categorical or continuous-valued. For instance, to compute P(X|Ci), we consider the following:

(a) If Ak is categorical, then P(xk |Ci) is the number of tuples of class Ci in D having the value xk for Ak , divided by |Ci,D|, the number of tuples of class Ci in D.

(b) If Ak is continuous-valued, then we need to do a bit more work, but the calculation is pretty straightforward. A continuous-valued attribute is typically assumed to have a Gaussian distribution with a mean μ and standard deviation σ, defined by

$$g(x, \mu, \sigma) = \frac{1}{\sqrt{2\pi}\sigma} e^{-\frac{(x-\mu)^2}{2\sigma^2}}$$

so that,

$$P(x_k|C_i) = g(x_k, \mu_{C_i}, \sigma_{C_i})$$

5. To predict the class label of X, P(X|Ci)P(Ci) is evaluated for each class Ci . The classifier predicts that the class label of tuple X is the class Ci if and only if

$$P(\boldsymbol{X}|C_i)P(C_i) > P(\boldsymbol{X}|C_j)P(C_j) \quad \text{for } 1 \le j \le m, j \ne i$$

In other words, the predicted class label is the class Ci for which P(X|Ci)P(Ci) is the maximum.

4.5 A Multilayer Feed-Forward Neural Network

A multilayer feed-forward neural network is trained using the backpropagation algorithm. It develops a set of weights for predicting the class label of tuples iteratively. One or more hidden layers, an output layer, and an input layer make up a multilayer feed-forward neural network as shown in figure 4.5.

Example:

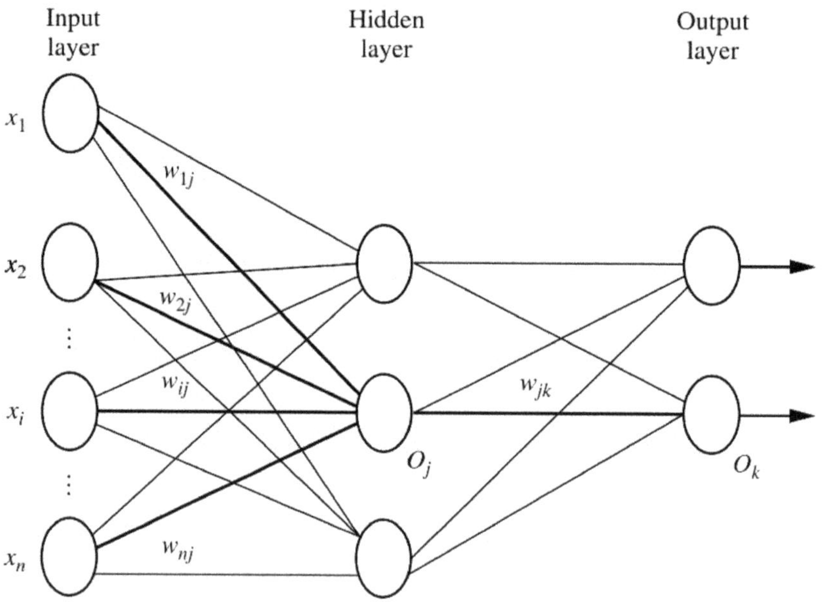

Figure 4. 5 Multilayer Feed-Forward Neural Network

The attributes that were measured for each training tuple correspond to the inputs to the network. The units that make up the input layer are simultaneously given the inputs. These inputs move through the input layer before being simultaneously weighted and routed to a subsequent layer known as the hidden layer. The hidden layer units' outputs can be fed into the input of a subsequent hidden layer, and so forth. The number of layers that are hidden is arbitrary. Units in the output layer receive the weighted outputs of the final hidden layer as input and emit the network's prediction for specific tuples.

4.6 ClassificationbyBackpropagation

A neural network learning algorithm is backpropagation. A neural network is made up of connected input/output units with weights assigned to each connection. In order to be able to anticipate the right class label of the input tuples, the network learns during the learning phase by modifying the weights. Due to the links between units, neural network learning is also known as connectionist learning.

For applications where this is practical, neural networks are better suited because they require lengthy training times. Backpropagation learns through the iterative processing of training tuples in a data set and the comparison of each tuple's predicted value by the network with the actual known target value. In situations involving classification, the goal value could either be a continuous value or the training tuple's known class label (for prediction). The weights are changed for every training tuple in order to reduce the mean squared error between the predicted value of the network and the actual target value. Back propagation gets its name from the fact that these changes are made going "backwards," or from the output layer via each hidden layer and down to the bottommost hidden layer.

Generally speaking, the weights will balance, though this is not a guarantee.

4.6.1 Advantages

The advantages of backpropagation neural network for classification are given below.

- They can distinguish between different types of patterns even when they haven't been trained to, and they have a high tolerance for noisy input.

- When you may not be familiar with the connections between characteristics and classes, you can use them.
- In contrast to most decision tree methods, they are suitable for continuous- valued inputs and outputs.
- Many different types of real-world data, such as handwritten character recognition, pathology and laboratory medicine, and teaching a computer to pronounce English text, have shown success in their research.
- Due to the inherent parallelism of neural network methods, parallelization techniques can be employed to accelerate computation.

4.6.2 Process

The classification task using backpropagation involves the following steps.

a. Initialize the weights

Initial weights for the network are small random integers between -1.0 and 1.0 or -0.5 and 0.5. There is a bias attached to each unit. The biases are initialised to small random integers in a similar way.

The following stages are used to process each training tuple, A.

b. Propagate the inputs forward:

The input layer of the network is first fed with the training tuple. The inputs proceed unmodified through the input units. That is, with an input value of 1, its output, Oj, is equal to the value of the input. Next, it is calculated what the net input and output are for each unit in the hidden and output layers. A unit in the hidden or output layers has a net input that is calculated as a linear combination of its inputs.

Each of these units has a number of inputs that are actually the outputs of the units connected to it in the layer above. Each link is supported by a weight. Each input connected to the unit is multiplied by its associated weight, and this sum is used to calculate the net input to the unit.

$$I_j = \sum_i w_{ij} O_i + \theta_j$$

where w,j is the weight of the connection between unit i in the previous layer and unit j; O, is the output of unit i from the previous layer; Qj is the bias of the unit; and it works as a threshold by allowing the unit's activity to be changed.

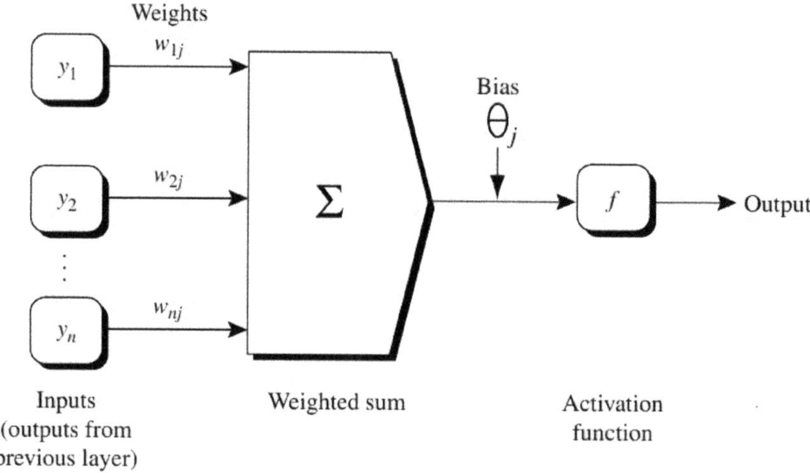

Figure 4.6 Hidden or Output Unit j

The hidden and output layers' individual units each take their net input and apply an activation function to it.

c. Back propagate the error

By changing the weights and biases to reflect the mistake of the network's prediction, the error is propagated backward. The error is calculated by using the output layer's unity as the input. where Tj is the known target value of the given training tuple and Oj is the actual output of unit j.

$$Err_j = O_j(1 - O_j)(T_j - O_j)$$

The mistake of a hidden layer is

$$Err_j = O_j(1 - O_j)\sum_k Err_k w_{jk}$$

where wt is the weight of the connection from unit j to a unit k in the next higher layer, and Errtis the error of unit k.

The weights and biases are updated to reflect the propagated errors. Weights are updated by the following equations, where Δwij is the change in weight wij:

$$\Delta w_{ij} = (l) Err_j O_i$$

$$w_{ij} = w_{ij} + \Delta w_{ij}.$$

Biases are updated by the following equations below

$$\Delta\theta_j = (l) Err_j$$

$$\theta_j = \theta_j + \Delta\theta_j$$

4.6.3 Backpropagation Algorithm

The backpropagation algorithm is given below.

Algorithm: Backpropagation. Neural network learning for classification or numeric prediction, using the backpropagation algorithm.

Input:

- *D*, a data set consisting of the training tuples and their associated target values;
- *l*, the learning rate;
- *network*, a multilayer feed-forward network.

Output: A trained neural network.

Method:

Initialize all weights and biases in *network*;

while terminating condition is not satisfied {

for each training tuple $\boldsymbol{X}$ in D {

// Propagate the inputs forward:

for each input layer unit j {

$O_j = I_j$; // output of an input unit is its actual input value

for each hidden or output layer unit j {

$I_j = \sum_i w_{ij} O_i + \theta_j$; //compute the net input of unit j with respect to the previous layer, i

$O_j = \frac{1}{1+e^{-I_j}}$; } // compute the output of each unit j

// Backpropagate the errors:

for each unit j in the output layer

$Err_j = O_j(1 - O_j)(T_j - O_j)$; // compute the error

for each unit j in the hidden layers, from the last to the first hidden layer

$Err_j = O_j(1 - O_j) \sum_k Err_k w_{jk}$; // compute the error with respect to the next higher layer, k

for each weight w_{ij} in *network* {

$\Delta w_{ij} = (l) Err_j O_i$; // weight increment

$w_{ij} = w_{ij} + \Delta w_{ij}$; } // weight update

for each bias θ_j in *network* {

$\Delta \theta_j = (l) Err_j$; // bias increment

$\theta_j = \theta_j + \Delta \theta_j$; } // bias update

} }

Enter Caption

4.7 k-Nearest-Neighbor Classifier

Nearest-neighbor Classifiers work by comparing a given test tuple with training tuples that are similar to it, which is a method known as learning by analogy. N attributes are used to describe the training tuples. An n-dimensional point in space is represented by each tuple. Thus, the entire training set of tuples is saved in an n-dimensional pattern space. A h-nearest-neighbor classifier looks for the k training tuples that are most similar to an unknown tuple when given an unknown tuple. The k closest neighbours of the unknown tuple are these k training tuples.

A distance metric, like Euclidean distance, is used to define proximity.

$$dist(X_1, X_2) = \sqrt{\sum_{i=1}^{n} (x_{1i} - x_{2i})^2}$$

In other words, we take the difference between each numeric attribute's corresponding values in tuple X1 and tuple X2, square that difference, and then add it up for each numeric attribute. The overall accumulated distance count is square-rooted. Normally, before applying the distance equation, we normalise the values of each attribute. This aids avoid letting characteristics with initially big ranges (like money) dominate characteristics with initially lower ranges (e.g., binary attributes). For instance, by computing the min-max normalisation coefficient, a value v of a numeric attribute A can be changed to v 0 in the range [0, 1].

$$v' = \frac{v - min_A}{max_A - min_A}$$

where min and m are attribute A's minimal and maximum values.The most prevalent class among the unknown tuple's k nearest neighbours is allocated for k-nearest neighbour categorization.When k — 1, the training tuple's class that is most similar to the unknown tuple in pattern space is given to it. In order to provide a real-valued forecast for a provided unknown tuple, nearest neighbour classifiers can also be utilised for prediction.The classifier then returns the average value of the real-valued labels connected to the k closest neighbours of the unknown tuple in this situation.

4.7.1 Accuracy and Error Measures

4.7.1.1 AccuracyMeasures

After training a classifier or predictor, you could have a lot of questions on your mind. Assume, for instance, that you trained a classifier to anticipate client purchase trends using data from previous sales. In other words, future customer data on which the classifier has not been trained, you would need an estimate of how accurately the classifier can forecast the purchase behaviour of future consumers.

You might even have experimented with various techniques to create many classifiers (or predictors) and now want to evaluate how accurate they are. What, though, is accuracy?How do we calculate it?Exist any methods to improve the trained model's accuracy? The next sections answer these queries. Measures for calculating classifier accuracy are described. Predictor error measurements are provided, and approaches for estimating accuracy, such as holdout, random subsampling, k-fold cross-validation, and bootstrap methods, can employ these measures.

classes	buy_computer = yes	buy_computer = no	total	recognition(%)
buy_computer = yes	6954	46	7000	99.34
buy_computer = no	412	2588	3000	86.27
total	7366	2634	10000	95.52

Accuracy of a classifier M, acc(M): percentage of test set tuples that are correctly classified by the model M

Error rate (misclassification rate) of M = 1 – acc(M)

Given m classes, CMi,j, an entry in a confusion matrix, indicates # of tuples in class i that are labeled by the classifier as class j

Alternative accuracy measures (e.g., for cancer diagnosis)

sensitivity = t-pos/pos /* true positive recognition rate */

specificity = t-neg/neg /* true negative recognition rate */

precision = t-pos/(t-pos + f-pos)

accuracy = sensitivity * pos/(pos + neg) + specificity * neg/(pos + neg)

This model can also be used for cost-benefit analysis

4.7.1.2 Classifier Accuracy Measures

Due to the overspecialization of the learning algorithm to the data, using training data to generate a classifier or predictor and then estimating the accuracy of the resulting learnt model can lead to deceptive overoptimistic predictions.(We'll elaborate on this a bit later!)Instead, a test set of class-labeled tuples that weren't used to train the model is a better place to gauge correctness. The proportion of test set tuples that are properly classified by a classifier on a certain test set is known as accuracy. This is also known as the classifier's overall recognition rate in the pattern recognition literature and measures how successfully the classifier detects tuples belonging to different classes.

4.7.1.3 ErrorMeasures

How can prediction accuracy be measured? Assume that DT is a test set with the elements (X1, y1), (X2, y2),:::, (Xd, yd), where Xi are the n-dimensional test tuples with known values (yi) for the response variable (y), and d is the total number of tuples in DT. It is challenging to determine with certainty whether the projected value, y0 I for Xi is accurate because predictors return a continuous value rather than a categorical label. We consider how distant the anticipated value is from the actual known value rather than whether y0 I is a "exact" match with yi. The difference between yi and the expected value, y0 I is measured by loss functions.

4.8 Evaluating the Accuracy of a Classifier and Predictor

How can we accurately quantify classifier accuracy (or predictor accuracy in terms of error) using the aforementioned measures? Common methods for judging accuracy based on data include holdout, random subsampling, cross validation, and the bootstrap.

4.8.1 Ensemble Methods—Increasing the Accuracy

Two strategies are bagging and boosting. They serve as illustrations of ensemble methods, or techniques that combine several models. Both bagging and boosting combine a set of k trained models (classifiers or predictors), M1, M2,::, and Mk, in an effort to produce a better composite model. Both techniques can be applied to both classification and prediction.

4.8.1.1 Bagging

First, we examine how bagging functions intuitively as a strategy for improving accuracy. We'll start off assuming that our model is a classifier to make the explanations easier. Take the example of a patient who wants a diagnosis based on their symptoms. You might decide to consult with numerous doctors rather than just one. You may decide to use a particular diagnosis as the final or best diagnosis if it manifests more frequently than any of the others. In other words, the final diagnosis is decided by a majority vote, with each doctor receiving an equal number of votes. The fundamental concept of bagging can be understood if each doctor is replaced by a classifier. It makes sense that a majority vote cast by a big number of doctors would be more trustworthy than one cast by a smaller number.

4.8.1.2 Boosting

Now let's examine the ensemble boosting technique. As in the last section, let's say you are a patient and you exhibit a few symptoms. You decide to see multiple doctors rather than just one. Consider giving each doctor's diagnosis different weights based on how accurately they have diagnosed patients in the past. The weighted diagnoses are then combined to form the final diagnosis. This is what boosting is all about. Each training tuple is given a weight in boosting. Iterative learning of k classifiers is used. The weights are changed when a classifier Mi is trained so that Mi+1 can "pay more attention" to the training tuples that Mi incorrectly classified.

Popular boosting method Adaboost. Let's say we want to increase a learning method's accuracy. We are given D, a data set of d class-labeled tuples, where yi is the class label of tupleXi, (X1, y1), (X2, y2),:::, and (Xd, yd). Adaboost initially gives each training tuple a weight of 1=d. It takes k rounds of the remaining method to create k classifiers for the ensemble. The tuples from D are sampled in round I to create a training set,Di, of size d. The same tuple may be selected more than once when sampling with replacement is employed. The probability of any tuple being chosen depends on its weight. The training tuples of Di are used to create the classifier model, Mi. Then, using Di as the test set, its error is determined. The training tuples' weights are then changed in accordance with how they were categorised. A tuple's weight is increased if the classification was erroneous. A tuple's weight is reduced if it was successfully categorised. The weight of a tuple indicates how difficult it is to classify; the higher the weight, the more frequently it has been incorrectly classified. The training samples for the classifier in the following round will be created using these weights. The essential premise is that we want a classifier to concentrate more on the incorrectly categorised tuples from the previous round.

4.9 Overview of clustering

Clustering is the process of organising a collection of concrete or abstract things into classes of related objects. A cluster is a group of data objects that are distinct from the objects in other clusters yet comparable to one another within the same cluster. When a collection of data objects is handled as a single unit, it can be said to be compressed data. Many statistical analysis software packages or systems, such as S- Plus, SPSS, and SAS, also include cluster analysis tools based on k-means, k-medoids, and various approaches.

4.9.1 Characteristics of Clustering

4.9.1.1 Clustering Scalability

Given the volume of data available today, massive databases should be used. The clustering algorithm must be scalable to accommodate large databases. Data must be scalable; otherwise, we won't be able to obtain the right answer, which would produce inaccurate findings.

4.9.1.2 High Dimensionality

The algorithm must be able to handle both small amounts of input and a high dimensional space.

4.9.1.3 Algorithm Usability with various data types

Clustering algorithms can be utilised with a variety of data types. It should be able to handle a variety of data kinds, including binary, discrete, categorical, and interval-based data.

4.9.1.4 Handling unstructured data

Some databases may contain noisy or inaccurate data, as well as missing values. If the algorithms are susceptible to such data, it could result in clusters of poor quality. Therefore, it should be able to handle unstructured data and give the data some structure by grouping related data objects together. In order to process the data and find novel patterns, this makes the job of the data expert simpler.

4.9.1.5 Interpretability

The grouping results ought to be clear, understandable, and useful. How simple it is to understand the data is shown by its interpretability.

4.10 Applications

1. A variety of applications, including as market research, pattern recognition, data analysis, and image processing, have extensively used cluster analysis.
2. In the commercial world, clustering can assist marketers in identifying unique client groups and describing customer groupings based on purchase trends.
3. In biology, it can be used to create taxonomies for plants and animals, group genes with similar functions, and understand the underlying structures of populations.
4. Clustering may also be useful in identifying areas of similar land use in an earth observation database, groups of houses in a city according to house type, value, and location, and groupings of car insurance policy holders with high average claim costs.
5. Because clustering divides enormous data sets into groups based on their similarity, it is also known as data segmentation in some applications.
6. The detection of credit card fraud and the observation of criminal activity in online commerce are two examples of applications for outlier detection, which may also be done using clusterin

4.10.1 **Type of data in clustering analysis**

1. Interval-scaled (numeric) variables
2. Binary variables
3. Categorical (nominal) variables
4. Ordinal variables
5. Ratio variables
6. Mixed types variables

Interval-valuedvariables

Interval-scaled (numeric) variables are continuous measurements of a roughly linear scale

Examples : weight and height, latitude and longitude coordinates (e.g., when clustering houses), and weather temperature.

Binary Variables

A binary variable has only two states: 0 or 1, where 0 means that the variable is absent, and 1 means that it is present. Given the variable smoker describing a patient, 1 indicates that the patient smokes and 0 indicates that the patient does not. Treating binary variables as if they are interval-scaled can lead to misleading clustering results. Therefore, methods specific to binary data are necessary for computing dissimilarities

Categorical Variables

A categorical (nominal) variable is a generalization of the binary variable in that it can take on more than two states.

Example: map_color is a categorical variable that may have five states: red, yellow, green, pink, and blue. The states can be denoted by letters, symbols, or a set of integers.

Ordinal Variables

A discrete ordinal variable resembles a categorical variable, except that the M states of the ordinal value are ordered in a meaningful sequence.

Example: professional ranks are often enumerated in a sequential order, such as assistant, associate, and full for professors.

Ordinal variables may also be obtained from the discretization of interval-scaled quantities by splitting the value range into a finite number of classes.

Variables of Mixed Types

A database may contain different types of variables interval-scaled, symmetric binary, asymmetric binary, nominal, and ordinal We can combine the different variables into a single dissimilarity matrix, bringing all of the meaningful variables onto a common scale of the interval [0.0, 1.0].

4.10.2 ClusteringMethods

1. Partitioning Methods
2. Hierarchical Methods
3. Density-Based Methods
4. Grid-Based Methods
5. Model-Based Methods

PartitioningMethods

A partitioning method divides the data into k divisions, each of which represents a cluster and where k = n. In other words, it divides the data into k groups that collectively meet the requirements listed below: At least one object must be present in each group, and each object must belong to exactly one group.

HierarchicalMethods

A hierarchical approach breaks down the supplied collection of data objects into levels. Depending on how the hierarchical breakdown is created, a hierarchical technique can be categorised as either agglomerative or divisive.

Density-BasedMethods

The majority of object clustering techniques use object distance to group things together. Such algorithms struggle to find clusters of any shape and can only locate spherical-shaped clusters. On the basis of the idea of density, other clustering techniques have been created.

The main idea is to develop the given cluster as long as the density in the surrounding area reaches a certain threshold; to put it another way, each data point within a given cluster must have at least a certain number of neighbours within a given radius. This technique can be used to remove noise (outliers) and find clusters of any shape.

DBSCAN and its extension, OPTICS, are typical density-based algorithms that create clusters in accordance with a connectivity-based density analysis. Through the examination of density function value distributions, the DENCLUE approach groups objects into clusters.

Grid-Based Methods

The object space is quantized by grid-based approaches into a finite number of cells that make up a grid structure. All clustering actions are carried out on the quantized space, or the grid structure.

The key benefit of this strategy is its quick processing time, which is usually unaffected by the quantity of data items and only depends on the number of cells in each dimension of the quantized space. A common illustration of a grid-based approach is STING. Wave Cluster uses both grid-based and density-based wavelet transformation for clustering analysis.

Model-BasedMethods

Model-based methods posit a model for every cluster and then determine which model best fits the data. By creating a density function that reflects the spatial distribution of the data points, a model-based method may detect clusters. It also results in a method for automatically calculating the number of clusters based on common statistics, accounting for "noise" or outliers, and producing reliable clustering techniques.

4.10.3 **PartitioningMethods**

The most well-known and commonly used partitioning methods are

1. The *k*-Means Method
2. k-Medoids Method **The K-Means Method** Using the input parameter k, the k-means algorithm divides a set of n items into k clusters, resulting in high intracluster similarity but low intercluster similarity. The average value of the objects in a cluster, also known as the centroid or centre of gravity of the cluster, is used to quantify how similar the objects are to one another. Following are the steps in the k-means algorithm.

    1. First, it chooses k objects at random, each of which at this point represents the cluster mean or centre.
    2. Based on the separation between each surviving object and the cluster mean, each object is then assigned to the cluster to which it is most comparable.
    3. The new mean for each cluster is then calculated.
    4. The criterion function is iterated through several times until convergence.

Typically, the square-error criterion is used, defined as

$$E = \sum_{i=1}^{k} \sum_{p \in C_i} |p - m_i|^2,$$

Where E is the sum of the square error for all objects in the data setp is the point in space representing a given object

Mi is the mean of cluster Ci

The k-means partitioning algorithm

The *k*-means algorithm for partitioning, where each cluster's center is represented by the meanvalue of the objects in the cluster

Input:

- k: the number of clusters,
- D: a data set containing n objects.

Output: A set of k clusters.

Method:

(1) arbitrarily choose k objects from D as the initial cluster centers;
(2) **repeat**
(3) (re)assign each object to the cluster to which the object is the most similar, based on the mean value of the objects in the cluster;
(4) update the cluster means, i.e., calculate the mean value of the objects for each cluster;
(5) **until** no change;

4.10.3 The k-Medoids Method

The k-means technique is vulnerable to outliers because an object with an extraordinarily big value may significantly alter the data's distribution. The square-error function is used, which significantly worsens this impact. We can choose actual items— one representative object per cluster—to symbolise the clusters rather than using the mean value of the objects in a cluster as a benchmark. The representative object that is most comparable to each remaining object is grouped with them. Following that, the partitioning procedure is carried out according to the guiding concept of reducing the total of the differences between each object and its corresponding reference point. Thus, the application of an absolute-error criterion is made.

$$E = \sum_{j=1}^{k} \sum_{p \in C_j} |p - o_j|,$$

Where E is the sum of the absolute error for all objects in the data set pis the point inspace representing a given object in cluster Cj

Ojis the representative object of Cj

Initially, representative objects are selected at random.

As long as the quality of the resulting clustering is improved, the iterative process of replacing representative objects with non-representative objects will continue.

A cost function that calculates the average dissimilarity between an object and the representative object of its cluster is used to estimate this quality.

The following four instances are looked at for each of the non representative objects to see if they would make a good substitute for the existing representative object, oj.

Case 1: 'p' currently belongs to representative object, oj. If ojis replaced by orandomasa representative object and p is closest to one of the other representative objects, oi,i≠j, then p is reassigned to oi.

Case 2: 'p' currently belongs to representative object, oj. If ojis replaced by orandomasa representative object and p is closest to one of the other representative objects, oi,i≠j, then p is reassigned to oi.

Case 3:'p' currently belongs to representative object, oj. If ojis replaced by orandom as a representative object and p is closest to orandom, then p is reassigned to Orandom.

Case 4: 'p' currently belongs to representative object, oi, i≠j. If ojis replaced byorandomas arepresentative object and p is closest to orandom, then p is reassigned toorandom.

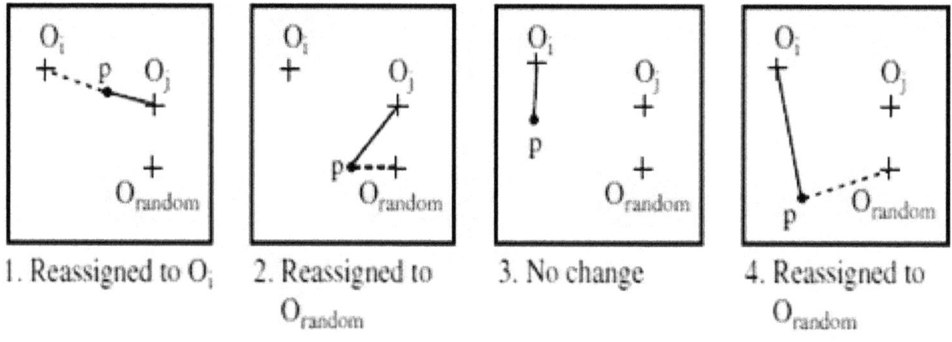

- • data object
- + cluster center
- — before swapping
- --- after swapping

Figure 4.7 Four cases of the cost function for *k*-medoids clustering

The k-Medoids Algorithm

The k-medoids algorithm for partitioning based on medoid or central objects.

Input:

- k: the number of clusters,
- D: a data set containing n objects.

Output: A set of k clusters.

Method:

(1) arbitrarily choose k objects in D as the initial representative objects or seeds;
(2) **repeat**
(3) assign each remaining object to the cluster with the nearest representative object;
(4) randomly select a nonrepresentative object, o_{random};
(5) compute the total cost, S, of swapping representative object, o_j, with o_{random};
(6) **if** $S < 0$ **then** swap o_j with o_{random} to form the new set of k representative objects;
(7) **until** no change;

In the presence of noise and outliers, the k-medoids approach is more reliable than the k-means method because a medoid is less susceptible to outliers or other extreme values than a mean is. Its processing, however, is more expensive than the k-means approach.

CHAPTER FIVE

MINING OF TIME SERIES

5.1 Trends Analysis

Data mining is one of the most popular techniques for gathering data from many sources and organising it for later use. Although there are numerous commercial methods for data mining, when they are used, various problems arise. Companies are expected to keep up with all the latest advancements given the data mining industry's quick progress.

Data segmentation can be used to spot trends and patterns, spot variations, and estimate the likelihood of certain events. This allows for the foundation of data mining to be provided by complex algorithms. Depending on the source of the data, the raw data may be presented in analogue or digital formats. To succeed in the market and outcompete fierce competition, businesses must stay informed on the most recent data mining developments.

Companies can utilise data mining to learn about client preferences, build strong customer relationships, boost sales, and lower risks. Data segmentation is based on sophisticated algorithms that enable the discovery of multiple trends and patterns, the detection of deviations, and the estimation of the probability of specific events occurring. The format of raw data, which can be analogue or digital, mostly depends on where the data came from. To compete in the market and outperform the competition, businesses must stay up to date with the most recent data mining trends.

One of the few emerging trends in data mining that data science professionals need to be aware of is data mining specialisation by vertical. These 5 additional emerging themes in data mining.

1. Data Mining Dominance in the Pharmaceutical and Health Care Industries.

In the field of data mining, the pharmaceutical and healthcare sectors have long been pioneers. In fact, improvements in data mining techniques for pharmaceutical testing, specifically in signal recognition during the clinical trial process for new medications, are directly responsible for the recent quick creation of coronavirus vaccines. Specialized data mining methods are being utilised in the medical field to examine DNA sequences in order to develop personalised treatments, generate more accurate diagnoses, and more.

2. Increasing Automation in Data Mining

Data mining used to be manually coded by experts with extensive backgrounds in statistics and programming. Modern methods for generating pattern-discovering algorithms are substantially automated, with AI/ML replacing the majority of these formerly manual operations. Modern data mining systems frequently combine ML with large data storage to offer sophisticated data analysis methods as well as comprehensive data management capabilities.

3. Embedded Data Mining

A wide range of enterprise software use cases, from sales forecasting in CRM SaaS platforms to cyber threat identification in intrusion detection/prevention systems, are increasingly incorporating data mining functionalities. Applications for vertical markets that incorporate data mining allow prediction capabilities for a variety of businesses, opening up new horizons for the development of distinctive value.

4. Rise of Spatial and Geographic Data Mining

With the current new space race, data mining has received more attention than ever for a variety of commercial space-related use cases, including asteroid mining, zero- gravity cancer research, spacecraft design/testing, and others. Back on Earth, geographic information system (GIS) services like Google Maps and GPS-powered navigation have already ingrained spatial and geographic data mining into everyday life. Data Mining Vendor Consolidation

5. Data Mining Vendor Consolidation

If the past is any guide, there will soon be a big product consolidation in the data mining market as larger database suppliers buy up data mining tool startups to expand their product lines with new capabilities. The current big data vendor environment, which is still undergoing consolidation, is similar to the fragmented big data market with its wide range of participants.

Data mining, once the domain of statisticians and number crunchers, is now attracting interest from a wider range of functional roles (such as developers and data mining APIs, and niche consumers and specialised data mining apps) and sectors. In terms of data mining technologies, improvements in pattern detection based on AI/ML in combination with feature sets tailored to certain verticals are driving the production of new value in sectors that haven't historically used data mining. This particular area of data science is one to watch in the upcoming months and years as a result of all these trends.

5.1.1 Regression and Trend Analysis in Time-Series Data

The fields of statistics and signal analysis have extensively researched time- series data regression. But sometimes it's necessary to go beyond simple regression.

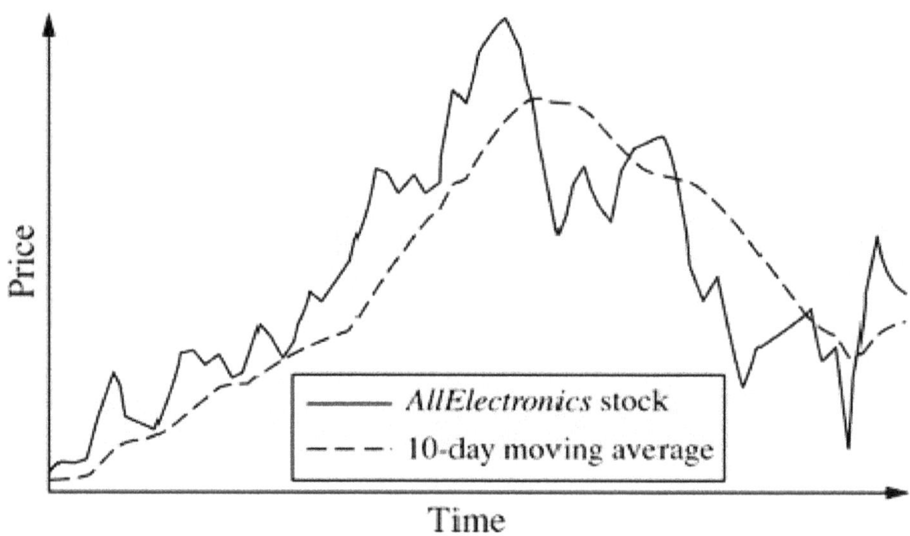

Figure. 5.1 Regression and Trend Analysis in Time-Series Data

Time-series data for the stock price of All Electronics over time. The trend is shown with a dashed curve, calculated by a moving average.

Analysis and perform trend analysis for many practical applications. Trend analysis builds an integrated model using the following four major components or movements to characterize time-series data:

Trend or long-term movements:

These show the general direction that a time-series graph is moving over time. For instance, trend curves can be found using the weighted moving average and least squares methods, as the dashed curve in Figure.

Cyclic movements

These are the long-term oscillations about a trend line or curve.

Seasonal variations

These are essentially same patterns that a time series seems to adhere to during relevant seasons in succeeding years, like the holiday shopping season. Often, data must be "deseasonalized" based on a seasonal index calculated using autocorrelation in order to do trend analysis effectively.

Random movements

These describe periodic shifts brought on by unplanned occurrences like labour disputes or publicly reported staff changes within corporations.

The process of developing a mathematical function that will roughly produce the historical trends in a time series and utilising it to create long- or short-term forecasts of future values is known as time-series forecasting. Popular techniques for this type of study include autoregression, long-memory time-series modelling, and ARIMA (auto-regressive integrated moving average).

5.2 Similarity Search in Time-Series Data

Sequences of numerical values gathered via repeated measurements of time make up a time-series data set. Typically, the values are measured at regular periods of time (e.g., every minute, hour, or day). Numerous applications, including stock market research, economic and sales forecasting, budgetary analysis, utility studies, inventory studies, yield estimates, workload projections, process and quality control, are common uses for time-series databases. They are also helpful for research into scientific and engineering experiments, medicinal procedures, and natural phenomena (such as the atmosphere, temperature, wind, and earthquake).

A similarity search identifies data sequences that deviate just slightly from the given query sequence, in contrast to regular database queries, which locate data that exactly matches a given query.Subsequence matching, or locating a group of sequences that contain subsequences that are similar to a particular query sequence, is necessary for many time-series similarity queries.

Time-series data transformation and data or dimensionality reduction are frequently required prior to similarity search. The discrete Fourier transform (DFT), discrete wavelet transformations (DWT), and singular value decomposition (SVD) based on principal components analysis are common dimensionality reduction techniques (PCA). We won't go into great detail here because we briefly discussed these ideas in Chapter 3 and because a comprehensive explanation would exceed the bounds of this book. The data or signal is mapped to a signal in a modified space using such techniques. The "strongest" transformed coefficients are only a small subset of those that are kept as features.

These features combine to create a feature space, which is a projection of the altered space. To expedite a search, indices can be created using the original or converted time-series data. Techniques for a query-based similarity search include normalisation transformation, atomic matching (i.e., finding pairs of gap-free windows of a small length that are similar), window stitching (i.e., sewing similar windows to form pairs of large similar subsequences, allowing gaps between atomic matches), and subsequence ordering (i.e., linearly ordering the subsequence matches to determine whether enough similar pieces exist). For a similarity search in time-series data, there are many software programmes available.

Time-series data can now be regarded as a succession of symbolic representations thanks to a recent proposal by researchers to turn the data into piecewise aggregate approximations. The similarity search issue is afterwards changed into a matching subsequences in symbolic sequence data issue. We can find motifs (often occurring sequential patterns), and then create indexes or hashing systems to enable effective search based on those motifs. Experiments demonstrate that this method has a similar search quality to DFT, DWT, and other dimensionality reduction techniques while being quick and easy to use.

5.3 Sequence patterns in transactional data bases

Sequence databases are collections of ordered objects or events that can be recorded with or without a specific sense of time. Applications for sequencing data are numerous. Examples of typical sequences of occurrences include customer shopping patterns, Web clickstreams, biological patterns, events in science and engineering, as well as patterns in natural and social processes.

5.3.1 Sequential Pattern Mining

Sequential pattern mining is the process of looking for patterns in frequently recurring ordered occurrences or subsequences. Customers who purchase a Canon digital camera are likely to purchase an HP colour printer within a month, to give one example of a sequential pattern. Sequential trends in retail data are useful for shelf layout and marketing. Sequential patterns can be used by this sector, telecoms, and other companies for a variety of purposes, including targeted marketing and customer retention. Observe that the majority of works on sequential pattern mining focus on categorical (or symbolic) patterns, while numerical curve analysis typically falls under the purview of trend analysis and forecasting in statistical time-series analysis.The analysis of Web access patterns, weather forecasting, production procedures, and network intrusion detection are further fields in which sequential patterns might be used.

According to Agrawal and Srikant's 1995 study of customer purchase sequences, "Given a set of sequences, where each sequence consists of a list of events (or elements) and each event consists of a set of items, and given a user-specified minimum support threshold of min sup, sequential pattern mining finds all frequent subsequences, that is, the subsequences whose occurrence frequency in the set is the highest.

Sequential pattern mining has focused extensively on mining symbolic sequences. A sequential pattern is a frequent subsequence existing in a single sequence or a set of sequences. A sequence $\alpha = \langle a1a2 \cdots an \rangle$ is a subsequence of another sequence $\beta = \langle b1b2 \cdots bm \rangle$ if there exist integers $1 \leq j1 < j2 < \cdots < jn \leq m$ such that $a1 \subseteq bj1$, $a2 \subseteq bj2, \ldots, an \subseteq bjn$. For example, if $\alpha = \langle \{ab\},d \rangle$ and $\beta = \langle \{abc\}, \{be\}, \{de\}, a \rangle$, where a, b, c, d, and e are items, then α is a subsequence of β. Mining of sequential patterns consists of mining the set of subsequences that are frequent in one sequence or a set of sequences. Many scalable algorithms have been developed as a result of extensive studies in this area. Alternatively, we can mine only the set of closed sequential patterns, where a sequential pattern s is closed if there exists no sequential pattern s′, where s is a proper subsequence of s′, and s′ has the same (frequency) support as s. Similar to its frequent pattern mining counterpart, there are also studies on efficient mining of multidimensional, multilevel sequential patterns.

As with constraint-based frequent pattern mining, user-specified constraints can be used to reduce the search space in sequential pattern mining and derive only the patterns that are of interest to the user. This is referred to as constraint-based sequential pattern mining. Moreover, we may relax constraints or enforce additional constraints on the problem of sequential pattern mining to derive different kinds of patterns from sequence data. For example, we can enforce gap constraints so that the patterns derived contain only consecutive subsequences or subsequences with very small gaps. Alternatively, we may derive periodic sequential patterns by folding events into proper- size windows and finding recurring subsequences in these windows. Another approach derives partial order patterns by relaxing the requirement of strict sequential ordering in the mining of subsequence patterns. Besides mining partial order patterns, sequential pattern mining methodology can also be extended to mining trees, lattices, episodes, and some other ordered patterns.

5.3.2 Scalable Methods for Mining Sequential Patterns

Sequential pattern mining may generate and/or test a combinatorially exploding number of intermediate subsequences, it presents computational challenges.

"How can we develop efficient and scalable methods for sequential pattern mining?" Recent developments have made progress in two directions: (1) efficient methods for mining the full set of sequential patterns, and (2) efficient methods for mining only the set of closed sequential patterns, where a sequential pattern s is closed if there exists no sequential pattern s′ where s′ is a proper supersequence of s, and s′ has the same (frequency) support as s.6 Because all of the subsequences of a frequent sequence are also frequent, mining the set of closed sequential patterns may avoid the generation of unnecessary subsequences and thus lead to more compact results as well as more efficient methods than mining the full set. We will first examine methods for mining the full set and then study how they can be extended for mining the closed set.

In addition, we discuss modifications for mining multilevel, multidimensional sequential patterns (i.e., with multiple levels of granularity).

The major approaches for mining the full set of sequential patterns are similar to those introduced for frequent itemset mining in Chapter 5. Here, we discuss three such approaches for sequential pattern mining, represented by the algorithms GSP, SPADE, and PrefixSpan, respectively. GSP adopts a candidate generate-and-test approach using horizonal data format (where the data are represented as ⟨sequence ID : sequence of itemsets⟩, as usual, where each itemset is an event). SPADE adopts a candidate generate-and-test approach using vertical data format (where the data are represented as ⟨itemset :(sequence ID, event ID)⟩). The vertical data format can be obtained by transforming from a horizontally formatted sequence database in just one scan. PrefixSpan is a pattern growth method, which does not require candidate generation.

5.3.3GSP: A Sequential Pattern Mining Algorithm Based on Candidate Generate-and-Test

GSP (Generalize Sequential Patterns) is a sequential pattern mining method that was developed by Srikant and Agrawal in 1996. It is an extension of their seminal algorithm for frequent itemset mining, known as Apriori (Section 5.2). GSP uses the downward-closure property of sequential patterns and adopts a multiple-pass, candidate generate-and-test approach. The algorithm is outlined as follows. In the first scan of the database, it finds all of the frequent items, that is, those with minimum support. Each such item yields a 1-event frequent sequence consisting of that item. Each subsequent pass starts with a seed set of sequential patterns— the set of sequential patterns found in the previous pass. This seed set is used to generate new potentially frequent patterns, called candidate sequences. Each candidate sequence contains one more item than the seed sequential pattern from which it was generated (where each event in the pattern may contain one or multiple items). Recall that the number of instances of items in a sequence is the length of the sequence. So, all of the candidate sequences in a given pass will have the same length. We refer to a sequence with length k as a k-sequence. Let Ck denote the set of candidate k-sequences. A pass over the database finds the support for each candidate k-sequence. The candidates in Ck with at least min sup form Lk, the set of all frequent k-sequences. This set then becomes the seed set for the next pass, k + 1. The algorithm terminates when no new sequential pattern is found in a pass, or no candidate sequence can be generated.

5.3.4 SPADE: An Apriori-Based Vertical Data Format Sequential Pattern Mining Algorithm

The Apriori-like sequential pattern mining approach (based on candidate generate-and-test) can also be explored by mapping a sequence database into vertical data format. In vertical data format, the database becomes a set of tuples of the form ⟨itemset : (sequence ID, event ID)⟩. That is, for a given itemset, we record the sequence identifier and corresponding event identifier for which the itemset occurs. The event identifier serves as a timestamp within a sequence. The event ID of the ith itemset (or event) in a sequence is i. Note than an item set can occur in more than one sequence. The set of (sequence ID, event ID) pairs for a given item set forms the ID list of the itemset. The mapping from horizontal to vertical format requires one scan of the database. A major advantage of using this format is that we can determine the support of any k-sequence by simply joining the ID lists of any two of its (k – 1)-length subsequences. The length of the resulting ID list (i.e., unique sequence ID values) is equal to the support of the k-sequence, which tells us whether the sequence is frequent.

SPADE (Sequential Pattern Discovery using Equivalent classes) is an Apriori- based sequential pattern mining algorithm that uses vertical data format. As with GSP, SPADE requires one scan to find the frequent 1-sequences. To find candidate 2- sequences, we join all pairs of single items if they are frequent (therein, it applies the Apriori property), share the same sequence identifier, and their event identifiers follow a sequential ordering. That is, the first item in the pair must occur as an event before the second item, where both occur in the same sequence. Similarly, we can grow the length of item sets from length 2 to length 3, and so on. The procedure stops when no frequent sequences can be found or no such sequences can be formed by such joins. The following example helps illustrate the process.

5.3.5 Sequence Classification

The majority of classification techniques build models using feature vectors. Sequences lack specific features, nevertheless. The dimensionality of potential features might still be quite high and the sequential nature of features is challenging to capture, even when using sophisticated feature selection techniques. Sequence classification becomes difficult as a result.

There are three types of methods for classifying sequences: (1) feature-based classification, which converts a sequence into a feature vector before applying conventional classification techniques; (2) sequence distance-based classification, where the distance function that gauges how similar two sequences are greatly influences the quality of the classification; and (3) model-based classification, which makes use of hidden Markov models (HMM) or other statistical models.

The feature selection methods for symbolic sequences cannot be easily applied to time-series data or other numeric-valued data without discretization. Discretization,however, may result in information loss. The time-series subsequences that can best describe a class are used as the features in a recently developed time-series shapelets approach. It produces accurate categorization outcomes.

5.3.6 Alignment of Biological Sequences

Nucleotide or amino acid sequences are the most common kind of biological sequences. Bioinformatics and contemporary biology both rely heavily on biological sequence analysis, which compares, aligns, indexes, and analyses biological sequences.

All living things are related to one another through evolution, which is the foundation for sequence alignment. This suggests that species that have evolved more recently should have nucleotide (DNA, RNA) and protein sequences that are more similar to one another. An alignment is the process of lining up sequences to produce a maximal identity level, which also represents the degree of similarity between sequences. If two sequences have a common ancestor, they are homologous. The level of homology between two sequences can be ascertained using the sequence alignment's measure of similarity. A phylogenetic tree, which represents the evolution of species, can be used to establish the relative positions of several species.

5.3.7 **Hidden Markov Model for Biological Sequence Analysis**

Biologists are interested in figuring out what a biological sequence means. Biologists create a variety of probabilistic models, including as Markov chains and hidden Markov models, to reflect the structure or statistical regularities of sequence classes. Both models are particularly helpful for the analysis of biological sequence data because the likelihood of a state simply depends on the probability of the previous state. The forward algorithm, Viterbi algorithm, and Baum-Welch algorithm are the most frequently used techniques for creating hidden Markov models. The forward algorithm calculates the likelihood that a given sequence of symbols, x, will appear in the model; the Viterbi algorithm determines the most likely path (corresponding to x) through the model; and the Baum-Welch algorithm learns or modifies the model's parameters to best explain a set of training sequences.

5.4 Mining Text Data

Information retrieval, data mining, machine learning, statistics, and computational linguistics are all applied in the interdisciplinary topic of text mining. The majority of information is saved as text, including news stories, technical papers, books, digital libraries, emails, blogs, and web pages. Consequently, text mining research has been quite busy. To extract trustworthy information from text is a crucial objective. This is often accomplished by the identification of patterns and trends using techniques like topic modelling, statistical language modelling, and statistical pattern learning. Text input must typically be organised for text mining (e.g., parsing, along with the addition of some derived linguistic features and the removal of others, and subsequent insertion into adatabase). Determining patterns within the structured data, output evaluation, and output interpretation come next. In text mining, "high quality" typically refers to a convergence of relevance, uniqueness, and interestingness.

Text categorization, text clustering, concept/entity extraction, creation of fine- grained taxonomies, sentiment analysis, document summarization, and entity-relation modelling are examples of common text mining tasks (i.e., learning relations between named entities). There are further text mining applications in security, biomedical literature analysis, online media analysis, and analytical customer relationship management, as well as multilingual data mining, multidimensional text analysis, contextual text mining, and trust and evolution analysis in text data. There are numerous types of text mining and analysis software and applications accessible in academic settings, open-source communities, and business. WordNet, Sematic Web, Wikipedia, and other information sources are frequently used in text mining to improve comprehension and data mining.

5.4.1 Text data analysis and information retrieval

Database systems and the discipline of information retrieval (IR) have long coexisted and developed simultaneously. Information retrieval has a wide range of uses because there is a wealth of text data. There are several information retrieval systems, including online document management systems, online library catalogue systems, and the more recently created Web search engines.

Basic Measures for Text Retrieval: Precision and Recall

Precision: This is the percentage of retrieved documents that are in fact relevant to the query (i.e., "correct" responses). It is formally defined as

$$\text{Precision} = \frac{|\{\text{Relevant}\} \cap \{\text{Retrieved}\}|}{|\{\text{Retrieved}\}|}$$

Recall: This is the percentage of documents that are relevant to the query and were, in fact, retrieved. It is formally defined as

$$\text{Recall} = \frac{|\{\text{relevant documents}\} \cap \{\text{retrieved documents}\}|}{|\{\text{relevant documents}\}|}$$

F-score, which is defined as the harmonic mean of recall and precision:

$$F = \frac{2.\text{precision}.\text{recall}}{(\text{precision} + \text{recall})}$$

The harmonic mean discourages a system that sacrifices one measure for another too drastically.

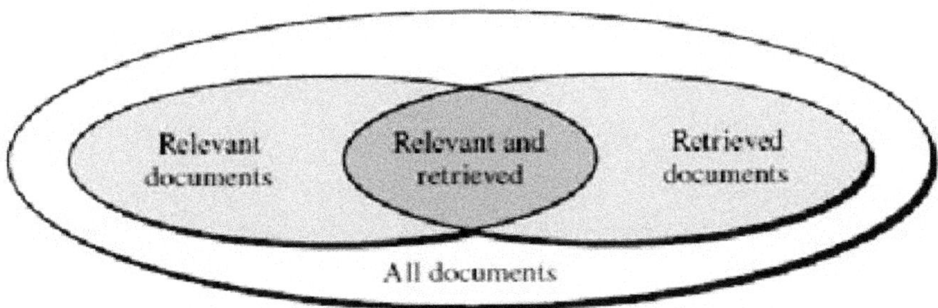

Figure 5.2 Relationship Between the set of Relevant Doucments and Retrieved Documents

Text Retrieval Methods

There are two types of retrieval techniques:

1. Document selection problem
2. Document ranking problem

In document selection methods, the query is regarded as specifying constraints for selecting relevant documents.

Document ranking methods use the query to rank all documents in the order of relevance. How can we model a document to facilitate information retrieval?" Starting with a set of d documents and a set of t terms, we can model each document as a vector v in the t dimensional space R t , which is why this method is called the vector-space model. Let the term frequency be the number of occurrences of term t in the document d, that is, freq(d; t). The (weighted) term-frequency matrix TF(d; t) measures the association of a term t with respect to the given document d: it is generally defined as 0 if the document does not contain the term, and nonzero otherwise. There are many ways to define the term- weighting for the nonzero entries in such a vector. For example, we can simply set TF(d; t) = 1 if the termt occurs in the document d, or use the term frequency freq(d; t), or the relative term frequency, that is, the term frequency versus the total number of occurrences of all the terms in the document. There are also other ways to normalize the term frequency. For example, the Cornell SMART system uses the following formula to compute the (normalized) term frequency:

$$\mathrm{wf}_{t,d} = \begin{cases} 1 + \log \mathrm{tf}_{t,d} & \text{if } \mathrm{tf}_{t,d} > 0 \\ 0 & \text{otherwise} \end{cases}.$$

Inverse document frequency (IDF), that represents the scaling factor, or the importance, of a term t. If a term t occurs in many documents.

where d is the document collection, and dt is the set of documents containing term t. If jdt j_jdj, the term t will have a large IDF scaling factor and vice versa.

$$IDF(t) = log\frac{N+1}{DF(t)+1} + 1$$

In a complete vector-space model, TF and IDF are combined together, which forms the TF-IDF measure:

$$TF\text{-}IDF\ (t) = TF(t) \times IDF(t)$$

Term frequency and inverse document frequency. Table 10.5 shows a term frequency matrix where each row represents a document vector, each column represents a term, and each entry registers freq(di; t j), the number of occurrences of term t j in document di. Based on this table we can calculate the TF-IDF value of a term in a document. For example, for t6 in d4, we have

$$TF(d_4, t_6) = 1 + \log(1 + \log(15)) = 1.3377$$

$$IDF(t_6) = \log \frac{1+5}{3} = 0.301.$$

$$TF\text{-}IDF(d_4, t_6) = 1.3377 \times 0.301 = 0.403$$

Enter Caption

A representative metric is the cosine measure, defined as follows. Let v1 and v2 be two document vectors. Their cosine similarity is defined as

$$sim(v_1, v_2) = \frac{v_1 \cdot v_2}{|v_1||v_2|},$$

where the inner product $v_1 \cdot v_2$ is the standard vector dot product, defined as $\sum_{i=1}^{t} v_{1i}v_{2i}$, and the norm $|v_1|$ in the denominator is defined as $|v_1| = \sqrt{v_1 \cdot v_1}$.

A term frequency matrix showing the frequency of terms per document.

document/term	t_1	t_2	t_3	t_4	t_5	t_6	t_7
d_1	0	4	10	8	0	5	0
d_2	5	19	7	16	0	0	32
d_3	15	0	0	4	9	0	17
d_4	22	3	12	0	5	15	0
d_5	0	7	0	9	2	4	12

Text Indexing Techniques

There are several popular text retrieval indexing techniques, including inverted indices and signature files. An inverted index is an index structure that maintains two hash indexed or B+-tree indexed tables: document table and term table, where

a. document table consists of a set of document records, each containing two fields: doc id and posting list, where posting list is a list of terms (or pointers to terms) that occur in the document, sorted according to some relevance measure.
b. Term table consists of a set of term records, each containing two fields: term id and posting list, where posting list specifies a list of document identifiers in which the term appears.

A signature file is a file that stores a signature record for each document in the database. Each signature has a fixed size of b bits representing terms. A simple encoding scheme goes as follows. Each bit of a document signature is initialized to 0. A bit is set to 1 if the term it represents appears in the document. A signature S1 matches another signature S2 if each bit that is set in signature S2 is also set in S1.

Query Processing Techniques

When a document collection's inverted index is built, a retrieval system can swiftly respond to a keyword query by determining which documents contain the query terms. To be more precise, we will keep score accumulators for each document and update them as we process each search word.

We will get all of the documents that match a certain search keyword and raise their scores. As we go through each search term, accumulators will appear. We will get all of the documents that match a certain search keyword and raise their scores.

Techniques for reducing the number of dimensions, including locality-preserving indexing, probabilistic latent semantic analysis, and latent semantic indexing

Latent Semantic Indexing

Latent semantic indexing (LSI) is one of the most popular algorithms for document dimensionality reduction. It is fundamentally based on SVD (singular value decomposition). Suppose the rank of the term-document X is r, then LSI decomposes X using SVD as follows:

$$X = U\Sigma V^T,$$

$$a_{opt} = \arg\min_a \|X - aa^T X\|^2 = \arg\max_a a^T X X^T a,$$

with the constraint,

$$a^T a = 1.$$

Since XX^T is symmetric, the basis functions of LSI are orthogonal.

Locality Preserving Indexing

The basic idea of LPI is to preserve the locality information (i.e., if two documents are near each other in the original document space, LPI tries to keep these two documents close together in the reduced dimensionality space).

$$a_{opt} = \arg\min_a \sum_{i,j} (a^T x_i - a^T x_j)^2 S_{ij} = \arg\min_a a^T X L X^T a,$$

Given the document set x1; : : : ;xn 2 Rm, LPI constructs a similarity matrix S 2 Rn_n. The transformation vectors of LPI can be obtained by solving the following minimization problem:

$$a^T X D X^T a = 1,$$

where L = DS is the Graph Laplacian and Dii = åj Si j. Dii measures the local density around xi. LPI constructs the similarity matrix S as where L = D-S is the Graph Laplacian and Dii = åj Si j. Dii measures the local density around xi. LPI constructs the similarity matrix S as

$$S_{ij} = \begin{cases} \frac{x_i^T x_j}{\|x_i^T x_j\|}, & \text{if } x_i \text{ is among the } p \text{ nearest neighbors of } x_j \\ & \text{or } x_j \text{ is among the } p \text{ nearest neighbors of } x_i \\ 0, & \text{otherwise.} \end{cases}$$

"close" then $y_i (= a^T x_i)$ and $y_j (= a^T x_j)$ are close as well. Finally, the basis functions of LPI are the eigenvectors associated with the smallest eigenvalues of the following generalized eigen-problem:

$$XLX^T a = \lambda XDX^T a.$$

Probabilistic Latent Semantic Indexing

The probabilistic latent semantic indexing (PLSI) method is similar to LSI, but achieves dimensionality reduction through a probabilistic mixture model. Specifically, we assume there are k latent common themes in the document collection, and each is characterized by a multinomial word distribution

$$p_{d_i}(w) = \sum_{j=1}^{k} [\pi_{d_i,j} p(w|\theta_j)]$$

Formally, let C = fd1;d2; : : : ;dng be a collection of n documents. Let q1; : : :
;qk be k theme multinomial distributions. A word w in document di is regarded as a sample of the following mixture model.

$$p_{d_i}(w) = \sum_{j=1}^{k} [\pi_{d_i,j} p(w|\theta_j)]$$

5.4.2 Data Reduction

Data reduction techniques can be used to produce a condensed version of the data set that is substantially lower in size while closely preserving the original data's integrity. In other words, mining on the smaller data set should be more effective while still yielding essentially the same analytical conclusions. This section begins with a summary of data reduction tactics and then takes a closer look at specific procedures.

Overview of Data Reduction Strategies

Data reduction strategies include dimensionality reduction, numerosity reduction, and data compression.

Dimensionality reduction refers to the process of lowering the number of random variables or qualities taken into account. The original data is transformed or projected into a smaller space using dimensionality reduction techniques like wavelet transforms and main components analysis. A dimensionality reduction technique called attribute subset selection identifies and eliminates features or dimensions that aren't significant, are just marginally relevant, or are redundant.

Numerous reduction strategies substitute different, more compact forms of data representation for the original data volume. Both parametric and nonparametric methods can be used. For parametric approaches, a model is used to estimate the data, which often results in the necessity to maintain only the data parameters rather than the actual data. Examples include regression and log-linear models. Histograms, clustering, sampling, and data cube aggregation are nonparametric techniques used to store condensed representations of the data.

In **data compression**, transformations are used to create a condensed or "compressed" version of the original data. The data reduction is referred to as lossless if the original data can be restored from the compressed data without any information being lost. Instead, lossy data reduction is used when we can only rebuild a rough version of the original data. There are various lossless string compression algorithms, but they typically only allow for a small amount of data manipulation. Techniques for reducing numerosity and dimensions can also be categorised as data compression techniques.

Dimensionality reduction

Dimensionality reduction approaches try to construct a much lower-dimensional space and search for clusters in such a space. Often, a method may construct new dimensions by combining some dimensions from the original data.

Dimensionality Reduction Methods and Spectral Clustering

Methods for subspace clustering look for clusters within the original data space's subspaces. Instead of employing subspaces of the original data, it may be more beneficial in some circumstances to create a new space. Dimensionality reduction techniques for clustering high-dimensional data are used for this purpose.

Clustering in a derived space. Consider the three clusters of points in Figure . It is not possible to cluster these points in any subspace of the original space, X × Y, because

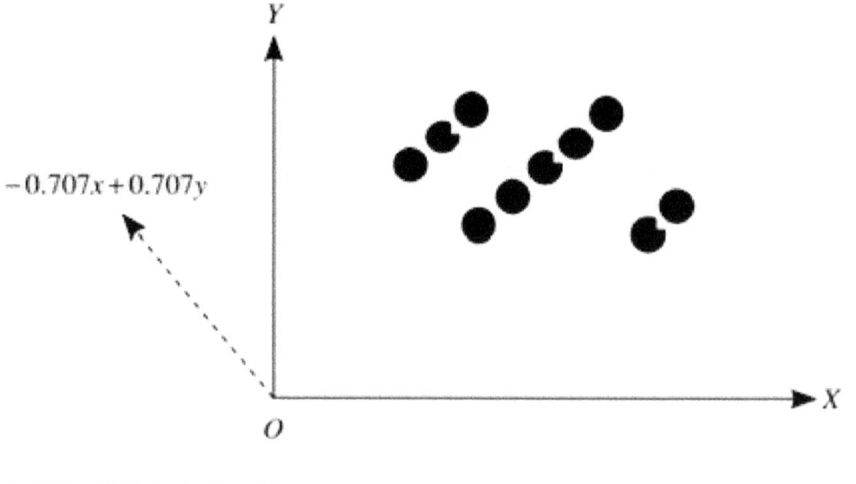

Figure 5.3 Dimensionality Reduction

Clustering in a derived space may be more effective.

all three clusters would end up being projected onto overlapping areas in the x and y axes. What if, instead, we construct a new dimension,– $\sqrt{2}/2X+ {}^{\sqrt{2}} /2$? (shown as a dashed line in the figure) By projecting the points onto this new dimension, the three clusters become apparent.

5.4.3 Text mining Approaches

Text Mining is one of the most critical ways of analyzing and processing unstructured data which forms nearly 80% of the world's data. Today a majority of organizations and institutions gather and store massive amounts of data in data warehouses, and cloud platforms and this data continues to grow exponentially by the minute as new data comes pouring in from multiple sources.

Text mining is nothing less than a multidisciplinary field because it combines and incorporates information retrieval, data mining, machine learning, statistics, and computational linguistics technologies. Natural language texts that have been saved in either semi-structured or unstructured formats are the focus of text mining.

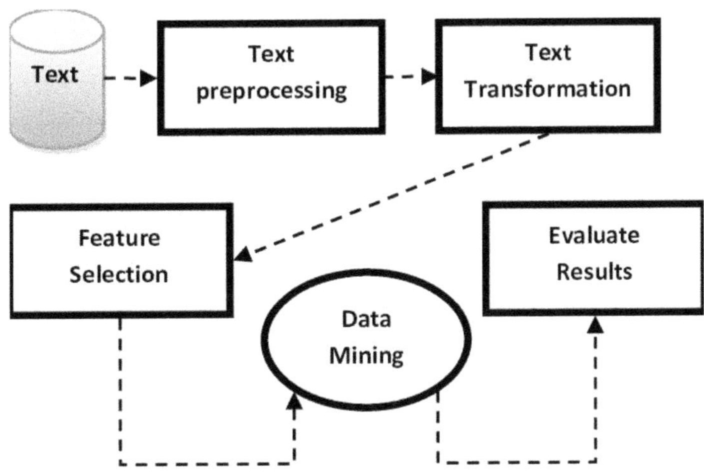

Figure 5.4 Text Mining Process

Most famous techniques used in text mining techniques:

1. **Information Extraction**

The most well-known text mining method is this one. The process of separating pertinent information from enormous quantities of textual material is referred to as information exchange. Identifying the extraction of entities, properties, and their relationships from unstructured or semi-structured texts is the main goal of this text mining technique. Whatever data is extracted is then kept in a database for retrieval and access in the future. Precision and recall techniques are used to check and assess the efficacy and relevance of the results.

2. **Information Retrieval**

The practise of collecting pertinent and related patterns from a particular set of words or phrases is known as information retrieval (IR). IR systems use several algorithms in this text mining technology to watch and analyse user actions and find pertinent data as a result. The two most well-known IR systems are Google and Yahoo.

3. **Categorization**

One of the "supervised" learning methods used in text mining, this method categorises natural language documents according to their content and assigns them to one of a predefined set of subjects. In order to find the appropriate subjects or indexes for each text document, categorization, or more precisely Natural Language Processing (NLP), is a process of gathering text documents and processing and analysing them. In NLP, the co-referencing technique is frequently used to extract pertinent synonyms and abbreviations from textual input. NLP is being employed as an automated process in a variety of applications, including the distribution of targeted advertisements, the detection of spam, the classification of web pages according to hierarchical criteria, and much more.

4. **Clustering**

The most essential text mining method is clustering. It looks for inherent structures in textual content and groups them into useful groupings or "clusters" for additional research. Making sense of unlabelled textual data clusters without any prior knowledge of them is a significant issue in the clustering process. A common text mining method, cluster analysis aids in data distribution or serves as a pre-processing stage for other text mining algorithms operating on identified clusters.

5. **Summarisation**

The practise of automatically creating a compressed version of a certain text that contains useful information for the end-user is known as text summarization. This text mining technique aims to browse through numerous text sources to provide succinct summaries of texts that contain a significant amount of information while essentially maintaining the overall content and intent of the original documents. The numerous text classification techniques, including as decision trees, neural networks, regression models, and swarm intelligence, are integrated and combined in text summarization.

Techniques	Characteristics	Tools
Retrieval	Retrievals Valuable information from unstructured text	Intelligent Miner, Text Analyser
Extraction	Extract information from structured database	Text finder clear forest text
Summarization	Reduce Length by keeping its main points and overall meaning as it is	Tropic tracking tool, sentence Ext Tool
Categorization	Document based categorization	Intelligent Miner
Cluster	Cluster Collection of documents, Clustering, Classification and analysis of text document	Carrot, Rapid Miner

Table 5.1 Sumarisation

5.5 Mining Multimedia Data

Multimedia databases that store and manage enormous collections of multimedia objects, including image, video, and audio data, as well as sequence data and hypertext data containing text, text markups, and links, are known as multimedia databases. Multimedia data mining is the process of finding interesting patterns in these databases. Image processing, image interpretation, computer vision, data mining, and pattern recognition are all combined in the interdisciplinary field of multimedia data mining. Content-based retrieval, similarity search, generalisation, and multidimensional analysis are all problems that arise in the analysis of multimedia data. Additional dimensions and measurements for multimedia data are contained in multimedia data cubes.

5.5.1 **Mining Multimedia Databases**

A multimedia database system collects and maintains a sizable collection of multimedia objects, including text- and markup-containing audio, image, video, sequence, and hypertext data. Due to the widespread usage of audio-visual equipment, CD-ROMs, and the Internet, multimedia database systems are becoming more and more prevalent. The Earth Observation System (EOS) of NASA, different image and audio- video databases, human genome databases, and Internet databases are examples of common multimedia database systems.

5.5.2 **Similarity search in multimedia data**

"When searching/or similarities in multimedia data, I suppose we can search based on either the data description or the data content?" That is correct. For similarity searching in multimedia data, we consider two main families of multimedia indexing and retrieval systems:

1. description-based retrieval systems, which build indices and perform object retrieval based on image descriptions, such as keywords, captions, size, and time of creation; and
2. Content-based retrieval systems, which support retrieval based on the image content, such as color histogram, texture, shape, objects, and wavelet transforms. Description- based retrieval is labor- intensive if performed manually. If automated, the results are typically of poor quality; for example, the assignment of keywords to images can be a tricky and arbitrary task. Content-based retrieval uses: visual features to index images and promotes object retrieval based on feature similarity, which is highly desirable in many applications.

There are typically two types of queries in a content-based retrieval system: image-sample-based queries and image-feature specification queries. Images that are similar to the provided image sample are found using image sample-based queries. The feature vector (or signature) that was derived from the sample is compared with feature vectors of previously extracted and indexed images in the image database in this search. Images that are similar to the example image are returned as a result of this comparison. The feature vectors of the images in the database are matched with the feature vectors specified in the image feature specification queries, which specify or sketch image properties like colour, texture, or shape. Numerous industries, such as e-commerce, television production, weather forecasting, and medical diagnosis, use content-based retrieval. There are certain systems that support both sample-based and image feature specification queries, such as QBIC (Query By Image Content). There are also systems that offer retrieval based on both content and description.

Several methods for similarity-based retrieval in picture databases based on image signature have been put forth and researched:

Color histogram-based signature: In this method, regardless of the size or orientation of the image, the signature of the image contains colour histograms based on the colour composition of the image. Two photos with identical colour compositions may have extremely distinct shapes or textures and so could be completely unconnected in semantics because this technique lacks information about shape, location, or texture.

Multifeature constructed signature: Using this method, an image's signature is made up of a variety of features, including the colour histogram, form, location, and texture. Frequently, distinct distance functions for each feature can be constructed and then merged to obtain the final results. One or more probe features are frequently used in multiple dimensional content-based searches to look for images with these (or comparable) features. Therefore, it can be used to look for photographs with comparable themes.

Wavelet-based signature: This method employs an image's predominate wavelet coefficients as its signature. Wavelets use a single, integrated framework to record shape, texture, and position data. Contrary to the second way described above, this increases efficiency and minimises the need to provide several search primitives. However, because this method computes a single signature for a whole image, it might not be able to distinguish between photos that have identical objects but with different shapes or sizes.

Wavelet-based signature with region-based granularity: With this method, computation and comparison of signatures are done at the level of individual areas rather than the full image. This is based on the observation that while portions in two photographs that are similar to one another may contain identical regions, they may also be translated or scaled differently. As a result, the percentage of the two images' surface area that is shared by matching pairings of regions from Q and T can be used to determine the similarity between the query image Q and the target image T. Such a region-based similarity search can locate pictures with comparable things, but these things might be resized or translated.

5.5.3 **Multidimensional Analysis of Multimedia Data**

Multimedia data cubes can be generated and built similarly to traditional data cubes using relational data in order to enable the multidimensional analysis of big multimedia datasets. Additional dimensions and measurements for multimedia information, such as colour, texture, and shape, can be included in a multimedia data cube.

Let's examine a multimedia data mining system prototype called MultiMediaMiner, which extends the DBMiner system by handling multimedia data. The example database tested in the MultiMediaMiner system is constructed as follows: Each image contains two descriptors: a feature descriptor and a layout descriptor. The original image is not stored directly in the database; only its descriptors are stored. The description information encompasses fields like image file name, image URL, image type (e.g., gif, jpeg, bmp, avi, mpeg, etc.), a list of all known Web pages referring to the image (i.e., parent URLs), a list of keywords, and a thumbnail used by the user interface for image and video browsing. The feature descriptor is a set of vectors for each visual characteristic. The main vectors are a color vector containing the color histogram quantized to 512 colors (8 x 8 x 8 for R x G x B), a MFC (Most Frequent Color) vector, and a MFO (Most Frequent Orientation) vector. The MFC and MFO contain five color centroids and five edge orientation centroids for the five most frequent colors and five most frequent orientations, respectively- The edge orientations used are 0°, 22.5°, 45°, 67.5°, 90°, and so on. The layout descriptor contains a color layout vector and an edge layout vector. Regardless of their original size, all images are assigned an 8 X 8 grid. The most frequent color for each of the 64 cells is stored in the color layout vector, and the number of edges for each orientation in each of the cells is stored in the edge layout vector. Other sizes of grids, like 4 x 4, 2 x 2 and 1x1, can easily be derived. Similar to HTML tags in Web pages, the Image Excavator part of MultiMediaMiner leverages contextual information about images to derive keywords. It is feasible to build hierarchies of keywords mapped onto the directories where the image was discovered by navigating online directory structures like the Yahoo! directory. In the multimedia data cube, these graphs serve as concept hierarchies for the dimension keyword.

Multimedia data cubes can come in a variety of sizes. These are a few instances: the Internet domain of the image or video, the Internet domain of pages referencing the image or video (parent URL), the keywords, a colour dimension, an edge-orientation dimension, and so forth. The size of the image or video in bytes; the width and height of the frames (or picture), constituting two dimensions; the date the image or video was created (or last modified); the format type of the image or video; the frame sequence duration in seconds. Concept hierarchies can be automatically defined for numerous numerical dimensions. Predefined hierarchies may be utilised for various dimensions, like Internet domains or colour.

The creation of a multimedia data cube will enable summarization, comparison, categorization, association, and grouping of knowledge, as well as various dimensional analysis of multimedia data focused mostly on visual content. For multidimensional analysis of multimedia data, the multimedia data cube appears to be an intriguing model. We should be aware, too, that a data cube's efficient implementation is challenging given the quantity of its dimensions. Multimedia data cubes suffer particularly from this dimensionality issue. In a multimedia data cube, we might like to model several dimensions for things like colour, orientation, texture, keywords, and so on. Instead of being single-valued, several of these properties are set-oriented.

One image, for instance, might be associated with a list of keywords. It might include a collection of things, each connected to a spectrum of colours. In the design of the data cube, there will be a tremendous number of dimensions if we utilise each term as a dimension or each finely detailed colour as a dimension. However, failing to do so could result in the modelling of a picture at a relatively crude, constrained, and inaccurate scale. A multimedia data cube's potential to establish a balance between effectiveness and representational strength requires further study.

5.5.4 **Classification and Prediction Analysis of Multimedia Data**

Especially in scientific studies involving astronomy, seismology, and geoscience, classification and predictive modelling have been employed for mining multimedia data. In previously documented applications for picture data mining, decision tree classification is a crucial data mining technique.

Example, We may create models for identifying galaxies, stars, and other stellar objects based on characteristics like magnitudes, areas, intensities, picture moments, and orientation using sky photographs that have been meticulously identified by astronomers as the training set. In order to find new celestial bodies, a huge number of sky photos captured by telescopes or spacecraft can be compared to the built-in models. Venusian volcanoes have been successfully identified by similar investigations.

When mining such picture data, data preprocessing—which can include data cleaning, data focussing, and feature extraction—is crucial. Techniques like the breakdown of images into eigenvectors or the use of probabilistic models to handle uncertainty can be studied in addition to classic pattern recognition techniques like edge detection and Hough transformations. Parallel and distributed processing are advantageous since picture data are sometimes in enormous amounts and may need significant processing resources. Image analysis and scientific data mining are closely related, and as a result, numerous image analysis and scientific data analysis methods can be used for image data mining classification and clustering.

5.5.5 **Mining Associations in Multimedia Data**

In picture and video databases, association rules involving multimedia elements can be found. It is possible to see at least three categories:

Associations between non-image content features and image content This category includes rules that relate the image content to the keyword sky, such as "if at least 50% of the upper section of the picture is blue, it is likely to represent sky."

Associations between picture contents unconnected to spatial relations Since the connections are all related to the contents of images, rules like "a picture contains two blue squares, it is likely to also contain one red circle" fall under this category. Associations between spatial relationship-related image contents: This category includes rules like "a red triangle is between two yellow squares, it's likely there's a big oval-shaped object underneath," which associates spatial relationships between the objects in the image.

We can regard each image as a transaction and look for recurring patterns among several photos to mine relationships among multimedia items.

First, there could be a lot of associations because each image might have several objects, each with a variety of properties like colour, shape, texture, a keyword, and spatial location. A feature may, in many circumstances, be regarded as being the same in two photographs of the same object at a particular resolution level but different at a finer resolution level. Promoting a progressive resolution refinement method is so crucial. In other words, while mining at a finer resolution level, we can only pay attention to patterns that have passed the minimal support criterion after first mining frequently occurring patterns at a somewhat rough resolution level. This is due to the fact that patterns that are uncommon at a coarse resolution level cannot be uncommon at finer resolution levels. A multi-resolution mining method like this significantly lowers the cost of data mining as a whole without sacrificing the accuracy and comprehensiveness of the results. This results in an approach that is effective for finding common itemsets and associations in huge multimedia databases.

Second, recurrence of the same objects should not be disregarded in association analysis because a picture with multiple recurrent objects is a crucial element in image analysis. For instance, a picture with two golden circles is handled very differently than one with just one. As opposed to transaction databases, where the fact that a person buys one gallon of milk or two may frequently be viewed as the same as "buys milk," this is very different. As a result, the concept of multimedia association as well as its metrics, including support and confidence, should be modified.

Third, multimedia objects frequently have significant relative spatial relationships, such as above, below, between, close, left-of, and so on. In order to investigate object relationships and correlations, these qualities are particularly helpful. Interesting associations can be created by combining spatial linkages with other multimedia aspects that are content-based, such as colour, shape, texture, and keywords. Thus, topological spatial linkages and spatial data mining techniques play a significant role in multimedia mining.

5.6 **Mining the World Wide Web**

The World Wide Web functions as a massive, broadly dispersed, and international information hub for news, advertisements, consumer information, financial management, education, government, and e-commerce. It includes a comprehensive and ever-changing database of data on the contents of web pages, including hypertext and multimedia, information on hyperlinks, access and usage data, and other useful information that may be mined for data. Data mining techniques are used to mine the web for patterns, structures, and information. Web content mining, web structure mining, and web use mining are the three primary categories that web mining can be categorised into, according on analytical aims.

Web material such as text, multimedia data, and structured data are examined through web content mining (within web pages or linked across web pages). To comprehend the content of web pages, provide scalable and informative keyword-based page indexing, entity/concept resolution, web page relevance and ranking, web page content summaries, and other important information linked to web search and analysis, this is done. Web pages may be found on the deep Web or the surface Web. The area of the Web that is indexed by common search engines is known as the surface web. Web content that is not a part of the surface web is referred to as the deep web (or hidden web). The underlying database engine provides its contents.

Web service providers, search engines, and researchers have all done substantial research on web content extraction. Web content mining has the ability to reveal personal information in an undesirable way since it can help people create links across different web pages. Studies on privacy-preserving data mining address this issue by creating methods to safeguard individual privacy on the Web.

Web structure mining is the process of examining the nodes and connection structures on the Web using graph and network mining theory and techniques. Links, which are structural elements that connect one web page to another, are used to extract patterns. It can also mine a page's document structure (e.g., analyse the treelike structure of page structures to describe HTML or XML tag usage). Both types of web structure mining aid in the comprehension of web contents and have the potential to convert them into reasonably structured data sets.

Extraction of relevant data (such as user click streams) from server logs is a process known as web usage mining. It identifies patterns associated with general or specific user groups, comprehends the search patterns, associations, and trends of users, and forecasts the online search behaviour of users. It promotes products or relevant information to various user groups at the appropriate moment while also assisting in enhancing search effectiveness and efficiency. In order to increase the quality of their services, web search companies frequently do web usage mining.

The World Wide Web acts as a sizable, broadly dispersed, international information service hub for news, advertisements, consumer information, financial management, education, government, e-commerce, and many other information services.

A vast and dynamic collection of hyperlink data as well as information on page access and usage can be found on the Web, making it a valuable resource for data mining. But as the following facts show, the Web also presents significant obstacles to efficient resource and knowledge discovery.

i. The Web seems to be too huge for effective data warehousing and data mining.
ii. The complexity of Web pages is far greater than that of any traditional text document Collection
iii. The Web is a highly dynamic information source.
iv. The Web serves a broad diversity of user communities
v. Only a small portion of the information on the Web is truly relevant or useful.

5.6.1 Mining the Web Page Layout Structure

The basic structure of a Web page is its DOM (Document Object Model) structure. The DOM structure of a Web page is a tree structure, where every HTML tag in the page corresponds to a node in the DOM tree.

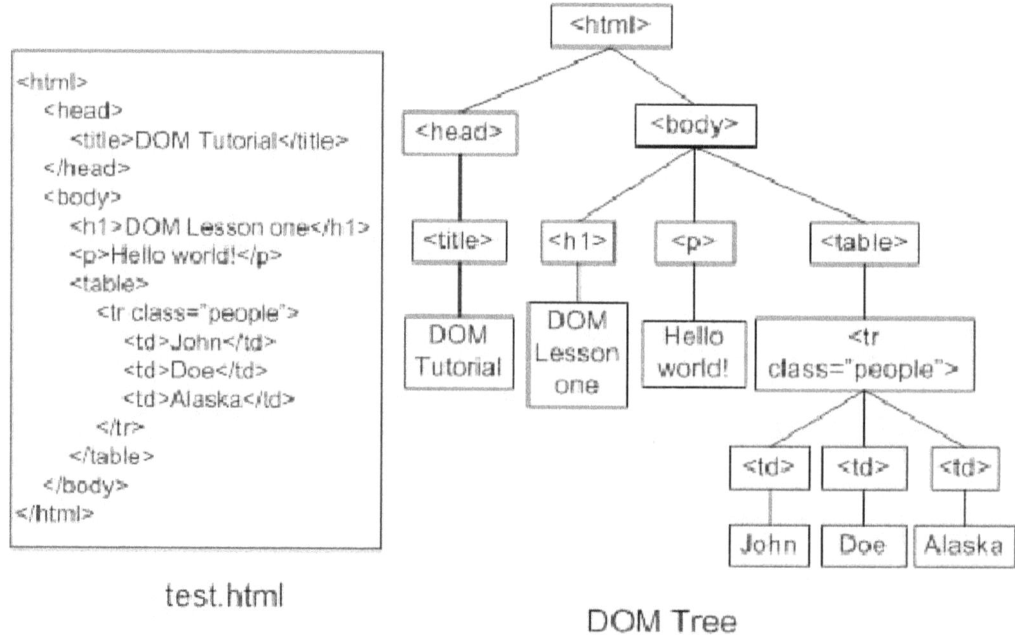

Figure 5.5 HTML Source and DOM Tree Structure

There are various Web search engines with indexes. These perform Web searches, index Web sites, and create and maintain sizable keyword-based indices that assist in locating collections of Web pages that include specific terms. Simple keyword- based search engines have a number of drawbacks. First off, there are probably hundreds of thousands of documents on any given topic. This can result in a search engine returning a massive number of document entries, many of which are only tangentially related to the subject or may contain low-quality content. Second, many highly relevant publications to a topic might not have keywords defining them. It's known as the polysemy problem.

5.6.2 Mining the Web's Link Structures to Identify Authoritative Web Pages

However, how can a search engine find reliable Web articles on my subject automatically? Curiously, links between Web pages conceal the authority's concealment. On the Web, there are hyperlinks connecting many pages as well as individual pages. Several intriguing experiments on mining authoritative Web resources have been inspired by this concept. These attributes of Web link systems have prompted scholars to take a closer look at a hub, a significant subcategory of Web pages. A hub is a single Web page or a collection of Web pages that offer links to authoritative sources. There may be few links leading to hub pages or they may not be very visible.

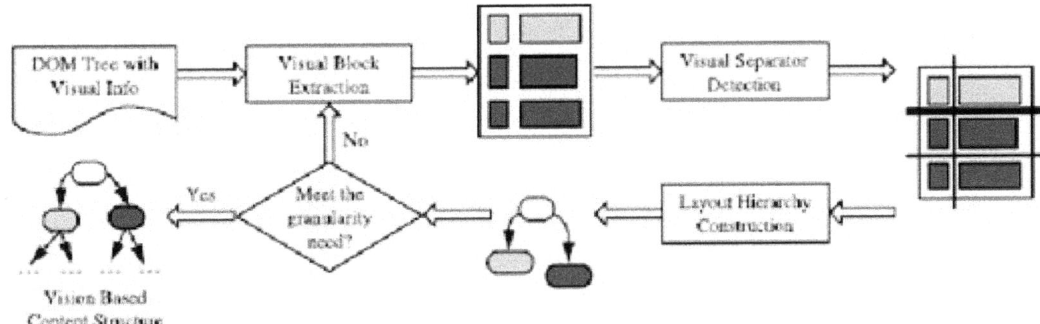

Figure 5.6 Vision Based Page Segmentation Algorithm

HITS (Hyperlink-Induced Topic Search), a hub-based algorithm, was created in the manner described below. Initially, HITS gathers a starter set of, let's say, 200 pages from an index-based search engine using the query terms. In the root set, these pages are found. There should be links to the majority of the well-known experts on some of these pages because many of them are undoubtedly relevant to the search topic. Therefore, the root set can be increased into a base set by include all of the pages that the root-set pages link to and all of the pages that link to a page in the root set, up to a defined size cutoff, such as 1,000 to 5,000 pages.

We first associate a non-negative authorityweight, ap, and a non-negative hubweight, hp, with each page p in the base set, and initialize all a and h values to a uniform constant

$$a_p = \sum (q \text{ such that } q \rightarrow p)\ h_q$$
$$h_p = \sum (q \text{ such that } q \leftarrow p)\ a_q$$

These equations can be written in matrix form as follows. Let us number the pages f1;2; : : : ;ng and define their adjacency matrix A to be an n_n matrix where A(i; j) is 1 if page i links to page j, or 0 otherwise. Similarly, we define the authority weight vector a = (a1;a2; : : : ;an), and the hub weight vector h = (h1;h2; : : : ;hn). Thus, we have

$$h = A.\ a$$
$$a = A^T.\ h_3$$

where AT is the transposition of matrix A. Unfolding these two equations k times, we have

$$h = A \cdot a = AA^T h = (AA^T)h = (AA^T)^2 h = \cdots = (AA^T)^k h$$
$$a = A^T \cdot h = A^T Aa = (A^T A)a = (A^T A)^2 a = \cdots = (A^T A)^k a.$$

Figure 5. 7 Web's Link Structures

The graph model in block-level link analysis is induced from two kinds of relationships ,that is, block-to-page (link structure) and page-to-block (page layout). The block-to-page relationship is obtained from link analysis. Let Z denote the block-to- page matrix with dimension n_k. Z can be formally defined as follows:

$$Z_{ij} = \begin{cases} 1/s_i, & \text{if there is a link from block } i \text{ to page } j \\ 0, & \text{otherwise,} \end{cases}$$

where si is the number of pages to which block i links. Zi j can also be viewed as a probability of jumping from block i to page. The page-to-block relationships are obtained from page layout analysis. Let X denote the page- to-block matrix with dimension k_n.

$$X_{ij} = \begin{cases} f_{p_i}(b_j), & \text{if } b_j \in p_i \\ 0, & \text{otherwise,} \end{cases}$$

5.6.3 **Automatic Classification of Web Documents**

Each document is given a class label in the automatic categorization of Web content based on a set of predefined topic categories and a set of samples of previously classified documents. The classification of documents on the Web can be done using keywords. A classification technique based on terms has produced effective results when used to categorise Web pages.

The semantic Web, a Web information infrastructure that is projected to give the Web structure based on the semantic meaning of the contents of Web sites, has been the subject of substantial research initiatives. The automatic extraction of the semantic meaning from web pages and the creation of an ontology for the semantic web will be made possible by the classification of web documents using web mining.

Figure 5.8 Six Image Categories

5.6.4 **Web Usage Mining**

Web usage mining, which analyses Weblog entries to determine how users visit Web pages, is another crucial activity for Web mining in addition to mining Web contents and Web linking architectures.

For each time a web page is accessed, a web server typically logs an item in its (Web) log or weblog. It provides a timestamp, the URL that was requested, and the IP address that made the request.

In developing techniques for Web usage mining, we may consider the following.

First, although it is inspiring and thrilling to consider the many potential uses of Weblog file analysis, it is crucial to understand that the success of such applications depends on what and how much true and reliable knowledge can be gleaned from the enormous raw log data. Raw Weblog data frequently has to be cleaned, compressed, and converted in order to extract and evaluate important and relevant information.

Second, a multidimensional view of the Weblog database can be created using the URL, time, IP address, and information about the Web page's content that is currently available. Multidimensional OLAP analysis can then be used to find the top N users, top N Web pages accessed, most frequently accessed time periods, and other information. This will help identify potential clients, users, markets, and other people.

Third, Web log information can be mined for association patterns, sequential patterns, and web accessing trends using data mining.

www.ingramcontent.com/pod-product-compliance
Ingram Content Group UK Ltd.
Pitfield, Milton Keynes, MK11 3LW, UK
UKHW061706190726
13853UKWH00008B/2438

9 798888 695128